THE FAMOUS, THE FAMILIAR AND THE FORGOTTEN
350 NOTABLE NEWARKERS

WITHDRAWN

GUY STERLING

XLIBRIS CORPORATION
1663 Liberty Drive • Bloomington, IN 47403
http://www.xlibris.com

Designed by Peter Ambush of Burnin' Bush Studios, www.peterambushart.com

On the cover, from left to right, top to bottom.
Queen Latifah, Thomas Edison, Mayor Kenneth Gibson and Frances Day
Photo of Guy Sterling: Mitsu Yasukawa

Print information available on the last page.

Rev. date: 11/17/2015

To order additional copies of this book, contact:
Xlibris
1-888-795-4274
www.Xlibris.com
Orders@Xlibris.com
663269

Still she haunts me, phantomwise,
Alice moving under skies
Never seen by waking eyes.

Lewis Carroll
"Through the Looking Glass"

To Maria
for her love, support and inspiration

CONTENTS

ACKNOWLEDGEMENT

Most of the research for this book was done online and at the Charles F. Cummings New Jersey Information Center in the main branch of The Newark Public Library on Washington Street.

I would like to extend my sincere appreciation to Wilma Grey and the entire library staff for their assistance, but special thanks goes to George Hawley and his team in the New Jersey Information Center, including Tom Ankner, Larissa Brookes, Dale Colston, John Goodnough and Kathryn Kauhl.

I am also grateful to the following people for the help they provided me in making this book possible: Phil Alagia; Peter Ambush; James Amemasor; Sam Arnold; Joe Bakes; Celeste Bateman; Andre Briod; Walter D. Chambers; Bill Chappel; Francis B. Coombs; Tim Crist; Father Augustine Curley; Bill Dane; Ulysses Dietz; Amanda Dios; Cristina Dios; Maria Dios; Bette M. Epstein; Sheriff Armando Fontoura; Linda Forgosh; Joe Fox; Glen Frieson; Roseanne Gasparinetti; Frank Giantomasi; Tom Giblin; Jim Goodness; Marcellus Green; Warren Grover; Larry Hazzard Sr.; Denise Holland; Sharpe James; George Kanzler; Don Karp; Bill Kleinknecht; Rich Koles; Father Edwin Leahy; James Lewis; Caryl Lucas; Kevin Lynch; Mrs. M; Gail Malmgreen; Stefanie Minatee; Antoinette Montague; Kevin Moriarty; Maureen Motherway; Stan Myers; Linda Nevells; the N.J. Historical Society; Dan O'Flaherty; Joe Parlavecchio; Dr. Victor Parsonnet; William Peniston, Ph.D.; Dr. Clement A. Price; Michael Redmond; Beverly Reid; Pat Restaino; Reginald Roberts; Dr. Mario Santos; Maria Spirito; Steve Tettamanti; Thomas Edison National Historic Park; Carolyn Whigham; Stephen Whitty; Kathleen Witcher; Phil Yourish and Zemin Zhang.

To those I may have forgotten, my deepest regrets, but also my heartfelt thanks for your help and cooperation.

INTRODUCTION

Midway through the fall of 2012, I began looking for a research project that I could tie into the celebration of Newark's 350th anniversary in 2016.

My initial inclination was to put together profiles of the city's most historic places, a guide I felt residents and visitors alike could put to good use during the anniversary year.

Once I started working on the project, however, I came upon a major dilemma —what to do about homes where notable people had lived in Newark over the course of its long history.

The issues I wrestled with were whether homes mattered strictly on the basis of who lived in them, how many of these residences there might be in Newark and what hurdles would exist in digging out their addresses.

It wasn't long before I decided to forgo cataloging historic places and instead took up the challenge of researching Newark's noteworthy residents and where they lived. It seemed like a more dynamic and singular project.

Thus was born *The Famous, The Familiar and The Forgotten: 350 Notable Newarkers*.

Information for the entries came from more than two dozen sources, everything from books and newspapers to official records such as U.S. Census data, military documents, rap sheets and birth certificates to items such as city directories, phone books and school yearbooks.

Some addresses came straight from the subjects themselves, or from family members, friends and neighbors. In almost every case, I attempted to confirm addresses using additional sources.

Where there were multiple addresses, I limited the number I listed to no more than four or five a person, giving the most weight to addresses showing up in official records. Length of time spent at residences was another key factor in those decisions.

So I am fully aware the addresses listed here may not be the only ones a notable person had in Newark. Another reason for this is because not every address a person has had is going to show up in print somewhere.

Also, being born in the city was not enough alone to make a person a Newarker. If it were, my list would surely be different. What I was looking for in deciding who qualified as a resident was an established address.

Just how many of the homes and buildings listed in the book remain standing is a question I did not try answering, though I have visited some and can say more than a few are still there.

I will leave it to readers with interests in particular names or addresses to do their own exploring on that front. But bear in mind, it's entirely possible for the number on a home or building, as well as a street name, to change over time, to say nothing of homes, buildings and streets disappearing.

Picking notables was a process unto itself and, by its very nature, purely subjective. The process was three-fold, with each step harder than the last: defining "notable," deciding who was notable and then contrasting the notables with each other to whittle down the list.

This balancing act included assessing just how noteworthy certain individuals were in their day or in their respective fields, which required more than a little study and is not what you would call an exact science.

There are certainly notable Newark residents we can all agree on — Sarah Vaughan, Philip Roth and Stephen Crane, to mention a few — and others whose degree of notoriety we might debate. By no means do I view my list as definitive.

My aim was to come up with a representative mix of people from different backgrounds and different times from a deep reservoir of candidates, and infamy was not a disqualifier.

I have no doubt others would compile lists distinct from mine and that there are deserving people I could well have missed, though it wasn't from a lack of trying to make the list of candidates as far-reaching as possible.

When I started out, I'd hoped to come up with a hundred names and, when I went beyond that, chose 350 as my target for no other reason than it matched the number of the city's anniversary celebration in 2016.

Ultimately, I came across so many noteworthy Newarkers that I compiled a second list of 400 names (in a nod to the city's next major anniversary), and will have even more people listed on the book's web site: www.famousfamiliarforgotten.com.

Beyond that, there are some people I'm still researching, and it's my intention to continue adding to the list. I wholeheartedly invite anyone with new names and addresses to offer to do so via the book's e-mail address: famousfamiliarforgotten@gmail.com.

Let's get a conversation going and have a shared experience!

Finally, it is my hope this book will serve several ends.

One is to stimulate interest in and add to the appreciation of Newark's rich past, especially in its buildings and homes that have stories of their own and are well worth researching.

If you think about it, where someone lived is often the last tangible connection we have to them, and maybe even the most revealing.

Perhaps such an effort will lead to more of these places being restored and preserved, as well as to Newark taking greater advantage of its unique past as the city seeks to enhance its image and plan its future.

I also hope the book will serve as a reminder to all that some really memorable people have lived and are living in Newark, an indication of just how special the city was and is.

I doubt many got to Newark by accident and, the fact is, a considerable number of them and their families were drawn to Newark or stayed because of what the city had to offer.

And the final goal is to give renewed recognition to some people whose significance, sadly, has diminished over time.

It gives me a great deal of satisfaction to be able to introduce to a new generation of Newark residents and those interested in the city's history the likes of Harland Bartholomew, Antoinette Brown Blackwell, Frances Day, Richard Watson Gilder, Lester B. Granger and Nicholas Longworth, among others.

It is to those we've lost sight of that I dedicate this book. They certainly did their part in putting Newark on the map and making it one of America's pre-eminent cities, if for no other reason than it was a place they called home, where they got their footing in life or where they did some pretty remarkable things.

May their memories live on as long as the hardscrabble city on the Passaic, exalted and embattled as it's been at times since its founding in 1666 by Puritans from Connecticut, continues to endure.

Guy Sterling
December 2015

350 NOTABLE
NEWARKERS

⨾⟋ Harriet Stratemeyer Adams: children's book author & editor ⟍⨾
Dec. 11, 1892 - March 27, 1982

Adams worked for a publishing syndicate her father owned, and then took it over in the 1930s upon his death. Using pen names shared by other authors, she wrote, edited or devised plots for dozens of books in the *Tom Swift*, *Nancy Drew*, *Bobbsey Twins* and *Hardy Boys* series. Though sometimes criticized as presenting a picture of the world too rosy, they are also among the most successful children's books ever printed, selling millions of copies in more than a dozen languages. Adams continued writing right up until her death, while the syndicate was bought out by Simon & Schuster in 1984.

LIVED: 99 & 171 N. 7th St.

⨾⟋ Hugh J. Addonizio: mayor & congressman ⟍⨾
Jan. 31, 1914 - Feb. 2, 1981

A graduate of St. Benedict's Prep and Fordham University, Addonizio was Newark's 33rd mayor, serving from 1962 to 1970. Prior to that, he was an executive at a clothing company and also spent 12 years as a Democratic congressman from Newark. Addonizio was the city's chief executive during the 1967 riots in Newark in which 26 people were killed and scores injured. The upheaval paved the way for the election of the city's first black mayor. In 1970, Addonizio was convicted on federal conspiracy and extortion charges at a trial in Newark and served five years of a 10-year prison term.

LIVED: 68 Hazelwood Ave.

⨾⟋ Stephen N. "Big Steve" Adubato Sr.: educator & politician ⟍⨾
Dec. 24, 1932 -

Adubato graduated from Barringer H.S. in 1949 and earned his bachelor and master's degrees from Seton Hall. He taught in the Newark schools for 15 years and served on the Newark Teachers' Union executive board. In 1970, he founded the North Ward Center, a nonprofit community development corporation now headquartered at the old Clark Mansion on Mount Prospect Avenue. It operates five institutions, including the Robert Treat Academy charter school. Adubato stepped down as the center's executive director in 2009. He has also been Democratic Party chairman in the city's North Ward.

LIVED: 59 Tiffany Blvd.; 3 Pine Lane S.; 400 Clifton Ave.; 57 Coeyman St.

Hugh J. Addonizio

༺ Armando "Ace" Alagna: photographer & publisher ༻
Feb. 17, 1925 - June 1, 2000

The son of Italian immigrants, Alagna was born in Newark and went to local schools. He pursued photography as a career after World War II, first as a freelancer and later working for *The Star-Ledger*. He covered presidential campaigns and was also the official photographer of the state Assembly and Senate. In 1968, Alagna bought the *Italian Tribune News* and spent many years as its publisher. He was the prime mover behind Newark's Columbus Day parade. The recipient of many awards, Alagna also recorded narrations of children's stories, appeared in films and produced documentaries on Italy.

LIVED: 352 N. 12th St.; 362 Highland Ave.

༺ Col. Richard T. Aldworth: war hero & Newark Airport manager ༻
Oct. 1, 1897 - Sept. 18, 1943

A member of the U.S. Army Air Corps, Aldworth flew with the celebrated commander Billy Mitchell in Europe during World War I. He was shot down behind German lines in 1918 and was held in a prison camp, only to escape and return to action. After the war, he served as manager of Newark Airport during a period of great industry growth. Aldworth later helped recruit the American Volunteer Group of the Chinese Air Force to fight the Japanese in China, a group that became the "Flying Tigers" of World War II fame. He received both the Legion of Merit award and Distinguished Flying Cross.

LIVED: 695 Clifton Ave.; 784 High St.; 715 Lake St.

༺ John Amos Jr.: actor ༻
Dec. 27, 1939 -

Born in Newark, Amos played football at Colorado State and had NFL ambitions but never made it much beyond the minor leagues. He started out in show business as a standup comic and variety show writer before landing small TV and movie roles, including one in the cult film *Sweet Sweetback's Baadasssss Song*. Amos is perhaps best known for playing "James Evans Sr." on the TV show *Good Times*. Among his other TV shows were *The Mary Tyler Moore Show*, the miniseries *Roots* and *The West Wing*. His films include *Die Hard 2*, *Coming to America* and *Let's Do it Again*.

LIVED: 28 Somerset St.

ᗒᐂ Louis V. Aronson: inventor & industrialist ᗕᐃ
Dec. 25, 1869 - Nov. 3, 1940

Aronson was the brains behind the Ronson lighter, but he had many other patents and inventions having to do with matches, lighters, fuses and toys. He was born and schooled in New York and, by the time he was 15, was an expert in metallurgy, drafting and design. He sold a patent to open up his own business, Art Metal Works, which operated a plant in Newark and became the largest firm of its kind in the world. Aronson was active in business, civic and political affairs in Newark and was especially benevolent toward children. In 1933, he hosted a banquet in Newark for Albert Einstein.

LIVED: 86 Clinton Ave.; 69 Nelson Place; 15 Sydney Place

ᗒᐂ William M. Ashby: social worker & civil rights advocate ᗕᐃ
Oct. 15, 1889 - May 17, 1991

Born in Virginia, Ashby came to Newark and worked as a waiter after graduating from Lincoln University in Pennsylvania. He returned to school and, after earning a divinity degree from Yale in 1916, became New Jersey's first black social worker. Within a few years, Ashby founded the first Urban League offices in the state and later played a key role in founding groups that were the forerunners of the United Way and Fuld Neighborhood House. The city held a day in Ashby's honor in 1974 and, in 1981, he published his autobiography. There's a monument in his honor in Newark's Central Ward.

LIVED: 12 Abington Ave.; 53; Irving St.; 214 W. Market St.

ᗒᐂ Joseph Atkinson: journalist & public official ᗕᐃ
Nov. 9, 1846 - Dec. 17, 1924

Atkinson came to the U.S. from Belfast, Ireland, and enjoyed a long career in America as a reporter and editor. He also served as city clerk in Newark and, from 1890-97, was clerk of the Essex County Board of Freeholders. He began his career on the staff of *The New York Herald*, serving as its Newark correspondent. He was also editor of *The Newark Journal, Free Press* and *Sunday Standard*, along with Prudential's in-house publication, *The Weekly Record*. He founded the *Orange Chronicle*. In 1878, Atkinson published a history of Newark that was used as a textbook in the city's school system.

LIVED: 439 Plane St.; 217 Fairmount Ave.; 785 Lake St.; 809 Clifton Ave.

⌒ Alvin A. "Al" Attles Jr.: basketball player & coach ⌒
Nov. 7, 1936 -

Attles played basketball at Weequahic H.S. and North Carolina A&T State University before becoming the 39th pick in the 1960 NBA draft. In a playing career that lasted 11 years with the Philadelphia and San Francisco Warriors, he averaged nine points a game and twice played in the NBA's championship series. Attles took over as head coach of the Warriors in 1970 and remained until 1983. His team, by this time the "Golden State Warriors," won the NBA title in 1975. When his coaching days ended, Attles moved into the Warriors' front office and had his jersey number (16) retired.

LIVED: 89 Monmouth St.

⌒ Paul B. Auster: writer ⌒
Feb. 3, 1947 -

Auster is best known for his novels, especially *The New York Trilogy*. But he has also written memoirs, poetry, essays, screenplays and translations. He grew up in South Orange but spent his early years in Newark, where his father was a shop owner and landlord. He wrote about his father in *The Invention of Solitude*. Auster studied at Columbia, moved to France and didn't get his career under way until he returned home at around age 30. He has written more than a dozen novels and won many awards in the U.S. and abroad. He was a finalist for the PEN/Faulkner Award for Fiction in 1991.

LIVED: 30 Vernon Ave.

⌒ George "Rev. M.J. Divine" Baker: evangelical preacher ⌒
c1870 - Sept. 10, 1965

"Father Divine," as he was known to his flock and in the papers, lived a life shrouded in mystery and one the established order looked upon with great skepticism. His "International Peace Mission Movement" raised millions in cash, much of it invested in real estate, usually large properties known as "heavens" where Father Divine's "angels" lived. There were a half-dozen in Newark, where he had an estimated 10,000 followers. The most prominent was the Divine Riviera Hotel, where Father Divine used an entire floor when in town. But for a time, he also lived and had his headquarters in Newark.

LIVED: 126 Howard St.; Divine Riviera Hotel, 169 Clinton Ave.

✍ Jacob Baker: publisher, economist & government official ✍
July 8, 1895 - Sept. 19, 1967

A native of Colorado, Baker began his career as an industrial engineer. He came east in the 1920s and helped found the Vanguard Press, an independent publishing house that issued the first books of Saul Bellow, Nelson Algren, Joyce Carol Oates, Dr. Seuss and others. Baker was an important federal relief administrator during the Depression and later with the WPA, getting credit for creating its art, music, theater and writers' projects. After his government service, he became a well-known economist, ending his career as chairman of the Economic Forecasting Institute in Mount Vernon, NY.

LIVED: 569 Mount Prospect Ave.

✍ Edward Balbach Jr.: industrialist & inventor ✍
July 4, 1840 - Dec. 30, 1910

Balbach came to the U.S. from Germany as a boy. His father was a gold refiner who started a business on the Passaic River in the city's Ironbound section processing precious metals. It became one of the largest enterprises of its kind in the country, largely due to a refining process the son invented that cut costs in separating gold and silver from other material. The business was important to the nation's jewelry industry, as well as to the early electric and telephone companies after the firm began producing copper. Balbach was a good friend of President Cleveland and lost a close race for Congress.

LIVED: 10 Ferguson St.; 107 & 109 Passaic Ave.

✍ Peter Ballantine: beer baron ✍
Nov. 16, 1791- Jan. 23, 1883

Ballantine was born in Scotland and came to Newark after first settling in Albany, NY, where he learned brewing. He and a partner founded a brewery in Newark in 1840 but, five years later, Ballantine set up his own brewery near the Passaic River. He took on his three sons as brewers at P. Ballantine & Sons, which became the nation's fourth largest brewery at its peak and was known for its ales. By then, the company was owned by brothers Carl and Otto Badenhausen. The brewery closed in 1972, but Ballantine, first TV sponsor of the Yankees, continued to be made and sold by other companies.

LIVED: 36 Broad St.; 55 Bridge St.; 15 Lumber St.; 594 Ogden

⤙ Louis A. Bamberger: department store founder & philanthropist ⤚
May 15, 1855 - March 11, 1944

Bamberger was born in Baltimore and came to Newark in 1892. He turned a failing general goods store on Market Street into one of the most successful department store in the U.S. named "L. Bamberger & Co." Though Bamberger sold the store in 1929 to Macy's, he remained as president. Revered by his workers, he funded many city institutions and charitable organizations. He and his sister gave $5 million to fund Princeton's Institute for Advanced Study, the academic home of Albert Einstein. He shunned the limelight and never married. Flags in Newark flew at half-staff for three days when he died.

LIVED: 6 West Park St.

⤙ Amiri Baraka: poet, playwright, critic & activist ⤚
Oct. 7, 1934 - Jan. 9, 2014

Perhaps no artist stuck his finger in the eye of authority more often or in more ways than Baraka. A champion of black causes who spared few words, he made a career of stirring the pot, all while creating a unique place for himself in American culture, one in which he was either revered or despised. Baraka went to Barringer H.S., attended Rutgers-Newark and made a name for himself in New York during the Beat era before returning to Newark to continue his writing and activism. He also taught, lectured, performed, acted, directed, produced, recorded, received awards and made appearances in court.

LIVED: 808 S. 10th St.; 33 Stirling St.; 19 Dey St.; 154 Belmont Ave.

⤙ Dr. William Nathan Barringer: educator ⤚
Sept. 23, 1826 - Feb. 4, 1907

Barringer was from upstate New York, where he studied at Troy Academy and Union College. After teaching school, he became a doctor but returned to education, coming to Newark in 1866 as principal of the Chestnut Street School. He stayed there until he was chosen superintendent in 1877, a job he held 19 years. Newark High School was renamed for him on July 21, 1907. Barringer High traces its origins as New Jersey's first public secondary school and third in a major American city to 1838, with its first building on Parker Street opening in 1899. A second Barringer High opened in 1964.

LIVED: 40 Baldwin St.; 1142A Broad St.

Louis A. Bamberger

➤ Harland Bartholomew: city planner ➤
Sept. 14, 1889 - Dec. 2, 1989

Bartholomew was hailed by *The New York Times* as "the dean of city planners" when he died. A native of Massachusetts, he was trained as a civil engineer and studied at Rutgers, later getting an honorary degree from the school. In Newark, Bartholomew served as the nation's first full-time city planner, and he worked in St. Louis before opening up his own consulting firm that prepared plans and ordinances for hundreds of cities in the U.S. and abroad. He served on federal planning committees under three presidents, taught at the University of Illinois and wrote extensively on city planning.

LIVED: 140 N. 12th St.

➤ Bernice Bass: radio host & show emcee ➤
June 15, 1926 - Jan. 18, 2000

Bass was a U.S. Customs official in Newark. But she was better known as host of a popular radio program, *News and Views*, which was broadcast on WNJR from the 1960s into the 1980s. The show was a mix of interviews, music and political commentary. Bass is credited with being the last person to interview Malcolm X before his 1965 assassination. She also served as an emcee and hosted the last show of famed gospel singer Mahalia Jackson, a friend of hers. Bass organized the Youth Cavalcade, a group of youngsters who made appearances in churches throughout New Jersey and New York.

LIVED: 109 Keer Ave.

➤ John F. Bateman: Rutgers head football coach ➤
Dec. 6, 1914 - Jan 1, 1998

Bateman attended Central H.S. and St. Benedict's Prep before graduating from Columbia University, where he was co-captain of the football team his senior year. He later got a doctorate in political science. He was an assistant coach at Columbia and Pennsylvania before taking over as head football coach at Rutgers in 1960, lasting until 1972. Bateman's overall record was 73 wins and 51 losses. With an undefeated team in 1961, he was named coach of the year by the Washington (DC) Touchdown Club. He played a key role in getting Paul Robeson inducted into the Football Hall of Fame.

LIVED: 55 Carteret St.; 8 Halleck St.; 127 3rd; 315 Chadwick Ave.; 77 Grafton Ave.

ᴥ James M. Baxter: educator ᴥ
1846 - Dec. 28, 1909

Born in Philadelphia, Baxter became the first black school principal in Newark. He began teaching in Newark in 1864 when he was only 19 and spent 45 years in the school system. When he retired in 1909, he was the dean of the city's public school principals. Baxter died the same year. He was instrumental in convincing the city that black grammar school pupils had the same rights as everyone and should be allowed to go to high school. Newark's first black high school graduates got their diplomas under him. One of Newark's first public housing complexes was named after Baxter.

LIVED: 22 Division Place; 15 Elm St.

ᴥ Bishop James Roosevelt Bayley: Newark's first Catholic bishop ᴥ
Aug. 23, 1814 - Oct. 3, 1877

Bayley was born in New York City to a family that included America's first native-born saint, Elizabeth Ann Seton. Teddy and Franklin Roosevelt were distant cousins. He abandoned early plans for a career at sea to become an Episcopalian minister only to convert to Catholicism in 1842. Bayley was ordained a priest in 1844, serving first as a college administrator and then a church official. He was consecrated Newark's first bishop in October 1853 and not only organized the new diocese but also got its college Seton Hall, with a seminary, off the ground. He later served as archbishop of Baltimore.

LIVED: 5 Nesbitt St.; 17, 25 & 43 Bleeker St.

ᴥ Hilda Belcher: artist ᴥ
Sept. 20, 1881 - April 27, 1963

Belcher was born in Vermont and moved to Newark with her family when she was in her teens. She graduated from Newark H.S. in 1900 and then moved to New York to pursue art. She was best known for her watercolors, exhibiting widely and winning several prestigious art awards. She later taught at the Art Students League. Belcher also had caricatures, cartoons and illustrations of hers published in popular magazines. She enjoyed a long association with the state of Georgia after painting a portrait in Savannah. Among her subjects were members of that area's black community.

LIVED: 247 Mount Prospect Ave.

➤ William "Bill" Bellamy: comedian & actor ➤
April 7, 1965 -

Bellamy graduated from Seton Hall Prep and Rutgers, where he majored in economics and got his start in comedy. He first came to the public's attention touring the country's comedy clubs and then on HBO's *Def Comedy Jam*. He was one of MTV's first VJs, and he also hosted several shows on the music network, including *MTV Jamz*. Bellamy has appeared as a featured actor in a number of movies — *Any Given Sunday* and *How To Be a Player*, among them — and been a regular on TV. He had his own show, co-starred in *Fastlane* and often appears on TV's day and night-time talk show circuits.

LIVED: 25 Underwood St.

➤ Morris "Moe" Berg: Major League catcher & spy ➤
March 2, 1902 - May 29, 1972

Berg was an all-star high school baseball player in Newark who graduated from Princeton and Columbia Law School. He played pro ball for 15 years, primarily as a catcher. During World War II, Berg served as a spy with the Office of Strategic Services, a CIA forerunner. He gathered intelligence on resistance groups in Yugoslavia and later interviewed European physicists about Nazi bomb-making capabilities. Berg's life after the war was largely unproductive. He rejected the Medal of Freedom, an award a sister accepted after his death. He is a member of the National Jewish Sports Hall of Fame.

LIVED: 92 S. 13th St.; 156 Roseville Ave.; 88 N. 6th St.

➤ Antoinette Brown Blackwell: minister & suffragette ➤
May 20, 1825 - Nov. 5, 1921

Blackwell was the first woman ordained in the U.S., but she was also widely known as an abolitionist and an advocate for women's rights. She preached and lectured throughout the country in an era when women were not thought of as equal to men. Blackwell graduated from Oberlin College, then studied theology there and took up the ministry. She also wrote for newspapers and magazines, authored books, got married and had seven children. She served as president of the New Jersey Suffrage Association and lived long enough to vote for president in 1920 after the enactment of the 19th Amendment.

LIVED: 1 Market St., above High; 150 Orange St.

⤳ Vivian Blaine: actress & singer ⤶
Nov. 11, 1921 - Dec. 9, 1995

Born "Vivian Stapleton," Blaine began singing for pay while in elementary school. By age 14, she was performing with orchestras and, after graduating from South Side H.S., toured with dance bands. In 1942, Blaine moved to Hollywood and appeared in a number of films. She debuted on Broadway as "Adelaide" in the 1950 musical *Guys and Dolls*, later reprising the role in the 1955 film version with Marlon Brando. Blaine continued making movies and also recorded for Decca and Mercury records. She appeared on TV as well and had a recurring role in the *Mary Hartman, Mary Hartman* series.

LIVED: 220 Van Buren St.; 77 Mount Prospect Ave.

⤳ Ruggiero "Richie the Boot" Boiardo: gangster ⤶
Dec. 8, 1890 - Nov. 17, 1984

Born in Italy, Boiardo came to the U.S. with his family, stopping first in Chicago before relocating to Newark in his late teens. He began his criminal career as a bookmaker but, during Prohibition, turned to bootlegging, butting heads with Newark's other major crime boss, "Longy" Zwillman, and survived a mob hit. After Zwillman's death, Boiardo was the undisputed king of the city's underworld. He was a Genovese crime family captain, had close ties with mob kingpin Lucky Luciano and served prison time. He also courted the press and came to be referred to in the papers of the day as just plain "Richie."

LIVED: 35 Newark Ave.; 242 Broad St.

⤳ Albert Boni: publisher ⤶
Oct. 21, 1892 - July 31, 1981

When Boni died, *The New York Times* called him "one of the historic and flamboyant figures in American publishing." He grew up in Newark, went to Barringer H.S. and gave up finishing college to enter business with an avant-garde bookstore in New York and the sale of classics in *The Little Leather Library* series. With Horace Liveright, he published the *Modern Library* series and works by some of the world's great authors. He and his brother launched a mail-order book program in 1929 called *Boni Paper Books*. In 1950, he created Readex, which printed books in a vastly reduced format.

LIVED: 104 Emmet St.; 116 Spruce St.

⚘ Cory A. Booker: mayor & U.S. senator ⚘
April 27, 1969 -

In the final year of his second term as Newark mayor, Booker won a special election for an open U.S. Senate seat from New Jersey and was re-elected in 2014. He grew up in Harrington Park, NJ, and earned bachelor and master's degrees from Stanford. He spent a year at Oxford as a Rhodes scholar and went to Yale Law School. Booker was elected to the Newark City Council from the Central Ward in 1998, lost a bid for mayor in 2002 but won the job in 2006. He was re-elected in 2010. He is best known for his use of social media to promote his causes and for his many TV appearances.

LIVED: Brick Towers Apts., 685-715 King Blvd.; 435 Hawthorne Ave.

⚘ Elisha Boudinot: lawyer, judge & patriot ⚘
Jan. 2, 1749 - Oct. 17, 1819

Brother of a president of the Continental Congress and head of the U.S. Mint, Boudinot studied and practiced law in Newark. He served as associate judge of the New Jersey Supreme Court from 1798 to 1804. Boudinot was a supporter of the Revolution and had a position of leadership in Newark's patriotic movement. As such, he entertained the likes of George Washington, Alexander Hamilton and the Marquis de Lafayette at his home, one of Newark's grandest mansions. He was president of Newark's first bank and also a trustee of the College of New Jersey, now Princeton University.

LIVED: 74 Park Place

⚘ Seth Boyden: inventor ⚘
Nov. 17, 1788 - March 31, 1870

Boyden was hailed by none other than Thomas Edison as one of America's great inventors, and his inventions fueled Newark's industrial rise in the 19th century. He was born in Massachusetts and came to Newark in 1815 because the city was a leather center. Boyden developed a process for making patent leather, invented a machine that cut the cost of making nails and introduced malleable iron. He also helped develop the telegraph, improved the steam engine, made one of America's first daguerreotypes and even created a strawberry hybrid. There is a statue of him in the center of Washington Park.

LIVED: 93 Lackawanna Ave.; 518 High St.; 60 Sheffield Drive

Home of Seth Boyden
93 Lackawanna Ave.

～ Joseph P. Bradley: U.S. Supreme Court justice ～
March 14, 1813 - Jan. 22, 1892

Bradley grew up in upstate New York but graduated from Rutgers. He studied law in Newark and was admitted to the bar in 1839. He spent 30 years practicing patent and railroad law, earning a national reputation as a commercial litigator. After losing a bid for a congressional seat, Bradley was nominated to the Supreme Court by President Grant and confirmed in March 1870. He served for 21 years. He cast the decisive vote on the commission that decided the disputed 1876 presidential election, making Rutherford B. Hayes president. A public housing complex in Newark was named for him.

LIVED: 131, 251 & 534 Broad St.; 1 Park Place

～ William J. Brennan Jr.: U.S. Supreme Court justice ～
April 25, 1906 - July 24, 1997

Brennan was the son of Irish immigrants who graduated from Barringer H.S., the University of Pennsylvania and Harvard Law School. Appointed to the Supreme Court by President Eisenhower, Brennan served on the high court from 1956 until 1990, authoring more than 1,300 opinions. He played a key role on the Warren Court in expanding the rights of individuals. He had previously served as a Superior Court and appellate court judge in New Jersey and was also a member of the N.J. Supreme Court. There is a bronze statue of him in front of the Hall of Records on King Boulevard in Newark.

LIVED: 119 N. Munn Ave.

～ William J. Brennan Sr.: labor leader & city commissioner ～
Dec. 26, 1872 - May 14, 1930

Brennan was born in County Roscommon, Ireland, and came to the U.S. in 1892. A Democrat, he was elected city commissioner in Newark four times, beginning in 1917. Twice he got the most votes. Brennan directed the Public Safety Department as city commissioner and had to enforce Prohibition. He also set up Newark's first family court and traffic court. Before entering politics, Brennan served as president of a union local and the Essex Trades Council. He was also on the executive board of the New Jersey Federation of Labor. Thousands viewed his body laid out in Newark City Hall upon his death.

LIVED: 155 Alexander St.; 212 1/2 Parker St.; 119 Munn Ave.

Home of William J. Brennan Jr.

119 Munn Ave.

➤ Fanny Brice: comedian, actress & singer ⤙
Oct. 29, 1891 - May 29, 1951

Born "Fania Borach," Brice was a stage, radio and film star in the first half of the twentieth century. She came to Newark as an infant with her parents, who were saloon keepers. The family stayed in Newark until around 1906. Brice went to school in Newark and credited the local theater with giving her the acting bug. She worked in burlesque and headlined the Ziegfeld Follies. *My Man* was her signature song, and it earned her a posthumous Grammy. Brice was also famous for her radio role of "Baby Snooks." Barbra Streisand played Brice in the Broadway play and film *Funny Girl*, winning an Academy Award.

LIVED: 78 William St.; 26 Lafayette St.

➤ Claude Brown: author ⤙
Feb. 23, 1937 - Feb. 2, 2002

Brown wrote *Manchild in the Promised Land*, one of the twentieth century's seminal books about growing up black in America. The book was praised by great writers and sold millions of copies after its release in 1965. But Brown failed to follow up on its success and published only one other book, though he did write essays and magazine articles. He also lectured and spent time mentoring students, helping them further their educations. Brown took his degree from Howard and attended law school. He avoided the limelight and spent many years living in Newark without people knowing who he was.

LIVED: The Pavilion, 138-162 King Blvd., #1605

➤ Victor J. "Buddy" Brown: promoter & roller skating enthusiast ⤙
1897 - Dec. 23, 1968

After operating Dreamland Park, Brown built the New Dreamland Arena in Newark, earning a reputation as the father of roller skating in America. He was a founder and first president of a national organization of rink operators formed in 1937 to regulate the sport of roller skating. The group became the Roller Skating Association International, and its annual rink operator of the year award is named in Brown's honor. He also labored to broaden skating's appeal as a form of family entertainment. In 1994, Brown was inducted into the USA Roller Sports Hall of Fame for distinguished service to skating.

LIVED: 25 Van Velsor Place; 18 Foster St.

Fanny Brice

✐ Mary B. Burch: teacher & social activist ✐
Aug. 5, 1906 - Aug. 12, 2001

Burch was born in Pennsylvania, graduated from Shippensburg State College and taught in Camden before moving to Newark in 1946. She and her husband, Reynold, an obstetrician, founded the Leaguers Inc. in their basement in 1949 to benefit the city's youth. It later expanded its services at six sites to include everyone from preschoolers to seniors. They also ran a summer camp in Maine. Burch was a founder of Essex County College and served on its board. The school's auditorium is named for her, as is a dorm at Kean University. She was awarded an honorary doctorate by Seton Hall.

LIVED: 102 S. 14th St.; 260 Meeker Ave.; 850 S. 11th St.

✐ Dr. William Burnet: physician & legislator ✐
Dec. 13, 1730 - Oct. 7, 1791

Burnet graduated from Princeton and studied medicine in New York before setting up a practice in Newark. He was a surgeon in the Continental Army, then started and served as superintendent of a military hospital in Newark. From 1776-83, he was surgeon general for the Eastern District of the U.S. Burnet was elected to the Continental Congress and was appointed Essex County's first judge. He also headed the New Jersey Medical Society. One of his sons, David, served as the first governor of the Republic of Texas, while another son, Jacob, is referred to as the "Father of the Ohio Constitution."

LIVED: 1020 Broad Street, Symphony Hall site

✐ Aaron Burr Jr.: vice president of the U.S. ✐
Feb. 6, 1756 - Sept. 14, 1836

Burr was born in Newark and barely walking when his parents died in successive years, leaving him an orphan. In 1772, he graduated from Princeton, where his father had been president. While most famous for his fatal 1804 gun duel with Alexander Hamilton, Burr was a lawyer in New York and had a distinguished public service career. He was a Continental Army officer during the Revolutionary War and a member of the Assembly, state attorney general and U.S. senator in and from New York. Burr served as the country's third vice president during Thomas Jefferson's first term as U.S. president.

LIVED: Broad & William streets, southwest corner

⌐ Rev. Aaron Burr Sr.: clergyman & educator ⌐
Jan. 4, 1716 - Sept. 24, 1757

Burr was born in Connecticut to a wealthy landowner. He studied for the divinity at Yale and became a Presbyterian minister in Newark, while also conducting a school for classical studies. He was a founder of the College of New Jersey, now Princeton. Burr served as the school's second president and remained 10 years until his early death. In his term, the college moved to Princeton from Newark. He was largely responsible for organizing Princeton into a school and traveled to raise money to keep it growing. Burr oversaw the construction of historic Nassau Hall, Princeton's best known building.

LIVED: Broad & William streets, southwest corner

⌐ Stephen Burrows, pioneering fashion designer ⌐
Sept. 15, 1943 -

Burrows attended elementary and high school in Newark before studying art and fashion in Philadelphia and New York. He began designing clothes in the mid-1960s and, by the '70s, was the first globally successful African-American designer. He was also one of five designers chosen to represent the U.S. at the historic "Battle of Versailles" fashion show in France in 1973 that broke color barriers. Burrows has won several Coty awards, one of the fashion world's most prestigious honors, while he and his work have been the subject of books, documentaries and exhibitions in the U.S. and Europe.

LIVED: 89 & 91 Bergen St.

⌐ William J. Campbell: TV & movie actor ⌐
Oct. 30, 1923 - April 28, 2011

Campbell is best remembered for his *Star Trek* TV and movie roles, most notably as a Klingon captain in the "The Trouble With Tribbles" episode. He broke into films in 1950, played the lead in a 1955 movie based on the life of Caryl Chessman and was the first person to sing opposite Elvis Presley in a film (*Love Me Tender*). His other movies included *The Naked and the Dead* and cult classics *Dementia 13* and *Blood Bath*. He also appeared on TV in shows such as *Gunsmoke, Perry Mason* and *Bonanza*. His first wife was Judith Exner, who later was a mistress of President John F. Kennedy.

LIVED: 357 Peshine Ave,; 191 Chadwick Ave.

⤛ Robinson Cano: Yankee & Mariner second baseman ⤜
Oct. 22, 1982 -

Cano was born in the Dominican Republic but lived in Newark for several years after his family moved to the U.S. His father had briefly been a Major League pitcher. Cano attended public school in Newark, including Barringer H.S. for a year, before the family returned to the Dominican. He signed with the Yankees in 2001 and made his big league debut in 2005. He was an all-star second baseman in 2006 and from 2010 through 2014, and won Golden Glove awards in 2010 and 2012. He was a member of the Yankees' world championship team in 2009 and MVP of the 2013 World Baseball Classic.

LIVED: 513 N. 6th St.

⤛ Lillie Mae "Betty Carter" Jones: jazz vocalist ⤜
May 16, 1929 - Sept. 26, 1998

Carter was one of the jazz world's pre-eminent singers. She began singing at 16 and joined Lionel Hampton's orchestra a couple years later in 1948. But by 1951, she'd decided to strike out on her own and moved to the New York area. Carter recorded for more than a half dozen labels in her career, one of them her own. She won a Grammy, was chosen *Down Beat's* female jazz singer of the year multiple times and was named an "American Jazz Master" by the National Endowment for the Arts. Known for nurturing young talent, she was awarded a National Medal of the Arts by President Clinton in 1997.

LIVED: 881 S. 15th St.; 139 Goodwin St.

⤛ Robert L. Carter: civil rights activist, lawyer & judge ⤜
March 11, 1917 - Jan. 3, 2012

Carter was born in Florida but moved to Newark with his mother while an infant. He attended Barringer but graduated from East Orange H.S. He took his undergraduate degree from Lincoln, his law degree from Howard and an advanced legal degree from Columbia. After military service in World War II, he joined the NAACP and was part of many landmark civil rights cases, including *Brown v. Board of Ed.* Carter took over for Thurgood Marshall as NAACP general counsel in 1956 but left in protest in 1968. He was named a federal judge in New York in 1972 and remained in the job until his death.

LIVED: 104 Boyden St.

Betty Carter

✎ Michael Caruso: champion wrestler ✎
May 23, 1946 -

Caruso's record as a high school wrestler at St. Benedict's was 81-0 and included three national prep championships. He graduated in 1963. From Newark, he went to Lehigh and compiled a 57-1 record, winning three consecutive NCAA wrestling championships at 123 pounds in the process. His only loss was to an opponent from West Point. Caruso graduated from Lehigh in 1967. He is a member of the National Collegiate Wrestling Hall of Fame, the U.S. Amateur Wrestling Hall of Fame and the Lehigh Hall of Fame. St. Benedict's hosts a wrestling tournament named in his honor.

LIVED: 363 Clifton Ave.

✎ Gerardo "Jerry" Catena: mob boss ✎
Jan. 8, 1902 - April 23, 2000

Catena was one of the highest ranking members of organized crime in New Jersey's history. He not only ran the Genovese crime family's operation in New Jersey, he was an acting boss when Vito Genovese was imprisoned and after his death. The son of Italian immigrants, Catena was born and spent his early years in Newark before moving elsewhere in Essex County. His first arrest was for gambling in 1923, but it wasn't his last, and he also spent time in prison. He attended the notorious mob convention in Apalachin, NY, in 1957. Catena preferred a low profile and lived quietly in Florida at life's end.

LIVED: 91 Delancy St.; 847 S. 18th St.; 176 Oliver St.; 284 Van Buren St.

✎ Peter A. Cavicchia: congressman & lawyer ✎
May 22, 1879 - Sept. 11, 1968

Cavicchia was born in Italy and came to the U.S. with his parents in 1888. He graduated from the American International College in Springfield, MA, and then studied law at NYU. He was admitted to the bar in 1908 and began practicing in Newark a year later. He also taught law and served on the Newark Board of Education for 14 years. A Republican, Cavicchia was elected to Congress three times, serving from 1931 to 1937. After losing a re-election bid, he returned to Newark to resume his legal practice. He also served as chairman of the city's Central Planning Board from 1946 to 1957.

LIVED: 108 Jefferson St.; 81 Longfellow Ave.; 140 Roseville Ave.

～ Richard A. "Rick" Cerone: Major League catcher ～
May 18, 1954 -

Cerone was born in Newark and played football and baseball at Essex Catholic H.S. He was an All-American catcher at Seton Hall. The Cleveland Indians made him the seventh overall pick in the 1975 amateur baseball draft, and he played for eight Major League teams in a 17-year career, including the New York Yankees and Mets. His career batting average was .245, with 59 home runs and 436 RBIs. His best year was with the Yankees in 1980, when he batted .277 in 147 games. Cerone was the original owner of the Newark Bears in the independent Atlantic League before selling to new owners in 2003.

LIVED: 322 & 332 Clifton Ave.

～ Diaz Victor "Dean" Cetrullo: fencer, actor, educator ～
Feb. 24, 1919 - May 9, 2010

Cetrullo was born in Newark into a family of accomplished fencers. He was a fencing star at Barringer H.S. and earned All-American honors at Seton Hall, finishing his career with 96 straight victories. He won a bronze medal at the 1948 London Olympics and several national championships. While serving in Europe with the Army Air Force in World War II, Cetrullo was shot down over enemy territory and escaped a German POW camp. He acted on Broadway, was the subject of a *Hardy Boys* mystery, was a grade school teacher and principal and also coached high school and college fencing.

LIVED: 113 Bloomfield Ave.; 234 Mount Prospect Ave.

～ Raymond G. Chambers: businessman & philanthropist ～
Aug. 7, 1942 -

Chambers was born and raised in Newark, graduating from West Side H.S. He earned an accounting degree from Rutgers-Newark in 1964 and later an MBA at Seton Hall. With partner William Simon, he made a fortune on Wall Street in leveraged buyouts before becoming one of the country's leading philanthropists. No one has invested more time, money and energy across a wider spectrum in improving Newark and its prospects for the future than Chambers. Education, sports, health care, business, religion, the arts and children's causes are some of the many areas to benefit from his generosity.

LIVED: 518 S. 20th St.

⟫⟫ Rear Adm. Alfred W. Chandler: presidential dentist ⟪⟪
June 17, 1890 - Sept. 24, 1978

Chandler graduated from Barringer H.S., where he excelled in sports and was captain of a state championship basketball team. He got a degree from the University of Pennsylvania dental school and was commissioned a U.S. naval officer in 1917. Chandler served on board the USS Saratoga and the USS Relief, the Navy's first hospital ship, and also at the U.S. Naval Academy. He was later named the Navy's senior dental officer and worked on the teeth of Presidents Coolidge, Hoover and Roosevelt. In the 1960s, he served as the president of the American Academy of the History of Dentistry.

LIVED: 717 Highland Ave.

⟫⟫ John M. Chapman: bicycle racer & promoter ⟪⟪
May 24, 1877 - March 20, 1947

Nicknamed "The Georgia Cyclone," Chapman was a champion cyclist, setting one world record that lasted 50 years. He later turned to organizing races and became cycling's leading promoter at a time when it was one of America's most popular sports. Chapman ran velodromes in Newark and New York and promoted annual six-day international races at Madison Square Garden, where he also served as assistant manager. For more than 20 years, he was president of the National Cycling Association, the country's pro circuit. He was inducted into the U.S. Bicycling Hall of Fame in 1993.

LIVED: 60 N. Munn Ave.; 82 Bleeker St.; 747 South Orange Ave.

⟫⟫ Christopher J. "Chris" Christie: governor & U.S. Attorney ⟪⟪
Sept. 6, 1962 -

Christie spent his early years in Newark before his family moved to the suburbs. He graduated from the University of Delaware and Seton Hall Law School and then headed into private practice. He served as a Morris County freeholder from 1995-98. Christie spent almost seven years as U.S. Attorney for N.J., gaining a national reputation for sending corrupt public officials to prison. He was elected governor in 2009 and re-elected in 2013. He almost ran for president in 2012 but delivered the keynote address at the GOP national convention instead. In 2015, Christie declared for the nomination.

LIVED: 402 S. 14th St.

Gov. Christopher J. "Chris" Christie

⟫ Minna Citron: artist ⟪
Oct. 15, 1896 - Dec. 21, 1991

Citron was born in Newark and began studying art in her 20s after moving to Brooklyn. A painter and a printmaker, she was first known as a social or urban realist. She had her first solo show in 1930 in New York. Later, Citron taught art, painted murals as part of the Federal Art Project and turned to abstract art. She had many exhibitions in the U.S. and abroad, and her work was collected by many major museums, including those in New York and Washington, DC. Citron was an outspoken critic of male dominance in the art world and identified strongly with the feminist movement of the 1970s.

LIVED: 67 Chestnut St.; 161 Lincoln Ave.

⟫ Joseph "Joe" Clark: educator & motivational speaker ⟪
May 7, 1938 -

Clark grew up in Newark and attended Central H.S. After earning degrees from William Paterson and Seton Hall, he began teaching. Toting a bullhorn and bat, he gained notoriety in the 1980s for the strict discipline he imposed as principal of Paterson's Eastside H.S. Clark was profiled on *60 Minutes*, was on the cover of *Time* magazine and was publicly lauded by President Ronald Reagan. He was also the subject of the film *Lean On Me*, in which he was portrayed by actor Morgan Freeman. He left education for the lecture circuit and also served as head of Essex County's juvenile detention center.

LIVED: 66 Seymour Ave.; 119 Quitman St.

⟫ William Clark: thread manufacturer ⟪
1841 - July 7, 1902

Clark was born in Scotland, a descendant of the inventor of spool thread. He came to the U.S. with his brother George in 1861 to set up a branch of their family's thread-making business. They began in Newark in a small building on the Passaic River and eventually built mills on each side of the river that employed thousands. The Clark Thread Co. later became one of the biggest operations of its kind in the world, processing raw baled cotton into finished spooled thread. Clark used his fortune from the business to construct one of Newark's grandest mansions. He retired and returned to Scotland in 1897.

LIVED: 342 Mount Prospect Ave.

✒ Rev. Lester H. Clee: pastor & politician ✒
July 1, 1888 - March 15, 1962

Clee was a successful minister and legislator. He served as pastor of the Second Presbyterian Church in Newark for almost 25 years, ensuring its survival at a time when its future was in question. But he was also elected a state assemblyman and state senator and served as Assembly speaker. Clee was Republican candidate for governor in 1937 but lost, despite capturing 15 of the state's 21 counties. Later, he was head of the state Mediation Board and Civil Service Commission and was a member of the state Parole Board. Clee was a big supporter of Bloomfield College and served as its president.

LIVED: 294 Mount Prospect Ave.

✒ Clarence A. Clemons Jr.: E Street Band saxophonist ✒
Jan. 11, 1942 - June 18, 2011

Known as "The Big Man," Clemons played a key role in Bruce Springsteen's E Street Band from 1972 until he died. He also owned a club, recorded a few solo albums and performed with several other groups, including the Grateful Dead and Ringo Starr's All-Star Band. Clemons acted in some films, made a series of cameo TV appearances and, in 2009, published a semi-fictional autobiography. A native of Virginia's Tidewater area, Clemons was married and lived in Newark in the mid-1960s while he worked as a counselor at a boys' training school and played his instrument on the side in local bars.

LIVED: 54 Boyd St.

✒ George Clinton: singer & record producer ✒
July 22, 1941 -

Clinton was born in North Carolina but spent much of his teens and 20s in Newark. His breakthrough came with the group Parliament. But he made his name as an originator of funk music in the 1970s with his band Parliament-Funkadelic, a musical collaboration that had a bunch of hits and was known for its elaborate stage shows. Clinton went solo in the early 1980s and later worked with some of the biggest names in the music world on their projects and his own. He has appeared in film and on TV and lent his voice to video games. P-Funk was inducted into the Rock and Roll Hall of Fame in 1997.

LIVED: 597 Bergen St.

ᴥ Katherine Coffey: Newark Museum director ᴥ
May 5, 1900 - April 4, 1972

Coffey graduated from Barnard College and took a job with The Newark Museum in 1923 when it was housed in The Newark Public Library. She left but returned in 1925 and stayed, first as head of exhibitions and educational programs and later as director, until retiring in 1968. Coffey upgraded the museum's collection, was in charge of its apprentice program, expanded its education program and added a planetarium in 1953. Rutgers and Seton Hall awarded her honorary degrees, and a museum fund was set up in her honor. Also, one of the most important awards in museum work was named for her.

LIVED: 569 Mount Prospect Ave.

ᴥ Willie Cole Jr.: artist ᴥ
Jan. 3, 1955 -

Cole graduated from the School of Visual Arts in New York in 1976 and had made a name for himself in the art world by the next decade from a base in Newark. He started out as a graphic designer and illustrator before moving into what he refers to as "three-dimensional" art that others call sculpture or assemblage art. In that style, Cole turns discarded items such as irons and high-heeled shoes into elaborately crafted pieces reflecting the modern urban experience. He has exhibited throughout the world and won awards, including the David C. Driskell Prize. Many major museums have collected his work.

LIVED: 7 Lum Lane; 56 Richmond St.; 293 Leslie St.; 55 Walcott Terrace

ᴥ Dr. Abraham Coles: physician, author & poet ᴥ
Dec. 26, 1813 - May 3, 1891

Coles was a man of many talents. He taught Latin and math before studying for the law, which he gave up to become a doctor and a surgeon. He got his medical degree in 1835 and set up a practice in Newark a year later, gaining a reputation in the U.S. and abroad. He was president of the Medical Society of N.J. Coles became famous in literary circles for his translations. He also wrote hymns and was a published poet. He served with the Newark Board of Education, Newark Library Association and N.J. Historical Society among many other civic groups. There's a bronze bust of him in Washington Park.

LIVED: 37 1/2, 172 & 222 Market St.; 49 Hamilton St.

⟩⟩ Moses N. Combs: merchant & educator ⟨⟨
Jan. 2, 1754 - 1834

Combs was a successful tanner who concentrated on making shoes and was credited with being the first merchant to create a market for Newark goods outside the city. Thus his nickname, "The Father of Newark Industries." He also led the effort to improve roads and set up efficient systems of banking and insurance. An ordained minister, Combs opposed slavery and split from the Presbyterian order to set up his own church, using half of a building at Plane and Market streets for worship and the rest as a free school to educate his apprentices. Established in 1794, it was the first of its kind in the nation.

LIVED: 77 Market St.

⟩⟩ William F. Cone: photographer ⟨⟨
1874 - May 12, 1966

No one did a better job of documenting Newark and its people with a camera than William F. Cone, one of the city's first commercial photographers. He spent his entire adult life, starting around 1895, taking photographs of the city, everything from parades to store windows. His client list included local businesses of all sizes and the city of Newark, as well as civic and charitable groups. Cone began taking pictures at age 13 during the blizzard of 1888. He took an estimated 75,000 photos over his lifetime, roughly 14,000 of them on glass plates. His work has been exhibited at the N.J. Historical Society.

LIVED: 237 1/2 & 239 1/2 S. 8th St.; 330 Summer Ave.

⟩⟩ Franklin Conklin Jr.: businessman & civic leader ⟨⟨
June 23, 1886 - July 28, 1966

Conklin came to Newark as a child and left college early to work in and later head a paint and varnish company started by his father. He also devoted himself to community work. He was president of the Essex County Park Commission and The Newark Museum Association, and founder and first president of the board of the University of Newark, now Rutgers. He was vice president of the Newark YMCA, a trustee of the Newark Welfare Foundation, industry representative on the state Mediation Board and active in Scouting. Conklin Hall on Rutgers-Newark campus was named for him.

LIVED: 57 Johnson Ave.; 874 S. 13th St.; 767 Ridge St.

⤜ James Connolly: labor organizer & Irish nationalist ⤛
June 5, 1868 - May 12, 1916

Connolly is a revered figure in Irish history, for his efforts on behalf of workers and an Ireland free from British rule, but also because he died for his beliefs in the 1916 uprising. He was born in Scotland to Irish parents and was an active socialist there, in Ireland and abroad. He came to the U.S. in 1903 and lived in Newark for several years — writing, speaking and working at the Singer plant in Elizabeth. In 1910, Connolly resumed his work in the labor movement in Ireland. There are statues of him in the U.S. and Ireland, and he was named one of the hundred greatest Britons in a BBC production.

LIVED: 146 & 152 Hawthorne Ave.

⤜ Stephen Crane: novelist, journalist & short story writer ⤛
Nov. 1, 1871 - June 5, 1900

A Newark native whose father was a Methodist minister, Crane was a major writer of the nineteenth century best known for his 1895 Civil War novel, *The Red Badge of Courage*. But he wrote four other novels, poetry, short stories, newspaper articles and was a war correspondent. He traveled widely and led a colorful life, at times a controversial one as he turned from polite society to the rough-and-tumble world. Most of the time that Crane spent in Newark was as a boy, and he was gone by the time his first known story was published. Plagued by ill health, he died of tuberculosis in a German sanatorium.

LIVED: 14 Mulberry Place

⤜ Robert S. "Bob" Crewe: songwriter & record producer ⤛
Nov. 12, 1930 - Sept. 11, 2014

Crewe was a recording artist who achieved his greatest success writing for and producing others, most notably Frankie Valli and The Four Seasons. He also worked with Michael Jackson, Bobby Darin, Mitch Ryder, Patti LaBelle and Roberta Flack and had a hit of his own in the mid-1960s — *Music to Watch Girls By*. Crewe had his own recording labels, wrote for film and Broadway and is credited as the lyricist of the hit musical *Jersey Boys*. He was inducted into the Songwriters Hall of Fame in 1985 and later formed his own foundation to nurture young artists and to support LGBT issues.

LIVED: 8 Orleans St.; 241 Peshine Ave.; 305 Jelliff Ave.

Home of Stephen Crane (*Crane, inset*)
14 Mulberry Place

Charles F. Cummings: librarian & historian
June 27, 1937 - Dec. 21, 2005

Few have known more about Newark's history than Cummings, a transplanted Southerner who was a librarian at The Newark Public Library for more than 40 years. Cummings was also the city's official historian from 1988 until his death, serving in that position in an unofficial capacity for many years earlier. In the latter part of his life, he wrote a weekly column on Newark history for *The Star-Ledger*. A bronze bust of Cummings is located in the small park off Springfield Avenue next to Essex County's historic courthouse, and the public library's New Jersey Information Center was named for him.

LIVED: 15 Branch Brook Place.; 54 Richmond St.

John T. Cunningham: journalist & historian
June 26, 1915 - June 7, 2012

Cunningham was born and lived in Newark for a few years before his family moved and ended up in Morris County, where he began his writing career and remained most of his life. A graduate of Drew, he was hired by the *Newark Evening News* in 1939 and returned to the paper after Army Air Corps service during World War II. One of Cunningham's newspaper jobs was writing a column called "Let's Explore." He left *The News* in 1963 to become a full-time author and wrote more than 50 books, one of them about the history of Newark. He is one of New Jersey's most beloved historians.

LIVED: 363 5th; 335 N. 6th St.

Richard D. Currier: attorney & law school founder
1877 - June 2, 1947

Currier was a New York attorney who founded the New Jersey Law School in Newark and served as its first president, remaining 26 years. It was the state's first law school. He was a native of Connecticut who studied at Yale and got his law degree from the New York Law School. He also founded Dana College and the Seth Boyden School of Business in Newark. In 1935, they, along with the law school, were folded into the University of Newark, which was absorbed into Rutgers after World War II. Currier also wrote several legal textbooks and co-founded Stoneleigh College in Rye, NH.

LIVED: 33 E. Park St.; 11 Thomas St.

⤙ Robert Curvin: educator & civil rights leader ⤚
Feb. 23, 1934 - Sept. 29, 2015

Curvin was born in Newark, grew up in Belleville and returned to Newark, where he was active in many local and national organizations. He earned two degrees from Rutgers and a Ph.D. in politics from Princeton. An Army veteran, he led Newark's CORE chapter in the 1960s and helped Kenneth Gibson get elected Newark's mayor in 1970. Curvin taught at Brooklyn College and Rutgers, was a dean at the New School and served as a Ford Foundation executive. He was also a member of *The New York Times* editorial board and as well as a board member at Princeton, Channel 13 and NJPAC.

LIVED: 709 Hunterdon St.; 106 Huntington Terrace; 28 Reynolds Place

⤙ John Cotton Dana: librarian ⤚
Aug. 19, 1856 - July 21, 1929

A lawyer by education, Dana was one of America's pre-eminent librarians. He promoted the benefits of reading and argued forcefully for libraries to have a connection to the lives of the common man. Dana joined the Newark library in 1902 after heading libraries in Denver and Springfield, MA. In 1909, he founded The Newark Museum inside the library and was its first director. Dana served as a president of the American Library Association, which gives an award in his honor, and he is a member of the Library Hall of Fame. The main library at the Rutgers-Newark campus was named for him.

LIVED: 226 Mount Prospect Ave.; 330 Clifton Ave.; 821 DeGraw Ave.

⤙ Raymond E. Dandridge: Hall of Fame third baseman ⤚
Aug. 31, 1913 - Feb. 12, 1994

Dandridge joined the Negro Leagues after he was discovered playing ball in his hometown of Richmond, VA. He made his pro debut with the Detroit Stars in 1933 and later played for the Newark Eagles. Considered one of the best third baseman ever to play the game, Dandridge was a three-time Negro Leagues all-star who also spent nine years in the Mexican League. He ended his career playing Triple-A baseball, batting .360 in his final season while in his early 40s. Dandridge was a longtime resident of Newark who worked in recreation. He was elected to the National Baseball Hall of Fame in 1987.

LIVED: 267 Littleton Ave.

⋙ Louis N. Danzig: lawyer & public housing official ⋘
May 5, 1907 - April 27, 1982

Danzig was a powerful but controversial figure in Newark's urban renewal efforts in the mid-20th century, an era of turmoil for American cities. He was to Newark what Robert Moses was to New York. He graduated from Central H.S. and New Jersey Law School and studied housing elsewhere. Danzig joined the Newark Housing Authority in 1941, became manager of a new public housing complex a year later and was named NHA executive director in 1947. He served for 20 years under three mayors, pushing for federal aid for affordable housing and expanding programs to clear slums.

LIVED: 825 S. 10th St.; 63 Oriental St.; 162 Mapes Ave.; 330 Hobson St.

⋙ Frances Day: singer & actress ⋘
Dec. 16, 1907 - April 29, 1984

Day grew up in Vailsburg with last names of "Schenk" and "Rowalski," according to city records. She began her show business career as a cabaret performer in the U.S. but became wildly popular overseas as Britain's first sex symbol. Blonde and shapely in the pre-Marilyn Monroe era, she appeared in her first film in 1928 and made her stage debut in London in 1932. Day continued acting and singing into the 1960s. She was said to have had affairs with four royal princes and a future British prime minister. The famed playwright George Bernard Shaw wrote one of his final plays for her.

LIVED: 207 Seymour Ave.; 82 West End Ave.

⋙ Robert J. Del Tufo: attorney & prosecutor ⋘
Nov. 18, 1933 -

Del Tufo spent a good part of his career in high-level law enforcement posts. A graduate of Princeton and Yale Law School, he was a law clerk for New Jersey's chief justice and then served as an assistant prosecutor in Morris County. He was U.S. Attorney for New Jersey from 1977 to 1980 and state attorney general from 1990 to 1993, when he took a job in private practice. Del Tufo was director of the state Division of Criminal Justice and a State Commission of Investigation commissioner. He has taught, been a member or trustee of many organizations and ran for governor in 1985.

LIVED: 315 Park Ave.; 216 Elwood Ave.

Frances Day

✒ Brian DePalma: movie director ✒
Sept. 11, 1940 -

DePalma, whose father was a respected orthopedic surgeon and medical director of Columbus Hospital in Newark, began as a physics student before turning to film in graduate school. He made documentaries in the 1960s and, after moving to Hollywood in the 1970s, became one of the leading directors of his generation. Known for building suspense and not shying away from violence, DePalma has directed movies such as *Carrie; Blow Out; Dressed to Kill; Scarface; The Untouchables; Mission: Impossible; Bonfire of the Vanities* and *Carlito's Way*. He has continued making movies into his 70s.

LIVED: 533 Mount Prospect Ave.

✒ Albert "Al" DeRogatis: football player & broadcaster ✒
May 5, 1927 - Dec. 26, 1995

DeRogatis was born and raised in Newark and was all-state in football at Central H.S. He was an All-American tackle at Duke before being drafted by the Giants in 1949. He played four years, earning all-pro honors twice, until a chronic knee injury forced him to retire. DeRogatis then began a long career at the Prudential Insurance Co., starting in sales and rising to vice president. For 20 years, he was also a highly praised radio and TV color commentator for college and pro football games, working several Super Bowls. He was inducted into the College Football Hall of Fame in 1986.

LIVED: 459 N. 12th St.

✒ Hugh Devore: football coach ✒
Nov. 25, 1910 - Dec. 8, 1992

Devore was born and raised in Newark and excelled in sports at St. Benedict's Prep. He was recruited to play football at Notre Dame by Knute Rockne and played end, serving as co-captain his senior year. He then began a long career as a football coach. Devore was Notre Dame's head coach in 1945 and 1963 and also head coach at NYU, Providence, Dayton and St. Bonaventure. In the pros, he was head coach of the Philadelphia Eagles and an assistant with the Green Bay Packers and Houston Oilers. He ended his career in Houston working for a group that brought events to the Astrodome.

LIVED: 52 N. 10th St.

➤ Joseph N. "Joe D" DiVincenzo Jr.: Essex County executive ➤
May 17, 1953 -

DiVincenzo was born and grew up in Newark and graduated from Barringer H.S., where he excelled in football and baseball. In the early 1970s, he was a quarterback at Jersey City State College (now New Jersey City University) and was picked by the Detroit Wheels in the 1974 draft of the short-lived World Football League but never played. DiVincenzo was later a recreation official in Newark who began serving as an Essex County freeholder in 1990 and was president for eight of his 13 years on the board. He was first elected Essex County executive in 2002 and elected again in 2006, 2010 and 2014.

LIVED: 149 Parker St.

➤ Msgr. George H. Doane: Catholic priest, rector & chaplain ➤
Sept. 5, 1830 - Jan. 20, 1905

Doane was born in Boston, son of the Trinity Church minister later named Episcopalian bishop of New Jersey. He graduated from medical college in Philadelphia in 1850 but gave up medicine and became an Episcopalian deacon in Newark. He later converted and in 1857 was ordained a Catholic priest at Newark's St. Patrick's Pro-Cathedral, where he served as rector for almost 50 years. He was a Union Army chaplain in the Civil War. Doane championed the cause of the old, sick and poor and took on many civic causes, often in newspaper letters. There's a statue of him in Military Park.

LIVED: 17, 25 & 35 Bleeker St.

➤ Amzi Dodd: Mutual Benefit Head, vice-chancellor & judge ➤
March 2, 1823 - Jan. 22, 1913

When he died, Dodd was the dean of New Jersey's lawyers and had been head of Mutual Benefit for two decades, serving as general counsel after retiring. He'd also been the state's vice-chancellor, a judge on New Jersey's highest court, clerk of the Newark Common Council and a state legislator. A descendant of one of Newark's founders, Dodd graduated from Princeton in 1841 and taught in Virginia before entering the law. He was admitted to the bar in 1848 and had a private practice. He was active in the formation of the Republican Party and campaigned for Abraham Lincoln as a party leader.

LIVED: 3 Park Place; 16 & 18 Cedar St.

⤳ Mary Mapes Dodge: author ⤨
Jan. 26, 1830- Aug. 21, 1905

Dodge and her family moved to Newark from New York in 1847. After her husband died eight years into their marriage, she relocated to her family's farm in what is now Weequahic Park to begin writing and working with her father publishing two magazines. She contributed to magazines such as *Harper's Weekly* and *The Atlantic Monthly*. Her first book was published in 1864. The next one, *Hans Brinker, or The Silver Skates*, was a bestseller and is today considered a classic of children's literature. Later, Dodge served as an editor of *Hearth and Home* and *St. Nicholas*, a children's magazine.

LIVED: Mapes Model Farm, near Renner and Elizabeth avenues

⤳ John J. "Jack" Dreyfus: mutual fund pioneer ⤨
Aug. 28, 1913 - March 27, 2009

Dreyfus and his family moved in with his mother's parents in Newark when he was a boy after his father's candy business in Alabama had failed. His grandfather owned a company in Newark that made the popular "John Ruskin" cigar. A Lehigh graduate, he bounced around in jobs until making his fortune selling mutual funds directly to the public, the company's TV ads famous for showing a lion leaving a Wall Street subway station. *Barron's* ranked Dreyfus the second most significant money manager of the twentieth century. He was also a champion bridge player and owned a racing stable.

LIVED: 48 Shanley Ave.

⤳ John F. Dryden: Prudential founder & U.S. senator ⤨
Aug. 7, 1839 - Nov. 24, 1911

Dryden was born in Maine, grew up in Massachusetts and came to Newark when he was 34 to found an insurance company to deal in industrial risks. Thus were the origins of the Prudential Insurance Co., which started in the basement of a Newark bank and grew into a worldwide corporation. For the first six years, Dryden was the firm's secretary, but he served as its president from 1881 until his death. He was also involved in setting up and managing financial institutions and street railways in New Jersey, New York and Pennsylvania. He served as a U.S. senator from New Jersey from 1902-07.

LIVED: 38 1/2 Walnut St.; 1020 Broad St.

⤞ William J. Dudley: footwear company founder ⤝
c1830 - March 1, 1881

Dudley came from England and was the founder of the Johnston & Murphy Shoe Co. that operated in Newark from 1850 until 1957 before moving to Nashville, TN. It started off making men's shoes and children's footwear. By 1870, the company was making 150,000 pairs of shoes a year; in three years, that number had doubled and firemen's boots, dress pumps and slippers were added to the line. In 1891, the "Johnston & Murphy" name was copyrighted. In its heyday, the company in Newark employed hundreds who made 50,000 pairs of shoes a week for a clientele that included presidents and celebrities.

LIVED: 281 & 397 Market St.; 24 Chestnut St.; 344 Broad St.

⤞ John Clement Dunn: career diplomat ⤝
Dec. 27, 1890 - April 10, 1979

Dunn enjoyed a long and remarkable career in the U.S. Foreign Service. He was ambassador to Brazil, France, Italy and Spain, U.S. charge d'affaires in Haiti and also assistant secretary of state for European, Far Eastern, Near Eastern and African Affairs. He studied the law and architecture but turned his attention to diplomatic service after serving in the Navy in World War I. Dunn was also chief of protocol in Washington, DC, settling delicate social disputes at high levels of government. At the end of World War II, he had key roles in peace conferences in Berlin, Paris, London and New York.

LIVED: 7 S. 9th St.; 13 N. 7th St.

⤞ Asher B. Durand: engraver & painter ⤝
Aug. 21, 1796 - Sept. 17, 1886

Durand began working in Newark as a teenager engraving book illustrations for the well-known Peter Maverick. He spent five years as an apprentice to Maverick and became so adept that Maverick later made him his partner. From engraving, Durand moved to oil painting, first with portraits of U.S. Presidents and other prominent Americans and then with landscapes. His nature paintings helped define the celebrated Hudson River School. His 1848 work, *Kindred Spirits,* sold for $35 million in 2005. He founded what became the National Academy of Design and was its second president.

LIVED: Drift Road, Woodside (North Newark)

🐛 Florence P. Eagleton: women's advocate & philanthropist 🐛
April 16, 1870 - Nov. 22, 1956

Eagleton spent her life advocating for women on issues from health care to voting rights to education. The daughter of a shoe dealer, she served as a Rutgers trustee for years and also helped organize the New Jersey College for Women. She was a leader in the suffragist movement, president of the Newark chapter of the N.J. League of Women Voters and first vice president of the state league. In her will, Eagleton left more than $1 million to set up a foundation in her name and that of her second husband, a noted surgeon in Newark. The money funded today's Eagleton Institute of Politics at Rutgers.

LIVED: 212 Elwood Ave.; 27 Rector St.; 39 LaGrange Place

🐛 Thomas A. Edison: inventor 🐛
Feb. 11, 1847 - Oct. 18, 1931

None other than Henry Ford said Edison was the person most responsible for the industrial age, and much of Edison's early work was in Newark. He came to Newark at 23 and set up shops for experiments and manufacturing. It was in Newark that he concluded electricity could pass through space, leading to the invention of the telegraph and radio, and perfected the forerunner of the copy machine. Edison moved in 1876, leaving for history to decide whether the life-changing discoveries he made later in Menlo Park and West Orange would have been possible without the knowledge he had gained in Newark.

LIVED: 854 Broad St.; 53 & 97 Wright St.; 65 Bank St.

🐛 Sherman Edwards: actor, pianist & songwriter 🐛
April 4, 1919 - March 30, 1981

Edwards wrote the music and lyrics for *1776*, a play about the country's founding fathers that ran on Broadway for more than 1,000 performances and won a Tony for best musical. He put himself through college playing the piano, served in World War II, taught history at Weequahic H.S. and then resumed a show business career that included acting and orchestra work. Edwards wrote pop songs at the Brill Building in the late 1950s and early 1960s. His hits included *Wonderful, Wonderful, See You in September* and *Flaming Star*, recorded by Elvis Presley for a movie of the same name.

LIVED: 14 Stuyvesant Ave.; 519 Clinton Place

Shop of Thomas Edison
Ward St.

⤳ Thomas Dunn English: physician, author & congressman ⤝
June 28, 1819 - April 1, 1902

English was born in Philadelphia and studied medicine and law before deciding on a career writing and editing. He wrote poems, stories, novels and plays and edited journals. He is best known for his 1843 poem *Ben Bolt,* which was printed in a New York newspaper before it was turned into a popular song. English moved to Newark in 1858 and was a member of the state Assembly in 1863-64. He also spent two terms as congressman. When his political days were over, he returned to Newark to resume his literary career. He had a lengthy feud with Edgar Allen Poe that included a fistfight.

LIVED: 57 State St.; 494 Washington St.; 311 1/2 High St.

⤳ Viola W. "Miss Rhapsody" Evans: jazz, blues & gospel singer ⤝
Dec. 14, 1902 - Dec. 22, 1984

Evans was born in Newark and had a singing career that began in her late teens and lasted six decades. By the 1930s, she was a headliner and toured the country, sometimes sharing top billing with the likes of Count Basie, Nat "King" Cole and Pearl Bailey. She performed in Kansas City in the heyday of Swing and was a regular at the clubs on New York's famed 52nd Street. In the 1970s, Evans performed with the Harlem Blues and Jazz Band, toured Europe and was the subject of a French documentary. She also recorded and appeared at clubs and festivals right up until several weeks before her death.

LIVED: 21 Scott St.; 801 N. 6th St., #1209

⤳ Gustave A. "Gus" Falzer: sportswriter & broadcaster ⤝
July 21, 1884 - Jan. 27, 1953

By the time Falzer graduated from Newark High School in 1902, he was already covering sports for the local papers, something he continued to do for the next 50 years. He worked for four papers in his career and became the dean of New Jersey sportswriters. He was best known for his coverage of high school sports and was one of the founders of the NJSIAA, the body that governs high school sports in the state. On Oct. 5, 1921, Falzer broadcast the first play-by-play radio account of a World Series game. The following year, he did the first coast-to-coast radio broadcast of a college football game.

LIVED: 219 Peshine Ave.; 792 S. 15th St.; 32 Elizabeth Ave.

✎ Gil Fates: TV game show host & producer ✎
Sept. 29, 1914 - May 1, 2000

Born "Joseph Gilbert Faatz," Fates graduated from West Side H.S. and the University of Virginia, where he studied drama. He began his career in the theater but then got interested in TV and went to work for CBS. Right before World War II, he served as the host of the *CBS Television Quiz*, TV's first regular game show. Fates returned to TV after the war, covering sports and elections and hosting other programs. He later produced game shows, among them *To Tell the Truth; Beat the Clock; I've Got a Secret* and *What's My Line?* He also wrote a book about the history of *What's My Line?*

LIVED: 422 Lafayette St.; 5 Howell Place; 5 Kenmore Ave.

✎ Christian W. Feigenspan: beer baron ✎
Dec. 7, 1876 - Feb. 7, 1939

Feigenspan took over the beer business his German-born father had founded in Newark after the Civil War, added to its holdings and became one of the nation's most highly regarded brewers. He went into the business right after graduating from Cornell and later also got involved in banking. Feigenspan felt Prohibition wouldn't last and contested the ban in the courts, never turning off his local brewery's "Pride of Newark" sign. A key U.S. Supreme Court Prohibition case carries his name. He was head of the U.S. Brewers Association and a trustee and major benefactor of the University of Newark.

LIVED: 39 Belmont Ave.; 121 Clinton Ave.; 53 Lincoln Park

✎ Leslie A. Fiedler: literary critic ✎
March 8, 1917 - Jan. 29, 2003

Fiedler wrote novels, stories and essays but is remembered most for his literary criticism, notably the book *Love and Death in the American Novel*. He took a Ph.D. from the University of Wisconsin-Madison and then began a life of teaching, lecturing and writing in the U.S. and abroad. Fiedler won several major awards for his contributions to the study of literature and was elected to the American Academy of Arts and Letters. He turned his focus to the criticism of pop culture in the 1970s and often appeared on TV. In 1997, he received a National Book Critics Circle lifetime achievement award.

LIVED: 60 Wolcott Terrace; 232 Jelliff Ave.

✿ Ted Fio Rito: pianist, orchestra leader & composer ✿
Dec. 20, 1900 - July 21, 1971

"Teodorico Salvatore Fiorito" was born in Newark and attended Barringer H.S. By his late teens, he was working in a New York recording studio. In 1921, he moved to Chicago and quickly became a band leader, performing locally and touring. He did his first radio remote in 1924 and before long was reaching a national audience. Fio Rito also appeared in films and on TV. He composed more than 100 songs and recorded for the Columbia, Victor, Brunswick and Decca labels. His two No. 1 hits were *My Little Grass Shack* and *I'll String Along with You*. He performed right up until he passed away.

LIVED: 293 15th Ave.; 185 Bruce St.

✿ Robert "Ruby Robert" Fitzsimmons: heavyweight champ ✿
May 26, 1863 - Oct. 22, 1917

Fitzsimmons won titles in three weight classes, including heavyweight, and is considered one of boxing's all-time great fighters. He was born in England and came to the U.S. after first relocating to Australia. He fought and gave exhibitions all over the country, including in Newark. But Newark was more than just another stop on the circuit for him. Fitzsimmons married and lived with his second wife in Newark and was around seemingly all the time for years. Later in life, he tried to marry his fourth and final wife in Newark but was denied when he couldn't produce proof he had divorced his third one.

LIVED: 204 Hunterdon St.; 64 Market St.

✿ E. Alma Flagg: teacher & school administrator ✿
Sept. 16, 1918 -

Flagg was born in Virginia and settled with her family in Newark. She graduated from East Side H.S. and Newark State College, got a master's from Montclair State and a doctorate from Columbia University's Teachers College. Flagg began teaching in Washington, DC, but returned to Newark in 1943, teaching and serving as a school administrator throughout the city. She was Newark's first black female school principal and later served as an assistant superintendent. Teachers College gave her its distinguished alumni award in 1986, the year after a school in Newark was named in her honor.

LIVED: 71 Kinney St.; 44 Stengel Ave.; 67 Vaughan Dr.; 61 Brunswick St.

Bob "Ruby Robert" Fitzsimmons

⌒ Armando Fontoura: Newark cop & Essex County sheriff ⌒
April 25, 1942 -

Fontoura was born in Portugal and moved to the U.S. with his family in 1954. After attending Newark schools and graduating from Newark State Teachers College, he began teaching. He joined the Newark police force in 1967, rising to the rank of captain and chief assistant to the director. He was appointed an Essex County undersheriff in 1986 and sheriff four years later, presiding over the state's largest and most active sheriff's department. With subsequent election victories, Fontoura became Essex County's longest serving sheriff. He's also been a commissioner of the N.J. Sports Authority.

LIVED: 83 McWhorter St.; 156 Lafayette St.

⌒ Dr. Albert Forsythe: physician & aviation pioneer ⌒
Feb. 25, 1897 - May 6, 1986

Forsythe was born in the Bahamas and came to the U.S. in 1912 to study at the Tuskegee Institute. He earned his medical degree at McGill University in Montreal and practiced in Atlantic City for many years. From 1933-35, he and C. Alfred Anderson undertook a series of historic flights to prove blacks could fly as well as whites, earning a parade in Newark. They were the first blacks to complete a cross-country trip. After a crash on a Caribbean and South America trip, he returned to medicine and later moved his practice to Newark, retiring in 1977. He is a member of the New Jersey Aviation Hall of Fame.

LIVED: The Colonnade, 51 Clifton Ave., #901

⌒ Connie Francis: singer ⌒
Dec. 12, 1938 -

Francis was born "Concetta Maria Franconero" in Newark and attended Arts H.S. before her family moved to Belleville. She began singing and playing the accordion as a child and appeared on Arthur Godfrey's TV show. She signed her first recording contract in 1955 at age 16 and became a major star within a few years. *Who's Sorry Now?* was the first of her many hits and the title of one of her autobiographies. With more than 70 LPs, Francis ranks as one of the biggest-selling female recording artists ever. She has been a guest star on countless TV shows, toured everywhere and acted on TV and in film.

LIVED: 228 Walnut St.; 466 Belmont Ave.

Connie Fransis

➤ Frederick T. Frelinghuysen: U.S. Secretary of State ◄
Aug. 4, 1817 - May 20, 1883

Frelinghuysen graduated from Rutgers College in New Brunswick in 1836, studied for the law, was admitted to the bar in 1839 and practiced in Newark. He was the city attorney and a member of the city council before serving as state attorney general. Frelinghuysen was elected to the U.S. Senate twice and twice lost re-election bids. In 1877, he returned to Newark to continue his legal practice. He turned down an appointment to be U.S. minister to England but did serve as secretary of state from 1881-85 under President Chester Arthur. He was also a longtime trustee of Rutgers College.

LIVED: 19 Washington St.; 7 & 18 Park Place

➤ Theodore Frelinghuysen: senator, college president & mayor ◄
March 28, 1787 - April 12, 1862

Frelinghuysen graduated from the College of New Jersey in 1804, studied for the law and was admitted to the bar in 1808. He practiced law in Newark, served as state attorney general and was elected to the U.S. Senate. He came back to Newark and was mayor from 1837-38. Frelinghuysen was Henry Clay's running mate in the 1844 presidential election. He became NYU's president before being named president of Rutgers College, serving from 1850 until 1862. Known as the "Christian Statesman," he opposed slavery, believed in temperance and was president of the American Bible Society.

LIVED: 31 Washington St.

➤ Felix Fuld: businessman & philanthropist ◄
July 19, 1868 - Jan. 20, 1929

Fuld was born in Germany and came to the U.S. at 14. His father was a banker, and he began his career as a traveling salesman. In 1893, he became partners with Louis Bamberger and together they built one of the country's great department stores in downtown Newark. They were also close friends, with Fuld marrying Bamberger's sister. Fuld was a patron of the arts who gave away millions to charity, hospitals, museums, scouting groups and Jewish causes. He served on the board of Prudential and several Jewish organizations. His memorial service was broadcast on the radio in Newark.

LIVED: 6 West Park St.

⌒ Howard R. Garis: children's book author & journalist ⌒
April 25, 1873 - Nov. 6, 1962

Garis was a reporter for the *Newark Evening News* who also wrote stories for the paper. In January 1910, the paper ran his first *Uncle Wiggily* story about a hero rabbit and, for almost 40 years thereafter, he pumped one out for every day's editions except Sunday. The series was later syndicated and made into a board game. Garis also authored 500 books using different pen names, many for the Stratemeyer Syndicate. As "Victor Appleton," he wrote the first 35 *Tom Swift* books, and he also contributed to the *Bobbsey Twins* series. His wife and fellow reporter, Lillian, also wrote children's books.

LIVED: 12 Myrtle Ave.; 46 N. 7th St.; 104 Peabody Place

⌒ Gloria Gaynor: Queen of Disco ⌒
Sept. 7, 1949 -

Gaynor was born "Gloria Fowles" in Newark, a member of a musical family. She began singing early and set out on a music career after graduating from South Side H.S., though she also took business and cosmetology courses just in case. She got her first recording deal in 1968. Gaynor hit it big in the 1970s disco era with the songs *Never Can Say Goodbye*, the first song to top *Billboard's* dance charts, and *I Will Survive*, a 1980 Grammy winner for best disco recording. She has recorded for MGM and Polydor among other labels, toured worldwide, appeared on TV and also done some acting.

LIVED: 321 15th Ave.; 150 1/2 Howard St.; 83 Waverly Ave.

⌒ Viola Gentry: pioneering female pilot ⌒
June 13, 1899 - June 23, 1988

A North Carolina native, Gentry was the first woman from that state to earn a pilot's license. In 1928, she set an endurance record — staying in the air for more than eight hours. The record was broken a year later and Gentry tried reclaiming it but never did, killing her co-pilot and almost killing herself in a 1931 attempt. She advocated flying for women all her life and was a charter member of the Ninety-Nines, a female pilots' organization. She also headed the Women's International Aeronautic Association. Gentry was recognized for her efforts with the Lady Day Drummond-Hay Air trophy in 1954.

LIVED: 193 N. 6th St.; 99 N. 6th St.

✎ John J. Gibbons: lawyer & judge ✎
Dec. 8, 1924 -

Gibbons was born and lived in Newark as a young boy. Raised in Belleville, he graduated from St. Benedict's, Holy Cross and Harvard Law School. He started his law career at a firm in Newark and, in 1969, was appointed to the 3rd U.S. Circuit Court of Appeals, serving as chief judge from 1987 to 1990, when he retired. Gibbons returned to Newark to work at a firm that bears his name and has taught at Seton Hall, Rutgers and other law schools. He has served as president of the state bar, founded a public interest legal fellowship program and was a leader in the fight against New Jersey's death penalty.

LIVED: 806 Parker St.; 284 Verona Ave.

✎ Thomas P. Giblin: labor leader & county and state legislator ✎
Jan. 15, 1947 -

Giblin followed his father, an Irish immigrant who settled in Newark, into organized labor and politics, becoming an official with the International Union of Operating Engineers. He was elected Essex County surrogate and an Essex County freeholder and served as state Democratic Party chairman from 1997-2001. Later, he was elected to the Assembly, where he has been deputy majority leader. Giblin graduated from Seton Hall Prep and Seton Hall University and graduate work at Rutgers. He has also served in the N.J. Air National Guard. His brother Vince served as IUOE president.

LIVED: 575 Sanford Ave.; 62 Eastern Pkwy.; 28 Hazelwood; 318 S.19th St.

✎ Kenneth A. Gibson: mayor ✎
May 15, 1932 -

A native of Alabama, Gibson was Newark's first African-American mayor, beating incumbent Hugh Addonizio in 1970. He served four terms as the city's 36th mayor until beaten in 1986 by Sharpe James. Gibson earned a degree in civil engineering from the Newark College of Engineering, now NJIT. He was an engineer for the state of New Jersey, the Newark Housing Authority and for the city before first running for mayor in 1966, losing but forcing a runoff. Gibson was the first black president of the U.S. Conference of Mayors and, in 1981, he lost the Democratic nomination for governor.

LIVED: 72 Tuxedo Parkway; 92 Rose Terrace

Kenneth A. Gibson

⤳ Richard Watson Gilder: journalist, editor & poet ⤺
Feb. 8, 1844 - Nov. 19, 1909

When Gilder died, *The New York Times* called him a national asset who'd "made his wise influence felt so strongly in many fields of endeavor." The son of a Methodist minister, he began a life of letters in Newark after serving in the Civil War. Gilder was a reporter and editor for the *Daily Advertiser* before co-founding the *Newark Morning Register,* which failed. He then became a magazine editor in New York at *Hours at Home, Scribner's* and *The Century.* He also wrote seven volumes of acclaimed poetry and fought to improve New York tenement house conditions, one of his many causes.

LIVED: 23 Fulton St.; 96 Halsey St.; 57 & 77 Brunswick St.

⤳ Willie Gilzenberg: sports promoter ⤺
Oct. 24, 1901 - Nov. 15, 1978

Gilzenberg was a boxing and wrestling promoter in the metropolitan area who also managed heavyweight Tony Galento and welterweight champ Freddie "Red" Cochrane. He was born in Newark and got his start in boxing as a corner man and trainer in local gyms. He put on his first show in 1926 and never stopped, promoting in Newark with his partner Babe Culnan at the Laurel Gardens and Meadowbrook Bowl. Gilzenberg was key in getting boxing and wrestling on early TV. In his later years, he joined with wrestling impressario Vince McMahon and served as WWWF president for 15 years.

LIVED: 495 Springfield Ave.; 528 S. 13th St.; 152 West End Ave.

⤳ Irwin Allen Ginsberg: poet & activist ⤺
June 3, 1926 - April 5, 1997

With the publication of *Howl* in 1956, Ginsberg moved to the forefront of living poets and embarked on a life full of exploration, experimentation and controversy. He was born and spent his early years in Newark and attended Montclair State briefly before going to Columbia. He was a leading figure in the Beat movement, a Buddhist and a critic of the Vietnam War, capitalism, the war on drugs and sexual repression. In 1974, he won the National Book Award for poetry, and he also taught. Ginsberg was cremated and some of his ashes were buried in the family's plot at a Jewish cemetery in Newark.

LIVED: 163 Quitman St.

On the Life-Mask of Abraham Lincoln

This bronze doth keep the very form and mould

Of our great martyr's face. Yes, this is he:

That brow all wisdom, all benignity;

That human, humorous mouth; those cheeks that hold

Like some harsh landscape all the summer's gold;

That spirit fit for sorrow, as the sea

For storms to beat on; the lone agony

Those silent, patient lips too well foretold.

Yes, this is he who ruled a world of men

As might some prophet of the elder day

Brooding above the tempest and the fray

With deep-eyed thought and more than mortal ken.

A power was his beyond the touch of art

Or armed strength: It was his mighty heart.

Richard Watson Gilder
reprinted from The Century
Vol. 33, issue 1
November 1886

✌ Herbert J. "Jackie" Gleason: comedian, actor & musician ✌
Feb. 26, 1916 - June 24, 1987

Gleason was born in Brooklyn, began a life in show business as a teen and became one of the country's most popular entertainers starting in the 1950s. Before he hit it big on TV and in the movies, he honed his skills in Newark — serving as an emcee and bouncer at clubs, house comedian at the Empire Burlesque and a part-time deejay at WAAT. Gleason married his first wife in Newark and joked that they honeymooned at the Empire. He won a Tony Award for *Take Me Along* and an Oscar for *The Hustler*. But he is best remembered as bus driver "Ralph Kramden" on TV's *The Honeymooners*.

LIVED: 108 Clinton Ave.

✌ Savion Glover: tap dancer, choreographer & actor ✌
Nov. 19, 1973 -

Glover showed musical ability as a toddler and began taking tap lessons at age 7. He was a student at the Newark School of the Arts, Arts H.S. and Broadway Dance Center. He debuted on Broadway in 1985 in *The Tap Dance Kid* and never looked back, performing throughout the world and appearing on TV and in the movies. Glover was nominated for a Tony in *Black and Blue* and won one for choreography in 1996 for *Bring in 'Da Noise, Bring in 'Da Funk*. He received a National Endowment for the Arts grant while still a teenager. Glover also started a school for tap dancing in Newark.

LIVED: 49 Rose Terrace; 236 Livingston St.

✌ Rudolph J. Goerke: department store owner ✌
Sept. 19, 1867 - April 13, 1938

At one point in his life, Goerke was said to control more department stores in the U.S. than anyone. He was born in Brooklyn and began work there in his father's home furnishings store. He came to Newark in 1896 and started building his empire. His stores operated under a variety of names, Goerke & Sons and R.J. Goerke & Co. among them. In 1925, Goerke got control of the City Store chain that had stores throughout the South. He once responded to criticism of his $75,000 salary by saying he was really worth $1 million. He had ties to numerous banks and was a trustee of Western Maryland College.

LIVED: 78 S. 11th; 135 & 156 Washington St.; 564 & 634 Clinton Ave.

⤳ Babs Gonzalez: bebop vocalist ⤲
Oct. 27, 1919 - Jan. 23, 1980

Gonzalez was born "Lee Brown" in Newark to a family whose brothers were all called "Babs." He studied and played the piano and drums early on before taking up singing. He worked in the big bands of Charlie Barnet and Lionel Hampton before striking out with his own group, "Three Bips and a Bop." The band recorded for Blue Note, backed by Sonny Rollins and Ray Haynes among other famous sidemen. Gonzalez was also road manager and vocalist for the James Moody Band. His biggest hit was *Oop-Pop-A-Da*, made famous by Dizzy Gillespie. He was also a poet and published three memoirs.

LIVED: 94 Milford Ave.

⤳ Rev. Hannibal Goodwin: clergyman & inventor ⤲
April 21, 1822 - Dec. 31, 1900

Goodwin was rector of the House of Prayer Episcopal Church in Newark who experimented with flexible photographic film around the same time as George Eastman of Eastman Kodak fame. In September 1898, however, Goodwin was granted a patent on his creation. He left the ministry to set up a business but died soon afterward from accident-related injuries. His patent was then sold and his heirs collected millions in a patent-infringement suit against Kodak, though Eastman could still use the new film in his cameras. Goodwin's invention helped pave the way for latter-day motion pictures.

LIVED: 556 Ferry St.; 15 Market St.; Plume House, 407 Broad St.

⤳ Alfred T. Goullet: champion bicycle racer ⤲
April 5, 1891 - March 11, 1995

Goullet was described by sportswriter Grantland Rice as "the Babe Ruth of six-day bike racing." He was a well-known cyclist in his native Australia before he came to the U.S. to begin racing in 1910. In his 15-year career in America, he won 400 races and set six world records. Goullet was as good in the sprints as he was in the six-day races. In one six-day event, he managed to cover 2,759 miles, while his record of 1 hour, 49 minutes and 8 seconds in the 50-mile race stood for decades. He is a member of the U.S. Bicycling, Australian, Madison Square Garden, New York and Newark halls of fame.

LIVED: 17 Noll Place; 49 N. Munn Ave.; 191 S. 7th St.

⤙ Lester B. Granger: civil rights leader ⤚
Sept. 16, 1896 - Jan. 9, 1976

Granger graduated from Barringer H.S. and Dartmouth College. After World War I military service, he took a job with the Urban League in Newark. He was named executive director of the National Urban League in 1941, serving 20 years. The group grew substantially during his tenure, and he is credited with helping integrate U.S. forces during World War II. He was awarded the President's Medal of Merit by Harry Truman and also received the Navy's highest civilian honor. A social worker by profession, Granger was head of the National Conference of Social Work and served on many commissions.

LIVED: 625 Warren St.; 27 Wallace Place

⤙ Dr. Gabriel Grant: surgeon & Medal of Honor winner ⤚
Sept. 4, 1826 - Nov. 8, 1909

A direct descendant of Newark founder Robert Treat, Grant graduated from Williams College and the College of Physicians and Surgeons in New York. He was Newark's health commissioner before enlisting with a New Jersey infantry regiment for service in the Civil War. Grant spent more than three years treating the wounded in a number of battles, including Antietam, Bull Run and Vicksburg, and was designated by Congress as the surgeon of U.S. Volunteers. He was awarded the Medal of Honor for the bravery he showed removing injured soldiers and officers from the battlefield under heavy fire.

LIVED: 107 Market St.; 43 & 65 Clinton Ave.; 1012 Broad St.

⤙ Ernest F. Guilbert: architect ⤚
July 23, 1869 - Dec. 1, 1916

Guilbert was born in Chicago and raised in Minneapolis before heading to Boston to begin his career. In 1899, he moved to New York and oversaw the preparation of drawings for a number of buildings, including Essex County's historic courthouse. Guilbert came to Newark in 1908 and was the Board of Education's supervising architect. He designed many of the city's grandest schools — the Newark State Normal School, Central H.S. and South Side H.S. among them. He was a consultant to school organizations around the country and often judged their building plans. He also had his own firm.

LIVED: 767 Ridge St.

⟶ William Stryker Gummere: N.J. Supreme Court chief justice ⟵
June 24, 1852 - Jan. 26, 1933

Gummere was New Jersey's longest-serving chief justice, sitting from 1901 until his death in 1933. Before that, he had been an associate justice of the N.J. Supreme Court for five years. He was captain of the Princeton team that played Rutgers in the first-ever college football game in New Brunswick in 1869 and graduated from Princeton in 1870 when he was 18. Gummere was admitted to the bar in 1873 after studying law with his father in Trenton, and he practiced law in Newark before his appointment to the bench. He also received a master's degree and an honorary doctorate from his alma mater.

LIVED: 45 Washington St.; 95 Clinton Ave.; 26 Camp St.; 391 Mt. Prospect

⟶ Bernard Gussow: artist ⟵
Dec. 1, 1879 - Feb. 8, 1957

Son of a rabbi, Gussow was born in Russia and moved to the U.S. when he was a boy. He studied at the Art Students League, National Academy of Design and Ecole des Beaux Arts in Paris. He taught at the Newark School of Fine and Industrial Art for many years. He exhibited two pieces at the famous International Armory Show in New York in 1913. His art was also shown at the 1939 New York World's Fair. Described as a modern realist, Gussow had his work collected by the Museum of Modern Art, Whitney Museum of American Art, Los Angeles Museum and The Newark Museum.

LIVED: 67 Hunterdon St.

⟶ Marvelous Marvin N. Hagler: boxing champion ⟵
May 23, 1954 -

Experts rate Hagler among the top middleweight fighters who ever lived. A lefthander, he was the undisputed champion from 1980 until 1987, and he successfully defended his title a dozen times. In a career spanning 14 years, Hagler won 62 fights (52 by KO) and lost three. In his final bout, he dropped a controversial decision to Sugar Ray Leonard in Las Vegas in April 1987. He grew up in Newark, but his mother relocated the family to New England in the late 1960s. Hagler legally changed his first name to "Marvelous," and he later moved to Italy, where he became an actor and a fight commentator.

LIVED: Hayes Homes; 227 Waverly Ave.; Lillie Street; Boyd Street

✈ Julius Hahne: department store founder ✈
1828 - Feb. 7, 1895

Hahne came to the U.S. from Germany as a teen and settled in Newark after residing in New York. His first job was making pocketbooks. But he saved his money and, in 1858, opened up a store with a partner selling birds, bird cages and Christmas items. The business prospered and grew and became Newark's first full-line department store — Hahne & Co. on Broad Street — in the early 20th century. For many years, the store served mostly an upscale clientele and later expanded to the suburbs. The Newark store closed in 1987. Hahne was said to be strict yet humble and a man of great integrity.

LIVED: 45 Lincoln Park; 51 Halsey St.

✈ William Halsey: Newark's first mayor ✈
1770 - Aug. 16, 1843

Newark was incorporated as a city in 1836, the year that Halsey was elected the city's first mayor. He was a member of the Whig Party, as were most of Newark's early mayors. A native of Short Hills and a lawyer, Halsey was 66 at the time he took office, and he served for two years. He later became a judge. Among his achievements were opening a central market, providing a jail and teaming up with Essex County to build a jointly-used courthouse. He also set up a "City Watch" to rid the streets of crime, Newark's first attempt at an organized police force. A street in Newark was named in his honor.

LIVED: 131 Broad St.

✈ Oliver Spencer Halsted: mayor & state chancellor ✈
Sept. 22, 1792 - Aug. 29, 1877

Halsted was born in Elizabeth, graduated from Princeton, became a lawyer and served as Newark's fourth mayor from 1840-41. Earlier, he had been surrogate of Essex and Union counties and a state legislator. In 1844, he was a member of the convention that revised the state's constitution and, the following year, he became chancellor under the new constitution. Halsted remained chancellor until 1852. In that job, he was ex-officio president of the Court of Errors and Appeals, the state's highest court. He later returned to the law but spent his final years reading, writing and studying the Bible.

LIVED: 417 Broad St.; Connecticut Farms; Prospect Ave., Lyons Farms

Julius Hahne

⤞ William H. "Sliding Billy" Hamilton: Hall of Fame outfielder ⤝
Feb. 15, 1866 - Dec. 15, 1940

Hamilton was a base-stealing whiz in an early baseball era who stayed in the game as a manager and scout after his playing days had ended. His prime years were in the 1890s, when he played for Philadelphia and Boston, won a batting title and set records in stealing bases and scoring runs. In 1891, he stole a career-best 115 bases and, three years later, scored 196 runs, still a Major League record. Hamilton once stole seven bases in a single game. He batted .390 or better in three seasons, and his lifetime average was .344. He was inducted into the National Baseball Hall of Fame posthumously in 1961.

LIVED: 15 Oxford St.

⤞ John R. Hardin: lawyer, insurance executive & civic leader ⤝
April 24, 1860 - Dec. 6, 1945

A Princeton graduate, Hardin studied for the law in Newark and was admitted to the bar in 1884. He set up his own practice in Newark and later formed a law firm that continues to this day. He was elected a city alderman and to the state Assembly but then gave up politics to return to law and take up insurance. Hardin became a director of Mutual Benefit Life in 1905 and its president in 1924, serving until his death. He was N.J. Bar Association president, treasurer of the Essex County Park Commission, a Princeton University trustee and a member of many civic and charitable organization boards.

LIVED: 171 Orange St.; 16 Saybrook Place; 40 Mt. Prospect Place

⤞ Jed Harris: theater producer & director ⤝
Feb. 25, 1900 - Nov. 15, 1979

Harris was born "Jacob Hirsch Horowitz" in Austria and came to the U.S. as an infant. He grew up in Newark and graduated from Central H.S. He dropped out of Yale but, by his mid-20s, was producing and directing hit shows on Broadway, including Thornton Wilder's award-winning *Our Town*. He reportedly earned as much as $40,000 a week. At 28, he was on the cover of *Time*. Harris worked with Laurence Olivier, Helen Hayes and Arthur Miller among other great actors and playwrights, though few called him a friend. He was inducted into the American Theatre Hall of Fame in 1981.

LIVED: 156 Spruce St.

🐦 Samuel A. Haynes Sr.: civil rights activist, editor & lyricist 🐦
Feb. 28, 1898 - July 1, 1971

Haynes was a Belizean soldier who fought for the British in World War I and then fought racism and discrimination at home. He was a key member of Marcus Garvey's movement, and he wrote the lyrics for the *Land of the Gods*, designated the national anthem when Belize gained its independence in 1981. Haynes was editor of the *New Jersey Afro-American*, head of Newark's ABC Board, president of Newark's NAACP chapter and co-chairman of the United Negro College Fund drive in the state. At one time, he was also the highest ranking black official in the state Labor Department.

LIVED: 15 Wallace St.; 334 Hillside Ave.

🐦 Larry Hazzard Sr.: boxing ref & athletic commissioner 🐦
Dec. 7, 1944 -

A Central H.S. graduate, Hazzard was a Golden Gloves and AAU boxing champion who began refereeing pro fights in 1967. He was the third man in the ring in more than 40 title bouts featuring some of the sport's biggest names, Marvin Hagler and Michael Spinks among them. Hazzard served as N.J. Athletic Control Board commissioner from 1986 until 2007. He is a member of the N.J. Boxing Hall of Fame and International Boxing Hall of Fame. Before taking the commissioner's job, Hazzard was a teacher and administrator in the Newark school system. He has a black belt in Ju-Jitsu.

LIVED: 334 15th Ave.; 199 Hillside Ave.; 725 Bergen St.; 889 S. 18th St.

🐦 Nathan C. "Bubi" Heard: novelist & poet 🐦
Nov. 7, 1936 - March 19, 2004

Heard grew up in Newark and was a school dropout, opting for life in the streets. He got interested in writing while serving time for armed robbery at the New Jersey State Prison in Trenton. In 1968, he published his first book, *Howard Street*, a gritty novel about his earlier years in Newark. It sold a million copies. Heard later published four more novels, but none was as successful as the first. He also wrote poems and taught creative writing at Fresno State College and Rutgers. He played "Big Pink" in *Gordon's War*, a 1973 film about a Vietnam veteran ridding his old neighborhood of drugs.

LIVED: 124 Broome St.; The Colonnade; 151 Lincoln Ave.

C. Willard Heckel: Rutgers Law School dean & church elder
May 1, 1913 - April 6, 1988

Heckel joined the Rutgers Law School faculty in Newark in 1946 and served as dean from 1963 to 1970, retiring in 1983. He was born in Bloomfield and took his bachelor's degree from Dartmouth, a master's from Columbia and a law degree from Rutgers. His specialty was government and municipal law. Heckel was chosen the equivalent of president of the United Presbyterian Church in this country in 1972 and remained a ruling church elder until his death. He was a leader in Newark's charter change movement and served as president of the United Community Corp., the city's anti-poverty agency.

LIVED: 352 & 375 Mount Prospect Ave.

Nathan Hedges: educator
Dec. 21, 1792 - Jan. 21, 1875

Hedges was the head of Newark's first high school, which was the first in New Jersey and third in the U.S. He was considered one of the nation's leading educators and regularly spoke at the major educational conferences of his day. He was an advocate of education beyond primary school for boys and girls, believing it made them better citizens and better parents. He also felt the Civil War might have been prevented had there been better education in the South. Hedges worked in Newark schools for 50 years. He was known for his expertise in math and grammar and for being a strict disciplinarian.

LIVED: 365 & 396 High St.

Elias George Heller: tool manufacturer & developer
April 27, 1837 - March 23, 1912

Heller's father was a German immigrant who made a name for himself in Newark with his hand-made files and rasps. Elias George joined the business in 1866 and, with his brothers, opened a new factory and took the business to a new level of prosperity. The company was so successful that it built a steel mill next to its plant to accommodate the demand for its products. The company later incorporated, closed its Newark operation, moved to Ohio and was bought out. But Heller products are still made. Elias George was also a pivotal figure in the development of Newark's Forest Hill section.

LIVED: 343 Elwood Ave.; Mount Prospect Ave., near Verona Avenue

Elias George Heller

⚬ **Bernard Hellring: lawyer** ⚬
May 7, 1916 - Jan. 4, 1991

Hellring came to the U.S. from Austria as a boy and grew up in Newark. He went to Lafayette College and graduated from Harvard Law School. He represented Newark Mayor Hugh Addonizio at his 1970 corruption trial and also an East German waitress accused in a 1978 airliner hijacking, a case turned into a book and a movie. Hellring was widely known for the years he spent helping simplify and standardize federal and state business, divorce and legislative apportionment laws. He was also an advisor to the American Law Institute and a special counsel on state economic development matters.

LIVED: 535 Hawthorne Ave.; 225 Meeker Ave.

⚬ **Rev. Ernest Helmstetter: abbot & St. Benedict's headmaster** ⚬
Oct. 7, 1859 - July 9, 1937

Helmstetter was born, raised and schooled in Newark and graduated from St. Vincent's College in Pennsylvania before heading off to the seminary. He was ordained a priest in 1884. He taught at St. Vincent's before returning to Newark when St. Mary's became an independent abbey. Helmstetter taught and was headmaster at St. Benedict's in a period when enrollment increased five-fold. He was president of the Benedictine Order in the U.S. from 1914 to 1929, a time in which the order grew in both size and prestige. He also had a role in St. Mary's buying the Delbarton estate and setting up a school.

LIVED: St. Mary's Abbey, 520 High St.

⚬ **Gustav "Gus" Heningburg: civil rights leader & TV host** ⚬
May 18, 1930 - Oct. 15, 2012

Heningburg was born in Alabama, went to high school in New York and graduated from Hampton Institute in Virginia in 1946. He served six years in the Army and was later a captain in the Army Reserves. He was an official with the NAACP Legal Defense Fund and the United Negro College Fund. In 1968, Heningburg was named first president of the Greater Newark Urban Coalition. He spent many years as an executive in the public relations field, some of it running his own firms, and he served as the host of the TV show *Positively Black*. He was also a commissioner of the N.J. Sports Authority.

LIVED: 311 Seymour Ave.; 555 Elizabeth Ave.

⤛ Henry William Herbert: writer & historian ⤜
April 7, 1807 - May 17, 1858

Herbert was an Englishman of noble blood and serious education who came to the U.S. in 1831 and became an author of some renown. He edited the *American Monthly Magazine*, contributed to the leading periodicals of the day and wrote books on history, sports and the outdoors, as well as historical fiction. He sometimes used the pen name "Frank Forrester." Herbert is best remembered for his books on game in America. He has been described as one of this country's first sportswriters and one of the first Americans to hunt for sport. His first job in his adopted homeland was teaching the classics.

LIVED: "The Cedars," Belleville Road (now Mt. Pleasant Cemetery)

⤛ Eugene V. "Gene" Hermanski: baseball player ⤜
May 11, 1920 - Aug. 9, 2010

Hermanski played baseball at East Side H.S. in Newark and then Seton Hall. An outfielder, he was signed into the pros in 1939 and made his big league debut with the Brooklyn Dodgers in 1943. After serving in the Coast Guard during World War II, he resumed playing with the Dodgers from 1946-51 and played on their 1947 and 1949 World Series teams. Hermanski was a Dodger when Jackie Robinson broke baseball's color line. He ended his career with the Cubs and Pirates. A lifetime .272 hitter, Hermanski enjoyed his best season in 1948 when he hit 15 home runs and knocked in 60 runs.

LIVED: 263 New York Ave.

⤛ Harry C. Hersey: horseman ⤜
1867 - April 23, 1940

Hersey was the trainer and driver of Dan Patch, often considered the greatest harness racehorse of all time. Dan Patch was foaled in Indiana in 1896 and lived until 1916. He was undefeated in three seasons and then was retired to perform in high-paying exhibitions across the U.S. Hersey managed those tours. In 1906, Dan Patch set a world record for a mile that stood more than 30 years. In his prime, the horse had his picture appearing on an assortment of objects, and a movie in 1949 was based on his life. Both Hersey and Dan Patch were elected to the Harness Racing Hall of Fame, Hersey in 1979.

LIVED: 35 Tichenor St.

✎ Max J. Herzberg: Weequahic principal, editor & author ✎
March 29, 1886 - Jan. 22, 1958

A graduate of Newark public schools and Columbia, Herzberg was the first principal of Weequahic H.S., serving from 1933 until his retirement in 1951. In all, he spent 44 years in the city schools, some as an English teacher or supervisor of English teachers. He was president of the National Council of English Teachers, as well as its director of publications. While he taught, Herzberg served for many years as a book reviewer and then literary editor at the *Newark Evening News*. He also wrote or edited a number of texts and books and was a member of the dictionary staff at G.&C. Merriam-Webster.

LIVED: 18 1/2 Thomas St.; 20 Ridgewood Ave.; 914 S. 19th; 24 Seymour

✎ William Earl Hidden: mineralogist & mining expert ✎
Feb. 16, 1853 - June 12, 1918

Hidden was an important mineralogist in the second half of the 19th century. From Rhode Island, he gave up a draughtsman's career to pursue an interest in minerals. He moved to Newark and had connections to Thomas Edison and George Westinghouse, both of whom were looking for minerals to use in electric light bulb filaments. In 1879, Edison sent Hidden to the southern Appalachians to search for platinum. He had no success, but he did discover a mineral that was named for him. *Hiddenite* is both a green transparent gemstone and the name of the town in North Carolina where it was found.

LIVED: 25 Orleans St.

✎ Frank J. Hill: basketball, player, coach & official ✎
Sept. 14, 1879 - Aug. 22, 1944

Hill was one of first players to take up basketball after the game was introduced in 1892, and he was active in the sport for the rest of his life. His playing career lasted almost 20 years before he was named the fourth head coach at Rutgers in New Brunswick in 1915, remaining until 1943. One of his players was Paul Robeson. In many of those same years, Hill coached at Seton Hall College and St. Benedict's Prep. He compiled a record of 222 wins and 165 losses at Rutgers, with 19 winning seasons. He also spent more than 40 years as an inspector with the Newark Water Department.

LIVED: 197 Plane St.; 17 Beverly St.; 18 Fabyan Place; 11 Shephard Ave.

➤ John P. Holland: father of the modern submarine ➤
Feb. 28, 1841 - Aug. 12, 1914

Holland gave up teaching to come to the U.S. from his native Ireland at age 27. He worked as a draughtsman in Boston and later moved to New Jersey to continue teaching. He began building submarines in Paterson, and several of his early models sank. But his 58-foot Holland No. 9 was the first submarine purchased by the U.S. government, and today it's considered the first modern submarine. Holland chose St. Patrick's Day in 1898 to give the vessel its first test in open waters, and it was primarily used for training. Holland died in obscurity, but his burial spot was finally marked with a headstone in 1976.

LIVED: 38 Newton St.; 116 & 209 Garside; 194 Fairmount; 349 13th Ave.

➤ Joseph C. Hornblower: lawyer & judge ➤
May 6, 1777 - June 11, 1864

Hornblower was the son of a prominent engineer who had served in the Continental Congress. He read for the law in Newark, was admitted to the bar in 1803 and became a well-known and politically active lawyer. He was a founder of the American Bible Society and a presidential elector for James Monroe in 1820. In 1832, Hornblower was named chief justice of the N.J. Supreme Court, staying until 1846 and taking an active role in the rewriting of the state Constitution in 1844. He later taught law at Princeton. He helped start up the N.J. Historical Society and served as its president until his death.

LIVED: 6 Park Place

➤ James Oliver Horton: educator & historian ➤
March 28, 1943 -

A longtime professor at George Washington University, Horton is one of the country's leading historians, with a specialty in African-American history. He has written a dozen books and lent his scholarly expertise to a host of cable and network TV shows and programs. Horton is historian emeritus of the Smithsonian Institution's National Museum of American History. He was chairman of the National Park System Advisory Board, president of the Organization of American Historians and a member of the Abraham Lincoln Bicentennial Commission, as well as the White House Millennium Council.

LIVED: 123 S. 12th St.; 30 Nairn Place

✐ Emily "Cissy" Houston: soul, disco & gospel singer ✐
Sept. 30, 1933 -

Houston began singing gospel with her siblings as a young girl, a group that evolved into the Drinkard Singers. She then formed the Sweet Inspirations, a group that recorded on its own and also backed many stars, including Elvis Presley and Otis Redding. Houston released her first solo album in 1970 and has continued performing and recording — on her own, on soundtracks and on the albums of Burt Bacharach and daughter Whitney among others. She has won Grammy awards for gospel albums, is the force behind McDonald's Gospelfest and has been choirmaster at Newark's New Hope Baptist Church.

LIVED: 199 Court St.; 82 S. Eighth St.; 35 Wainwright St.

✐ Whitney E. Houston: singer, actress & model ✐
Aug. 3, 1963 - Feb. 11, 2012

Houston spent her early years in Newark, where her father was a City Hall employee and where she learned the piano and began singing as a soloist in a church choir at age 11. As a teen, she sometimes performed at her mother Cissy's nightclub dates, sang backup on albums and was a magazine fashion model. Houston released her first album in 1985 and then became one of the top recording artists of all time, as well as a movie star. She once had seven consecutive No. 1 hits. Houston won two Emmys and six Grammy awards and sang *The Star-Spangled Banner* at Super Bowl XXV in Tampa, FL.

LIVED: 35 Wainwright St.

✐ John W. Howell: engineer, inventor & Edison associate ✐
Dec. 22, 1857 - July 28, 1937

Howell was a close associate of Thomas Edison and a key figure in the development of the electric light bulb. He studied at Rutgers, City College and Stevens Institute before spending his entire 50-year career with the famed inventor. Howell developed many upgrades in the incandescent lamp and provided crucial technical testimony in Edison's patent infringement suits. In 1924, he received the prestigious Edison Medal awarded by an electrical engineering society. Among his inventions was the first reliable voltmeter. He also co-authored a book on the history of incandescent lamps.

LIVED: 211 Ballantine Parkway

Whitney Houston

⤳ Frank L. Howley: military commander ⤨
Feb. 3, 1903 - July 30, 1993

Howley was a U.S. Army brigadier general who was put in charge of the American zone in Berlin after World War II. He wrote about the experience in *Berlin Command*, one of his several books. He was an athlete at South Side H.S. and NYU, nicknamed the "Golden Toe" for his ability to kick a football. In the 1930s, Howley had his own ad agency and was called into active military duty in 1940 after serving in the Officers Reserve Corps. He served as NYU's vice chancellor from 1950 to 1969. He was awarded the Distinguished Service Medal, and the city of Berlin named a street for him.

LIVED: 11 Thomas St.

⤳ Charles Evans Hughes: judge & statesman ⤨
April 11, 1862 - Aug. 27, 1948

Hughes occupied almost every high office in the land and would have had them all had he not narrowly lost a challenge to the incumbent Woodrow Wilson in the 1916 presidential election. He served as governor of New York, chief justice of the U.S. Supreme Court and was secretary of state under two presidents. Hughes spent some of his boyhood in Newark, where he attended local schools and where his father served as pastor of the Fifth Baptist Church. He took his undergraduate degree from Brown and his law degree from Columbia. He also practiced and taught law in New York.

LIVED: 164 Elm St.

⤳ William Tallmage Hunt: newsman & government official ⤨
Nov. 14, 1854 - May 22, 1916

Hunt worked his way up in the newspaper business in Newark from the age of 17 to become editor-in-chief of *The Sunday Call*, and one of its owners. While covering the state legislature, he worked for several papers, including the *New York Tribune*. Hunt also served as secretary to U.S. Sen. Frederick Frelinghuysen in Washington, DC, secretary of the U.S. Senate's Agriculture Committee, assistant secretary of the N.J. Senate and president of the state Sewerage Commission. His father was a Civil War doctor who gave up medicine to settle in Newark and became editor of the *Newark Advertiser*.

LIVED: 40 Park Place; Stratford Place; 29 Ninth Ave.

Charles Evans Hughes (with parents)

ᴥ John Wesley Hyatt: inventor ᴥ
Nov. 28, 1837 - May 10, 1920

Hyatt was born in upstate New York and began his working life as a printer. In 1868, he invented and later patented the process for making celluloid, the first commercially successful plastic. His first company produced dental plates in Albany, NY, but he later established several firms in Newark to make his products. Hyatt also got patents on a popular roller bearing, an improved sugarcane mill and an industrial sewing machine, among many others. He was given the Perkin Medal, the U.S. chemical industry's highest award, and he was also inducted into the National Inventors Hall of Fame.

LIVED: 793 High St.; 936 Broad; 239a Mount Prospect Ave.; 724 Ridge St.

ᴥ Anthony M. Imperiale: activist and legislator ᴥ
July 10, 1931 - Dec. 26, 1999

Imperiale was a former Marine who came to the nation's attention for the street patrols he formed during Newark's 1967 riots that policed his mostly Italian neighborhood. His efforts inspired a movie glorifying vigilantism. Imperiale attended Newark schools and took a variety of jobs after his father died when he was a boy. For years, he operated his own private detective agency, but he also served as a Newark city councilman, an assemblyman and a state senator from Essex County, director of the county's emergency management office and director of the state Office of Community Safety.

LIVED: 110 Summer Ave.; 760 DeGraw Ave.

ᴥ Laura Ingalls: pilot ᴥ
Dec. 14, 1903 - Jan. 10, 1967

Ingalls was an early American aviatrix who flew in the shadow of Amelia Earhart. But in September 1935, she broke Earhart's record of flying nonstop across the country. Earlier in her career, she'd also set records for loops and barrel rolls. Ingalls' most famous flight was in 1934 when she flew from New York to Chile and back, taking almost two months. In so doing, she became the first woman to fly over the Andes mountains and first to fly from North to South America. The trip also set a distance record. Ingalls was later convicted of serving as a Nazi publicity agent and served time in prison.

LIVED: 29 Stratford Place

🙬 Washington Irving: writer & diplomat 🙤
April 3, 1783 - Nov. 28, 1859

Irving was one of the first Americans to make a living solely by writing and also one of the first to be acknowledged for his talents in Europe. He is best known for *The Legend of Sleepy Hollow* and *Rip Van Winkle*, stories that brought him international fame. But throughout his life, Irving wrote in a variety of forms. One of his last projects was a five-volume biography of George Washington, for whom he was named. For health reasons, Irving spent extended periods at a mansion in Newark's Woodside section, where he continued his writing. He served as ambassador to Spain for four years.

LIVED: "Cockloft Hall," 208 Mt. Pleasant Ave.

🙬 Jerry Izenberg: sportswriter, author, documentary filmmaker 🙤
Sept. 10, 1930 -

Izenberg was born in Newark and graduated in 1952 from Rutgers-Newark, where he was the paper's sports editor. He wrote for a number of daily papers but spent most of his career at *The Star-Ledger*, retiring in 2007. He traveled the world covering many of the major sporting events of the last half of the 20th century. Izenberg published nine books and produced dozens of TV documentaries. Among his honors, he was inducted into the National Sportscasters and Sportswriters Hall of Fame and won the Red Smith Award from the AP Sports Editors in 2010 for his contribution to sports journalism.

LIVED: 80 Shanley Ave.

🙬 John P. Jackson: lawyer & railroad executive 🙤
June 8, 1805 - Dec. 10, 1861

Jackson graduated from the College of New Jersey (Princeton) and studied law in Connecticut. He was admitted to the bar in 1827 and then practiced in Newark. He was elected to the Assembly in 1831 and served as speaker. He was elected Essex County clerk in 1859 and held the job for 10 years. At the same time, Jackson got involved with the N.J. Railroad and Transportation Co., serving as treasurer and vice president and general superintendent. The company added lines in his tenure, including one between Newark and New York. President Fillmore appointed him to West Point's Board of Visitors.

LIVED: 384 Broad St.

⟫⟩ Sharpe James: mayor & state senator ⟨⟨
Feb. 20, 1936 -

James was born in Jacksonville, FL, and moved to Newark as a baby. He attended local schools and graduated from South Side H.S. A physical education major in college, James taught in Newark schools and later joined the Essex County College faculty. He was elected a city councilman in 1970 and served until 1986, when he was elected Newark's 35th mayor. James served five terms, becoming the city's longest-serving mayor. He was also elected to the state Senate. In 2008, he was convicted on charges in connection with the sale of city property and sentenced to 27 months in federal prison.

LIVED: 188 Renner St.; 43 Emmet St.; 38 & 59 Wilbur Ave.

⟫⟩ Vasco S. Jardim: newspaper publisher ⟨⟨
Jan. 22, 1900 - Oct. 5, 1983

In 1939, Jardim revived *Luso-Americano,* one of the largest and oldest Portuguese-language papers in the U.S., with readers on three continents. The paper was founded in 1928 but declined during the Depression. A native of Portugal, Jardim was owner and publisher for 40 years before retiring in 1979 and handing the reins over to relatives. The Portuguese government awarded him the Order of Prince Henry Medal in 1965 for his efforts on behalf of Portuguese fraternal groups and immigrants. He was also a founder of the first Catholic church in New Jersey to offer services in Portuguese.

LIVED: 107 Jefferson St.; 88 & 165 Ferry St.

⟫⟩ Wyclef Jean: singer-songwriter & record producer ⟨⟨
Oct. 17, 1969 -

Jean came to the U.S. with his family from Haiti while a boy. His father was a Nazarene pastor, and the family eventually settled in Newark in a spot that also served as a church. He gained his first success as a founding member of the Fugees, a hip-hop group whose 1996 album *The Score* made it to No. 1 on *Billboard's* top 200 chart and won two Grammys. Jean later embarked on a solo career, appeared on TV and in films and wrote for soundtracks, also producing and recording with other artists. His 2010 run for the presidency of his native Haiti was ruled invalid. In 2012, Jean published his life story.

LIVED: 1108 South Orange Ave.

Sharpe James in front of his home
59 Wilbur Ave.

ஊ John Jelliff: furniture maker ஊ
July 30, 1813 - July 2, 1893

Jelliff was born in Connecticut and moved to Newark to apprentice in cabinet making before opening his own business. He and his partner Henry H. Miller, a boyhood friend, operated at 301-303 Broad St. before moving to 794-796 Broad St. Jelliff furniture was considered one of the leading brands of its day, with pieces mainly in the Empire, Gothic, French and Italian Renaissance styles. They were shipped across the country. Even though his competitors moved to manufacturing by machine, Jelliff insisted work in his factory be done by hand. The company closed after Miller died in 1901.

LIVED: 70 Johnson Ave.; 9 Court; 13 Fair; 381 Broad; 206 Washington St.

ஊ Maria Jeritza: opera singer ஊ
Oct. 6, 1887 - July 10, 1982

One of opera's most celebrated figures, Jeritza lived the last half of her life in Newark after marrying a local businessman. She often had some of music's biggest names to her home for dinner or a recital. Jeritza was born "Marie Jedlickova" in Europe and rose to fame early in her career. She enjoyed a long association with the Vienna State Opera and the Metropolitan Opera in New York, both creating titles and as a leading soprano. *Tosca* and *Carmen* were two of her most popular roles. She performed her last *Tosca* at the Mosque Theatre in Newark in 1965 before an invitation-only audience.

LIVED: 200 Elwood Ave.

ஊ Jotham Johnson: archeologist ஊ
Oct. 21, 1905 - Feb. 8, 1967

The son of a physician, Johnson was born in Newark, graduated from Princeton in 1926 and received his doctorate from the University of Pennsylvania. He was part of important digs on the Appian Way in Italy, as well as in Turkey. He taught at Pitt and then served as chairman of NYU's classics department. With a specialty in ancient calendars, he came up with a date the ancient Egyptians used as the starting point of their calendar in 3251 B.C. In 1961, Johnson was chosen president of the Archeological Institute of America, and he served as the first editor of its magazine, *Archaeology*.

LIVED: 11 Tichenor St.; 10 Chestnut St.

⌘ Michael B. Jordan: TV & movie actor ⌘
Feb. 9, 1987 -

Jordan had local modeling jobs but got his first big break in the 2001 movie *Hardball*. That led to prime-time TV roles on *The Wire*, *Friday Night Lights* and *Parenthood*, as well as a stint on the long-running soap opera *All My Children*. He also appeared in music videos. In 2013, Jordan was praised for his role as the shooting victim in the critically acclaimed film *Fruitvale Station*. His 2015 movies included *Fantastic Four* and *Rocky*-spinoff *Creed*. Jordan graduated from Arts H.S., where he was a member of the varsity basketball team while commuting to acting jobs in New York City.

LIVED: 16 Beverly St.

⌘ Joseph M. Kasberger: St. Benedict's football & baseball coach ⌘
Jan. 31, 1896 - Oct. 1, 1969

Kasberger was raised on a farm in Oregon, the son of German immigrants. He got a degree from the Oregon Agricultural College, where he played three sports and was a student leader. He came east to study for a master's at Columbia, only to take a coaching and teaching job at St. Benedict's instead. He coached in Newark from 1930 until 1968, becoming a legend in New Jersey sports circles. His football teams won 203 games, lost 61 and tied 15. His baseball record was even more impressive: 610 wins, 150 defeats and 3 ties. At one point, his baseball teams enjoyed a 64-game winning streak.

LIVED: 17 Halsted St.

⌘ Maj. Gen. Philip Kearny Jr.: Army officer & Civil War general ⌘
June 2, 1815 - Sept. 1, 1862

Kearny was born in New York City to one of the wealthiest families in the country and spent much of his youth at the family's homestead in Newark. He got a law degree from Columbia College but later followed a lifelong dream and chose the Army as his profession. Kearny served on the western frontier and in the Mexican-American War; he studied cavalry tactics in France and fought with the French in North Africa. Fearless in battle, he commanded Union forces in the Civil War and was killed in action. His statue stands in Newark's Military Park, while a Newark street is named for the family.

LIVED: 207 Belleville Ave.

↣ Maj. Gen. Stephen W. Kearny: U.S. Army commander ↢
Aug. 30, 1794 - Oct. 31, 1848

Kearny was born in Newark and attended local schools. He left Columbia College to fight in the War of 1812 and remained in the Army, serving on the country's western frontier. When war with Mexico broke out, Kearny was put in command of the U.S. Army in the West and seized the province of New Mexico in August 1846, setting up a territorial government. He later led his troops to Texas and California and had a short stint as the military governor of California. He was promoted to major general and made head of the garrison at the Mexican port of Vera Cruz before dying from malaria.

LIVED: 207 Belleville Ave.

↣ Jerome D. Kern: Academy Award-winning composer ↢
Jan. 27, 1885 - Nov. 11, 1945

Kern was born in New York but spent his early years in Newark, where his father owned a store. He went to Newark H.S. but left several months before graduation to begin his songwriting career in New York. When sound came to film, he moved to Hollywood to write for the movies. Kern's career lasted four decades, and he wrote hundreds of songs. He is considered one of the country's greatest composers, as well as the father of the American popular theater song. His best-known musical was *Showboat*. He won two Oscars for best song: *The Way You Look Tonight* and *The Last Time I Saw Paris*.

LIVED: 39 Nelson Place

↣ Dr. Henry H. Kessler: founder of renowned rehab center ↢
April 10, 1896 - Jan. 18, 1978

Kessler founded the Kessler Institute for Rehabilitation in 1948 and was its medical director. He graduated from Cornell Medical School in 1919, got advanced degrees from Columbia and was introduced to rehab work while an intern at Newark's City Hospital and at a state clinic. Kessler continued his rehabilitation work as a World War II Navy captain and later traveled the globe as a UN consultant inspecting rehab programs. Patients from all over the world seek rehabilitation at Kessler's three campuses in New Jersey. The institute also trains specialists and helps develop new rehabilitation methods.

LIVED: 53 Lincoln Park; 29 & 168 Hillside Ave.; 91 Clinton Ave.

Jerome D. Kern with Oscar Hammerstein II, (on left)

⟫ William B. Kinney: editor & diplomat ⟪
Sept. 4, 1799 - Oct. 21, 1880

Kinney was educated at Princeton and studied for the law but got interested in publishing, working in both New York and New Jersey. He was editor of the *New Jersey Eagle*, a weekly, and later editor and majority owner of the *Newark Daily Advertiser*, the state's only daily paper at the time. Active in politics, he played a key role in getting Newarker Theodore Frelinghuysen picked to run for vice president with Henry Clay on the Whig Party's 1844 ticket. From 1850 to 1853, Kinney served as charge d'affaires at the Court of Sardinia and remained in Italy another 10 years before returning to Newark.

LIVED: 457 & 1062 Broad St.; 27 Park Place

⟫ Allen Klein: Beatles & Rolling Stones business manager ⟪
Dec. 18, 1931 - July 4, 2009

Klein became an accountant after graduating from Weequahic H.S. and Upsala College. Helping recording artists recover unpaid royalties led him to manage the business affairs of Sam Cooke and later The Beatles and Rolling Stones, among other groups. But many of those relationships broke apart in lawsuits, claims of fraud and accusations the outspoken Klein was strictly in it for himself. One of the prized possessions he kept in the settlements was control of the Stones' song catalog from the 1960s. He also produced and distributed films, and he spent two months in prison for income tax evasion.

LIVED: Hebrew Orphanage, 141 Lincoln Ave.; 374 Schley St.

⟫ Marie Knight: gospel, R&B singer ⟪
c1920 - Aug. 30, 2009

Knight rose to become a soloist in her church youth choir after her family moved to Newark from Florida. She toured nationally and began recording as a solo artist and with a male backup group in the early 1940s. But she gained her greatest fame touring and recording into the 1950s with gospel legend Sister Rosetta Tharpe. They were one of gospel's biggest acts and broke new ground when their records crossed over to the R&B charts. After they parted ways, Knight turned to an R&B career before returning to gospel music later in life after appearing on a Sister Rosetta Tharpe tribute album.

LIVED: 204 & 257 Broome St.

⤙ Edward I. Koch: New York City mayor ⤚
Dec. 12, 1924 - Feb. 1, 2013

A Bronx native, Koch grew up in Newark and graduated from South Side H.S. in 1941. His father worked in a Newark theater. He served in the Army during World War II and, after returning from duty, got his college degree from CCNY and law degree from NYU. Koch first practiced law by himself and then joined a firm. He was a member of the New York City Council before winning a seat to the House of Representatives, serving in the nation's capital from 1969 to 1977. Koch then served three terms as mayor of New York, ending in 1990. He was also a judge on TV's *The People's Court.*

LIVED: 61 Milford Ave.

⤙ Irving Kolodin: music critic, author & teacher ⤚
Feb. 21, 1908 - April 29, 1988

Kolodin was one of America's greatest music critics and is credited with being one of the first to recognize the importance of phonographic music. He studied music and then worked as a newspaper critic, eventually becoming music editor of *The New York Sun.* He later wrote for *The Saturday Review* for many years. Kolodin published a number of books, one being a history of the Metropolitan Opera. He also taught at Juilliard, wrote program notes for the New York Philharmonic, selected pieces for compilation albums and chose the classical music for the first official White House music library.

LIVED: 520 Clinton Ave.

⤙ Adolf F. Konrad: artist ⤚
Feb. 21, 1915 - Jan. 14, 2004

Born in Germany, Konrad came to America with his family as a boy. He studied at the Newark School of Fine and Industrial Art and later taught at Newark State College. He kept a studio in Newark into the 1960s before moving to Warren County. Called the "painter laureate of Newark," Konrad was best known for his landscapes and his scenes of Newark in the 1950s and '60s. His work is owned by corporations and museums. The Newark Museum has one of his better known paintings, *Reflections*, that depicts the front window of an old music store. Konrad's wife Adair was also a painter.

LIVED: 18 Orchard St.; 20 Fulton St.

⤞ George Krementz: jewelry manufacturer ⤝
1838 - March 5, 1918

Krementz came to the U.S. from Germany as a boy in 1849. His family settled in Indiana before he traveled to New York City to apprentice in the jewelry trade. In 1866, he and a cousin opened a business in Newark that made men's jewelry. Women's items were added later, and Krementz & Co. became one of the country's largest jewelry makers. Krementz began using gold overlay in the 1880s; he got a patent for collar buttons that survived a court fight, and his plant was one of the first to generate its own electricity. The firm stayed in Newark through the 20th century, family still at the helm.

LIVED: 347 & 470 Washington St.; 1072 Broad St.

⤞ Gottfried E. Krueger: beer baron ⤝
Nov. 4, 1837 - Nov. 7, 1926

Krueger came to Newark from Germany as a teen and worked in his uncle's brewery, eventually becoming a brewmaster and owning his own beer company. He became one of Newark's most powerful men, serving as a city alderman, county freeholder, state assemblyman, presidential elector, bank president and lay judge on the state's highest court. Krueger was best known as founder of a brewery bearing his name that opened in 1858 and, years after he died, was the first to sell beer in a can. He had interests in several other Newark brewing concerns, as well as significant real estate holdings.

LIVED: 63 Charlton St.; 266 W. Kinney St.; 601 High St.; 73 Lincoln Park

⤞ Frederick B. Lacey: federal prosecutor & judge ⤝
Sept. 8, 1920 -

The son of a city police chief, Lacey went to West Side H.S. He graduated from Rutgers and served in the U.S. Naval Reserve before going to Cornell Law School. He then worked in private practice in Newark and New York. From 1953 to 1955, Lacey served as an assistant U.S. Attorney in Newark. He returned to the office as the U.S. Attorney for New Jersey from 1969 to 1971, leading major cases against organized crime and public corruption. Lacey served as a federal judge in Newark from 1971 to 1986, when he retired and went back into private practice. He retired from the law in 2011.

LIVED: 583 S. 12th St.; 602 S. 12th St.; 127 Pine Grove Terrace

Home of Gottfried Krueger *(Krueger, inset)*
601 High St.

ᐳᡊᡤ David Lasser: labor organizer & space prophet ᡊᡤᐸ
March 20, 1902 - May 5, 1996

When Lasser died, *The New York Times* called him a "space and social visionary." During the Depression, he organized the Workers Alliance of America, hundreds of thousands of unemployed who pushed for government relief and better WPA pay. Earlier, with an MIT engineering degree, he was editor of a book series that promoted space travel, inspiring a host of science fiction writers including Arthur C. Clarke. Lasser also formed the American Interplanetary Society to advance the idea of space travel through rocketry. Today, the group is the American Institute of Aeronautics and Astronautics.

LIVED: 92 Brunswick St.; 795 S. 13th St.

ᐳᡊᡤ Solomon D. Lauter: piano maker ᡊᡤᐸ
Dec. 2, 1827 - June 3, 1885

Lauter established a company in Newark that made high-end pianos, including an early player piano. They were shipped all over the U.S. and throughout Europe and South America. The firm had showrooms in Newark and around New Jersey, and a factory in Newark. The business continued into the 1960s, under the direction of Charles E. Cameron Sr. and later his son, long after Lauter's death. The Lauter concert grand piano was used for recording at Thomas Edison's studio in New York and plant in West Orange. The first recordings of Rachmaninoff were made by Edison on a Lauter.

LIVED: 143 Washington St.

ᐳᡊᡤ Josephine Lawrence: newspaper editor & author ᡊᡤᐸ
March 13, 1889 - Feb. 22, 1978

Lawrence spent her early years in Newark and attended local schools. The family moved in her teens, but she returned to take an editor's job at *The Sunday Call* in 1915 and stayed until the paper closed. She then worked for the *Newark Sunday News*, retiring around 1970. Starting in 1919, Lawrence wrote 100 girls' and children's books, many in series and most of them under pen names. She moved to adult fiction in 1932 and wrote several dozen novels, focusing on ordinary people and their everyday lives. *Years Are So Long*, a bestseller, was made into the 1934 movie, *Make Way for Tomorrow*.

LIVED: 45 Halsey St.; 338 Belleville Ave.; 77 Mount Pleasant Ave.

⤙ Frederick R. Lehlbach: lawyer, prosecutor & congressman ⤚
Jan. 31, 1876 - Aug. 4, 1937

Lehlbach was born in New York City and moved to Newark with his parents as a boy. He graduated from Yale and the New York Law School. He was admitted to the bar in 1899 and then began his legal practice in Newark. He served on the Newark Board of Education and in the state Assembly and was an Essex County assistant prosecutor before returning to private practice. A Republican, Lehlbach was elected to Congress from the state's 10th district, serving from 1915 to 1933, and from the 12th district from 1933 to 1937. After finally losing an election, he remained in Washington to practice law.

LIVED: 881 S. 17th St; 2 Stratford Place; 16 Johnson Ave.

⤙ Michael Lenson: artist, muralist & art critic ⤚
Feb. 21, 1903 - June 9, 1971

Lenson was born in Russia and came to the U.S. as a teenager. He became a citizen and enrolled at the National Academy of Design, later winning the coveted Chanoler Prize. He used his $10,000 prize to travel and study in Europe for four years. Lenson had his first one-man show in 1933. During the Depression, he was in charge of murals for the WPA in New Jersey and afterward returned to painting and served as director of the Newark School of Fine and Industrial Art. He also taught at Rutgers, FDU and the Montclair Art Museum. For 15 years, he was art critic for the *Newark Sunday News*.

LIVED: 99 Lincoln Park

⤙ Jerry Lewis: comedian, actor, director & telethon host ⤚
March 16, 1926 -

Born "Joseph Levitch" to show business parents, Lewis began performing at age 5 and developed his own act by 15. He later partnered with Dean Martin to form one of the twentieth century's most popular comedy teams. He has acted in and directed dozens of films in a Hollywood career that has spanned more than 60 years, *The Nutty Professor* being one of the better known ones. Lewis has had his own TV show, acted on stage and, for years, he hosted a Labor Day telethon to benefit muscular dystrophy research. He received an Oscar for his humanitarian work and an Emmy for his contribution to TV.

LIVED: 10 Lehigh Ave.

➤ Msgr. William J. Linder: priest & community activist ➤
June 15, 1936 -

A Jersey City native, Linder is a Catholic priest who graduated from Seton Hall and took advance degrees from Fordham. After the 1967 Newark riots, he founded New Community Corp. to provide housing, job training, health care and other services to the city's disadvantaged. In 1991, Linder received a MacArthur Award for extraordinary accomplishment. He was pastor of St. Rose of Lima Church in Newark for more than 30 years. He received many honorary degrees, served on government boards, given expert testimony at hearings and written extensively. He has taught at Rutgers and Columbia.

LIVED: 11 Gray St.; 221 W. Market St.; 44 Belmont Ave.

➤ Mort Lindsey: pianist, composer & conductor ➤
March 21, 1923 - May 4, 2012

Born "Morton Lippman," Lindsey began taking piano lessons as a boy, graduated from Weequahic H.S. and later earned a doctorate in musical education from Columbia. He led Merv Griffin's TV orchestra for almost 25 years, wrote movie scores and worked in the studio and on stage with artists as diverse as Pat Boone and Willie Nelson. Lindsey was also Judy Garland's musical director, most notably at her Carnegie Hall appearance on April 23, 1961. An album of that show won four Grammys. He won an Emmy for his musical direction of Barbra Streisand's 1969 TV special from Central Park.

LIVED: 296 Meeker Ave.; 290 Seymour Ave.

➤ Wynona M. Lipman: first black female state senator ➤
1923 - May 9, 1999

Lipman was born in Georgia, studied French at Talladega College and got a Ph.D. from Columbia. She studied in France as a Fulbright scholar. She taught at Morehouse University in Atlanta, where she tutored Martin Luther King Jr. In 1971, Lipman was the first black woman elected to the N.J. Senate. For a while, she was the only woman and only black in the Senate. She was also an Essex County freeholder, serving as board president, and she taught at Montclair H.S. and Essex County College. As a state legislator, Lipman was an advocate for women, children, minorities and small business.

LIVED: Bel Air Towers, 555 Elizabeth Ave.

Wynona M. Lipman

Harold Lockwood: silent film star
April 17, 1887 - October 19, 1918

Before his life was cut short in the flu epidemic of 1918, Lockwood was one of the screen's biggest draws, rivaling Douglas Fairbanks and Mary Pickford. He was born and went to school in Newark but moved to New York in his late teens, working first as a dry goods salesman before trying his hand at musical comedy and vaudeville and then the movies. Lockwood made dozens of films in a career that lasted only 10 years, two dozen with May Allison in one of Hollywood's first celebrated on-screen romances. A bona fide matinee idol, he also played opposite Pickford in several movies.

LIVED: 18 Grant St.; 24 Breintnall Place

Nicholas Longworth: winemaker & Cincinnati forefather
Jan. 16, 1783 - Feb. 10, 1863

Longworth was born and lived in Newark as a boy, moved and came back before leaving again in 1804 for Cincinnati, essentially a frontier outpost at the time. There, he became a lawyer and banker, made a fortune and stayed the remainder of his life. He was a key figure in Cincinnati's early history and the city's development. Longworth was a savvy real estate investor who, in his devotion to growing the Catawba grape and making wine, has been called the father of the American wine industry. He also gained notoriety cultivating strawberries. His Ohio mansion is now the Taft Museum of Art.

LIVED: "Mount Quiet:" 77 High St., southeast corner with Longworth

Alan V. Lowenstein: lawyer
Aug. 30,1913 - May 8, 2007

Lowenstein was chairman of the Newark Charter Commission that urged a restructuring of city government to provide for the direct election of a mayor and city council. The plan was adopted by voters in 1953. Born in Newark, Lowenstein graduated from the University of Michigan and Harvard Law School. He worked for a law firm in Newark before starting his own firm that still carries his name. He was chairman of Hyatt-Clark Industries and president of the New Jersey Symphony. He also helped modernize New Jersey's corporate law and founded the Institute for Social Justice in Newark.

LIVED: 12 Baldwin Ave.

᠁ Herman Lubinsky: founder of Savoy records ᠁
Aug. 30, 1896 - March 16, 1974

A native of Connecticut, Lubinsky fixed radios, sold parts and operated a radio station in Newark before branching out into record production and sales. He founded the Savoy label in Newark in 1942, a company that issued jazz, blues, black gospel and R&B records by artists as important as Charlie Parker, Lester Young, Miles Davis, Charles Mingus, Dexter Gordon and Johnny Otis. Mostly a businessman, Lubinsky was notorious for cutting costs. But he expanded Savoy across the country by opening new offices and buying smaller labels. He stayed with the company right up until he died.

LIVED: 230 Garside St.; 89 Lehigh Ave.

᠁ Dominic N. "Nick Lucas" Lucanese: performer & guitarist ᠁
Aug. 22, 1897 - July 28, 1982

Lucas was known as "The Crooning Troubadour" and "Grandfather of the Jazz Guitar." He sang on the radio, recorded, appeared in movies and was a featured nightclub and vaudeville performer. He hit his peak in popularity in the 1920s and early '30s. Lucas headlined the last vaudeville show at New York's Palace Theater. Gibson also issued a model of one of its guitars in his name. His renditions of several songs were used in the 1974 film *The Great Gatsby* with Robert Redford. He sang one of his hits, *Tiptoe Through the Tulips,* when Tiny Tim got married on Johnny Carson's TV show in 1969.

LIVED: 139 Clifton Ave.; 331 N. 10th St.; 495 Highland Ave.

᠁ Robert Ludlum: novelist ᠁
May 25, 1927 - March 12, 2001

Ludlum was born in New York and went to Wesleyan University in Connecticut. After a stint in the Marines and as an actor and theater producer, he began writing thrillers at age 42 and eventually published more than two dozen. It is estimated there are 300 million copies of Ludlum's books in print worldwide. Featuring multi-layered plots and righteous heroes, they've also been translated into many languages. Some of his books have been made into TV miniseries or movies, including the Bourne series starring Matt Damon. *The Bourne Ultimatum* won three Oscars in 2008.

LIVED: 376 Ridge St.

⊱ Leon Lumpkins: choirmaster & gospel standout ⊰
April 26, 1934 - Oct. 14, 2007

Lumpkins was the founder of Leon Lumpkins & the Gospel Clefs, an influential all-male quartet that recorded and performed throughout the country in gospel's golden era of the 1950s and beyond. His song, "Open Our Eyes," is regularly listed among gospel's 10 greatest recordings and was covered by Earth, Wind & Fire, as well as Funkadelic and others. "Wings of a Dove" was another of his hits. Lumpkins was born in Newark and served as the musical director of a funeral home and several churches, where he also played the organ. He is a member of the New Jersey Gospel Hall of Fame.

LIVED: 65 Summit St.

⊱ Bertram "Bert" Lytell: actor ⊰
Feb. 24, 1885 - Sept. 28, 1954

Lytell lived briefly in Newark before making a name for himself. He was the host of radio's *Stage Door Canteen* during World War I, a matinee idol on Broadway and a star in the silent film era. His first screen appearance was in 1917 in *The Lone Wolf.* In 1924, he was in *Born Rich* with the film legend Claire Windsor, whom he married. Lytell was in more than 30 movies in the 1920s, but his career suffered when films added sound. He continued on the stage and on radio, and he was on early TV in *One Man's Family.* Lytell was president of the Actors' Equity Association and The Lambs, an actors' club.

LIVED: 107 Halsey St.

⊱ Clara Maass: nurse ⊰
June 28, 1876 - Aug. 24, 1901

Maass graduated from the Newark German Hospital's nursing school in 1895 and was head nurse there within three years. She served in the South, Cuba and the Philippines during the Spanish-American War and returned to Cuba for yellow fever studies in 1901. She died of the disease after letting herself be bitten by an infected mosquito. Maass was buried in Cuba, but her body was later moved to Newark. The U.S. and Cuba issued postage stamps in her honor, and she's in the nursing hall of fame. The hospital in Newark where she worked was named for her, as is a hospital in Belleville today.

LIVED: 9 Sussex Ave.

Clara Maass

⤙ Effa Manley: Negro Leagues team owner ⤚
March 27, 1897 - April 16, 1981

Manley was born in Philadelphia and met Abe, her husband-to-be, at a Yankees game in New York. They married in 1935 and she moved with him to Newark to serve as co-owner and business manager of the Newark Eagles of the Negro Leagues, a position she held until 1948. The Eagles won the Negro Leagues World Series in 1946. The only female owner in the league, Manley was a social activist and used the team to advance civic causes. She also labored to improve conditions for all Negro Leagues players. In 2006, she was the first woman inducted into the National Baseball Hall of Fame.

LIVED: 55 Somerset St.; 71 Crawford St.

⤙ James J. Mapes: chemist, inventor & educator ⤚
May 29, 1806 - Jan. 10, 1866

Born in New York, Mapes was self-educated yet became a professor of chemistry at prestigious institutions. He invented a system for refining sugar in the early 1830s, as well as a machine to make sugar from cane and a process for making sugar from molasses. In 1859, Mapes was awarded the first U.S. patent for artificial fertilizer. He held public exhibitions at his farm in Newark to popularize his agricultural methods, and he also organized the Franklin Institute in Newark. He was the father of celebrated children's story author Mary Mapes Dodge. The family had a street in Newark named for it.

LIVED: Mapes Model Farm, near Renner and Elizabeth avenues

⤙ Bernard "Bernie" Marcus: Home Depot co-founder ⤚
May 12, 1929 -

The son of Russian immigrants who settled in Newark, Marcus graduated from South Side H.S. and Rutgers. With a pharmacy degree, he started out as a druggist, but his interests lay elsewhere and he eventually became head of an L.A.-based home improvement business. Fired from that job, Marcus and his partner, Arthur Blank, founded The Home Depot in 1979 and turned it into the world's largest home improvement chain. Marcus was CEO for 19 years and board chairman until retiring in 2002. A billionaire, he is one of the top charitable donors in the U.S. and routinely cited for his philanthropy.

LIVED: 86 Rose St.

Home of Effa Manley
71 Crawford St.

↣ Anthony J. "Tony" Marenghi: sportswriter ↢
Jan. 14, 1904 - Feb. 21, 1979

Marenghi was one of the country's most revered sportswriters who covered many sports but was best known for his boxing stories. His "From Pillar to Post" column was required reading for area sports fans for years. Marenghi left school at 16 to take an office boy's job at the *Newark Star-Eagle* and remained with the paper almost six decades, the last 40 years after it was renamed a couple of times. He was the N.J. Boxing Writers Association's first president, and he was honored for his length of service by the national Boxing Writers Association at its annual dinner in New York City in 1960.

LIVED: 41 Stirling St.; 27 13th Ave.; 535 Hawthorne Ave.

↣ Dr. Harrison S. Martland: pathologist ↢
Sept. 10, 1883 - 1954

A native of Newark, Martland earned his medical degree from the College of Physicians and Surgeons of Columbia University after going to college in Maryland. In 1909, he was the first full-time paid pathologist at Newark City Hospital, a job he held for 45 years. Martland also served as Essex County's medical examiner for 25 years and was a professor of forensic medicine at NYU. He served on numerous boards and was honored many times for his work in pathology, forensic medicine and occupational safety, especially the effects of radiation. Newark's new city hospital was named for him in 1954.

LIVED: 180 Clinton Ave.

↣ Seymour "Swede" Masin: star athlete ↢
July 7, 1920 - Sept. 10, 2005

Masin is considered Newark's premier home-grown athlete of the pre-World War II era. He starred in football, basketball and track & field at Weequahic H.S. and later excelled in three sports at Panzer College, a small physical education teachers college in East Orange. He was a soccer All-American and a key player on a basketball team that won 44 consecutive games, a U.S. record at the time. Masin later played in the American Basketball League, a forerunner of the NBA. He was also the inspiration for the main character in Philip Roth's 1998 Pulitzer Prize-winning novel, *American Pastoral*.

LIVED: 434 S. 18th St.; 179 Keer Ave; 119 Maple Ave.; 123 Grumman Ave.

"Swede" Masin

⤳ Sherman L. "Jocko" Maxwell: sportswriter & sportscaster ⤲
Dec. 18, 1907 - July 16, 2008

Maxwell spent much of his life in Newark and made his mark covering local sports. He is thought to be America's first black sportscaster. He achieved that distinction with a weekly sports show on Newark radio station WNJR in the late 1920s. By the 1930s, Maxwell was heard on a number of North Jersey stations. He also contributed stories to the local papers, especially on the Newark Eagles of the Negro Leagues, as well as to *Baseball Digest*. A postal clerk by day, he became the announcer for the Eagles' games at Ruppert Stadium and, in 1940, published a book of his baseball interviews.

LIVED: 519 Hawthorne Ave.; 60 Greenwood Ave.; 17 Stengel Ave.

⤳ Cardinal Theodore E. McCarrick: Roman Catholic priest ⤲
July 7, 1930 -

Cardinal McCarrick was born in New York City and ordained a priest in 1958. He held a number of positions in the church, including dean of students at Catholic University in Washington, DC, where he'd earned a doctorate, before being named bishop of Metuchen, NJ, in 1981. Five years later, McCarrick was promoted to Archbishop of Newark. In that post, he traveled widely, served on many church committees and hosted Mother Teresa and Pope John Paul II in Newark. He was appointed archbishop of Washington, DC, in 2000, retiring in 2006 at the customary age of 75.

LIVED: 89 Ridge St.

⤳ Thomas N. McCarter: lawyer & Public Service president ⤲
Oct. 20, 1867 - Oct. 22, 1955

McCarter was born in Newark and attended Newark Academy before graduating from Princeton and Columbia Law School. He started his law career at his father's firm in Newark. He served as a judge, a state senator and, for a year, state attorney general. He organized the Public Service Corp. of NJ and served as president for 36 years, expanding its scope significantly before resigning in 1945. McCarter also served as general counsel to the Fidelity Trust Co. of Newark. McCarter Highway and Princeton's McCarter Theatre are named for him, while a Newark law firm bears the family name.

LIVED: 1044 Broad St.

⊱ Walter McDougall: cartoonist ⊰
Feb. 10, 1858 - March 6, 1938

McDougall was the dean of American cartoonists. Born in Newark, he began his career as an engraver at the *New York Graphic* in the 1870s and then contributed to some of the biggest magazines of the day before being hired by *The New York Herald*. McDougall was prolific, turning out a half-dozen daily newspaper comic strips and single cartoons for Sunday. One of his cartoons helped elect Grover Cleveland president; another was criticized by the U.S. Supreme Court. He also covered the White House as a newsman during the presidency of Teddy Roosevelt, who was a personal friend of his.

LIVED: 446 High St.; 161 Garside St.; 151 W. Kinney St.; 39 E. Kinney St.

⊱ Rachel K. McDowell: journalist ⊰
Jan. 11, 1880 - Aug. 30, 1949

McDowell started her newspaper career as a society reporter in Newark before joining *The New York Herald* and *The New York Times*. She worked at *The Times* from 1920 to 1948 and was the paper's first religion editor, developing a national reputation and getting nicknamed the "Lady Bishop." McDowell also had a radio program on religion and lectured on religious issues around the country. A strict Presbyterian who never married, she was an outspoken critic of profanity and started the Pure Language League to keep newspaper stories clean. Her father was William Osborne McDowell.

LIVED: 20 Spruce St.; 447 Summer Ave.; 201 Grafton Ave.

⊱ William O. McDowell: patriot & peace advocate ⊰
April 10, 1848 - March 1927

McDowell made his money from a variety of business ventures but was better known for his numerous projects that promoted freedom, democracy and world peace. He founded the national committee of the Sons of the American Revolution, helped start the DAR, raised money for the Statue of Liberty pedestal and initiated an effort to cast a Liberty Bell replica and send it on national tour. He also organized a flag-raising event where the "Pledge of Allegiance" was first recited. McDowell founded the League of Peace, a UN forerunner, and drafted a "United Nations of the World" constitution.

LIVED: 20 Spruce St.; 447 Summer Ave.; 201 Grafton Ave.

ᐧᐧ Joseph J. "Iron Man" McGinnity: Hall of Fame pitcher ᐧᐧ
March 20, 1871 - Nov. 14, 1929

McGinnity picked up his nickname from working in a foundry in the off-season and also for pitching into midlife. A righthander, he won 246 games and lost 142 in a Major League career that spanned 10 years, leading the league in wins five times and winning 30 games twice. He played on a team that captured the World Series in 1905. After leaving the majors, McGinnity owned and played for a series of minor league teams, including the Newark Indians of the Eastern League from 1909-12. He retired from playing when he was 54 and was elected to the National Baseball Hall of Fame in 1946.

LIVED: 21 Burnet St.; 243 Meeker Ave.; 454 Broad St.

ᐧᐧ Frank J. McGovern: bar owner ᐧᐧ
May 1902 - Nov. 18, 1989

McGovern was a laborer when he came to the U.S. from Ireland in the 1920s, working around Port Newark. In 1936, he opened a pub on New Street that became Newark's most revered tavern and one that is known worldwide. He remained at the helm until he retired in 1968 and family members took over the place. McGovern established a social and charitable organization that carried his name and helped young Irish immigrants. He was a strong supporter of the Irish Republican Army and was said as a youth to have taken part in the 1916 uprising that led to Irish independence.

LIVED: 17 Huntington Terrace; 71 S. 9th St.

ᐧᐧ A. Malcolm McGregor: actor ᐧᐧ
Oct. 13, 1892 - April 29, 1945

McGregor was born in Newark and educated at private schools and Yale, where he was an intercollegiate swimming and diving champion. He and a Yale classmate were the first persons to sail a wind-driven vessel through the Panama Canal. Intent on becoming an actor at an early age, McGregor traveled to Hollywood in 1920 and landed his first role two years later in *The Prisoner of Zenda*. He played in 55 movies between 1922 and 1937, usually supporting leading ladies. His career ebbed when sound came to film. His last film was as a gangster in the low-budget *Special Agent K-7*.

LIVED: 1066 Broad St.; 850 Broad St.

✒ James H. "Jimmy" McGriff: jazz organist ✒
April 3, 1936 - May 24, 2008

McGriff was a native of Pennsylvania who picked up the piano at age 5, studied music in college and bought his first Hammond B-3 organ in 1956. Primarily known as a soul-jazz artist, he recorded nearly 100 albums and played in concert halls and clubs all over the world, performing with artists as renowned as Buddy Rich, Wynton Marsalis, Junior Parker and Hank Crawford. An instrumental version of *I've Got a Woman* and *All About My Girl* were two of his hits. In the early 1970s, McGriff was owner of a club in Newark called the "Golden Slipper" and recorded two live albums there.

LIVED: 99 Lincoln Ave.

✒ George N. Mehnert: champion wrestler ✒
Nov. 3, 1881 - July 8, 1948

Mehnert is considered one of America's greatest wrestlers and one of the country's first wrestling superstars. He began wrestling as a amateur in 1898 and, while competing for a sporting club in Newark, won six national AAU titles starting in 1902. Along the way, he ran up a 59-match winning streak. Mehnert is one of only a handful of American wrestlers to win two Olympic gold medals. He captured his first one as a flyweight in St. Louis in 1904 and his second four years later in London as a bantamweight. He wrestled as a professional when his Olympic days ended and also promoted the sport.

LIVED: 184 N. 11th St.; 138 S. 10th St.; 155 W. Kinney St.

✒ William G. Mennen: founder, consumer products business ✒
Dec. 20, 1884 - Feb. 17, 1968

Mennen took a personal care business that his father, a German immigrant, started from a drugstore he bought in Newark in 1878 and built it into a global corporation with thousands of workers. He attended the Burnet Street School and Newark High School before going to Cornell, where he earned an engineering degree. The Mennen Co. was a pioneer in the development, packaging and advertising of products such as talcum powder, toothpaste, shaving cream and deodorant. It was sold to Colgate-Palmolive in 1992 for $670 million. A sports arena in Morris County carries the family's name.

LIVED: 38 Fulton St.; 727 High St.; 261 Grafton Ave.; 510 Ridge St.

⌒ Francis J. "Frank" Mertz: university president ⌒
Sept. 24, 1937 -

A native of Newark, Mertz graduated from St. Peter's Prep in Jersey City, St. Peter's College and NYU Law School. He held a variety of jobs at St. Peter's College, including executive vice president. In 1990, he was appointed interim president of Fairleigh Dickinson University and was officially installed as the school's fifth president two years later, remaining until 1999. Mertz was brought in to restore the university to financial stability. He served as chairman of the N.J. Commission on Higher Education and has been on the boards of a number of educational groups and institutions of higher learning.

LIVED: 11-3-1A Hawkins Court

⌒ Samuel C. Miller: Newark Museum director ⌒
May 6, 1930 - Nov. 7, 2013

A native of Oregon, Miller was born into a ranching family and headed east to do graduate work in fine arts at NYU. After working at an art gallery in Buffalo, he was named fifth director of The Newark Museum in 1968. He retired in 1993. During his tenure, the museum enlarged its American and Tibetan folk-art collections, opened its first permanent African art gallery, restored the 1885 Ballantine House and added paintings by European and American artists. Miller and his wife were celebrated for their lavish fund-raising parties, helping to raise millions for the museum's 1989 renovation.

LIVED: 375 Mount Prospect Ave.

⌒ Anthony S. "Skippy" Minisi: Hall of Fame halfback ⌒
Sept. 18, 1926 - May 5, 2005

Minisi was a three-sport star at Newark Academy who played football at the University of Pennsylvania and U.S. Naval Academy. In 1945, he caught a touchdown pass in the final seconds to help Navy beat Penn while, the next year, he scored three touchdowns to help Penn beat Navy before a crowd of 78,000 in Philadelphia. Minisi was elected to the College Football Hall of Fame in 1985. He played a year in the pros before going to law school and spending his career as a lawyer in Philadelphia. He was a college football official, president of the Maxwell Football Club and served on Penn's board.

LIVED: 336 Clifton Ave.

❧ Henry E. "Hank" Mobley: jazz saxophonist & composer ❧
July 7, 1930 - May 30, 1986

Mobley was born in Georgia and raised in Elizabeth. He came from a family of musicians, particularly pianists, and piano was his first instrument. He began playing professionally at 19 and recorded for Savoy, Prestige and Blue Note. He recorded 20 albums alone for Blue Note between 1955 and 1970. *Soul Station* is often cited as his best recording. Among those Mobley worked or recorded with were Miles Davis, Horace Silver, Art Blakey, Lee Morgan, Dizzy Gillespie, Elvin Jones, McCoy Tyner and Max Roach. He largely retired in his mid-40s because of bad lungs and died of pneumonia.

LIVED: 440 Jelliff Ave.

❧ Hortense Monath: concert pianist ❧
Jan. 16, 1905 - May 21, 1956

A leading American classical pianist of the mid-20th century, Monath was known as "Newark's gift to music." She grew up in Newark, studied with Arthur Schnabel and made her professional debut at 19 and New York debut seven years later. She performed abroad and appeared regularly with the New York Philharmonic. Monath was the first American woman to perform as a soloist with the NBC Symphony under Toscanini. She also had her own performing company in New York. A critic once wrote that listening to Monath was like communing with Schumann, Liszt and Beethoven.

LIVED: 777 Clinton Ave.

❧ James Moody: jazz saxophonist & flutist ❧
March 26, 1925 - Dec. 9, 2010

Moody was born in Savannah, GA, but grew up in Newark and lived in Newark well into his life. He began his career after playing in a segregated military band during World War II. At war's end, he joined Dizzy Gillespie and began a recording career as a leader and sideman that lasted until right before he died. Moody recorded for a dozen labels and is best known for *Moody's Mood for Love*, a hit in the 1950s. He lived and played in Europe for several years and, in the 1970s, played in Las Vegas show bands. He was an NEA Jazz Master, and his last album won a Grammy award after he died.

LIVED: 183 Pennington Court; The Colonnade

⤛ Melba Moore: singer & actress ⤜
Oct. 29, 1945 -

Moore was born "Beatrice Melba Smith" in New York and shortened her stepfather's last name for her stage name after her mother remarried and they moved to Newark. She graduated from Arts H.S. and Montclair State with a teaching degree but soon pursued a career in music, her first love. Moore was in the original cast of the play *Hair* and won a Tony in 1970 for *Purlie*. She has appeared in other Broadway productions, in movies and on TV, as well as recording for Mercury, Capitol and other major labels. She has been nominated for four Grammys and also had a long-running one-woman show.

LIVED: 283 Rose St.

⤛ Thomas Moran: painter ⤜
Feb. 12, 1837 - Aug. 25, 1926

Moran was one of America's greatest landscape artists, belonging to both the Hudson River School and Rocky Mountain School. He was born in England and was first employed in Philadelphia as a wood-engraver. His work as an illustrator for *Scribner's Weekly* and other publications helped launch his painting career. Moran was a member of one of the first official expeditions to Yellowstone, and his sketchings helped convince the government to make the area a national park. There are spots named for him in Yellowstone and the Grand Teton National Park. His wife, Mary, was an etcher and painter.

LIVED: 166 Brunswick St.; 9 Thomas St.

⤛ Charles Stewart Mott: businessman & philanthropist ⤜
June 2, 1875 - Feb. 18, 1973

Mott was one of the wealthiest men of his time, making his money largely through his association with General Motors. He was one of GM's biggest shareholders, a vice president and a company director for 60 years. He also set up and later funded his foundation with GM stock. It has given millions to causes throughout the country. Mott graduated from Stevens and was a Spanish-American War veteran who headed a family-owned company that made wire wheels and axles before it was sold to and he took a position with GM. He had other business interests and also served as mayor of Flint, MI.

LIVED: 964 Broad St.; 77 Thomas St.

Charles Stewart Mott

⌒ Franklin Murphy: governor & businessman ⌒
Jan. 3, 1846 - Feb. 24, 1920

Murphy was born in Jersey City and attended Newark Academy at the outset of the Civil War. Though a teen, he enlisted for duty and served three years with the Union forces. He returned to Newark, founded the Murphy Varnish Co. and got involved in local politics. A Republican, Murphy served on the common council and won a state Assembly seat. He was elected governor in 1902, serving until 1905. He remained active in politics and was a delegate to five national GOP conventions. Murphy was an unsuccessful candidate for vice president in 1908. There is a statue of him in Newark's Weequahic Park.

LIVED: 52 Pennsylvania Ave.; 12 Chestnut St.; 1027 Broad St.

⌒ Vincent J. Murphy: mayor & labor leader ⌒
Aug. 1, 1893 - June 8, 1976

Murphy was born in Newark, the oldest of 10 children. At 15, he took a job as a plumber's apprentice and then began ascending through the labor ranks, first in a local plumbers' union. In 1933, he became secretary-treasurer of the state American Federation of Labor. He was elected a city commissioner in Newark in 1937 and served as Newark mayor from 1941 to 1949. Murphy was an unsuccessful Democratic candidate for governor in 1943. After he was beaten in the 1949 city election, he returned to labor circles and became president of the N.J. AFL-CIO in 1961, serving until his 1970 retirement.

LIVED: 154 Hudson St.; 174 S. 11th St.; 45 Finlay Place

⌒ Don "Newk" Newcombe: Dodgers pitcher & NL MVP ⌒
June 14, 1926 -

Newcombe, who grew up in Elizabeth, pitched for the Newark Eagles before joining the Brooklyn Dodgers. He played for three teams in a big league career that lasted from 1949 to 1960, with two years off for military duty. His overall record was 149 wins and 90 losses. Newcombe's best season was in 1956, when he won 27 games and was named the National League's Most Valuable Player and Cy Young Award winner. He was Rookie of the Year in 1949, was named to the all-star team four times and was the first black pitcher to start a World Series game. Newcombe also owned a bar in Newark.

LIVED: 455 Elizabeth Ave.

Franklin Murphy

✨ John K. "Jack" Northrop: engineer & airplane designer ✨
Nov. 10, 1895 - Feb. 18, 1981

At one time it was said that Northrop had something to do with every major plane in the air. He began working in the aviation industry in 1916 and, by 1929, was running his own companies. Northrop was chief designer of the aircraft that early aviation legends Wiley Post and Amelia Earhart flew, as well as some of those used by the military during and after World War II. He also helped design airliners that brought air travel to the general public and was a proponent of the flying wing design. When the Northrop Corp. bought Grumman, it became one of the leading defense contractors in the world.

LIVED: 95 Halsey St.; 194 Fairmount Ave.

✨ Dr. Paul A. "Bucky" O'Connor: physician & halfback ✨
Oct. 24, 1907 - Jan. 2, 1998

O'Connor played for the legendary Knute Rockne and rushed for more than 100 yards in Rockne's final game, Notre Dame's victory over USC ending the 1930 season. The win capped the team's second consecutive perfect season and clintched the mythical college championship. He played himself in a 1931 film, *The Spirit of Notre Dame*. O'Connor later took a medical degree from Yale and had a private practice in Newark for more than a half-century. A World War II veteran, he was on the staffs of several hospitals and served as a Newark Police Department surgeon for many years. He retired in 1989.

LIVED: 157 & 342 Roseville Ave.

✨ Dr. William O'Gorman: physician & surgeon ✨
July 1824 - 1891?

O'Gorman made international news in 1885 when he sent four Newark boys to France for Louis Pasteur's newly discovered rabies treatment. But he was already well known in the states. Born and trained as a doctor in Ireland, he came to the U.S. in 1849 and later set up his practice in Newark. During the Civil War, he was appointed the chief physician for New Jersey soldiers returning from battle. O'Gorman diagnosed the first patient at St. Michael's Hospital in 1867 and served as its first medical director. He was elected Essex County physician, as well as president of the county's medical society.

LIVED: 67, 81 & 172 Market St.; 903 & 905 Broad St.

Jack Northrop

～ Hazel R. O'Leary: U.S. cabinet official & college president ～
May 17, 1937 -

O'Leary served as U.S. Energy Department secretary from 1993-97, the first black woman to do so, and later as president of Fisk University. In between, she headed an investment banking firm and her own consulting business. O'Leary was born in Virginia, lived in Newark with an aunt and graduated from Arts H.S. She took a bachelor's degree from Fisk and law degree from Rutgers-Newark. She was an assistant prosecutor in Essex County, worked for an accounting firm and then moved into the energy field. She was also a utility company official and held jobs President Jimmy Carter's administration.

LIVED: 734 S. 19th St.

～ Shaquille "Shaq" O'Neal: NBA player & media celebrity ～
March 6, 1972 -

O'Neal was one of basketball's biggest stars, earning All-America honors at LSU before turning pro. He played for six teams in a 19-year NBA career, winning four championships, two scoring titles and an MVP award. He was also a member of the 1996 Olympic basketball team that won a gold medal. O'Neal was born in and spent his early years in Newark. He credits the Boys and Girls Club with keeping him focused and off the streets. He made his name as a high school player in Texas, where his stepfather was stationed in the service. O'Neal frequently visits and has business interests in Newark.

LIVED: 296 Littleton Ave.; 139 Vassar Ave.

～ Jeremiah O'Rourke: architect ～
Feb. 6, 1833 - April 22, 1915

O'Rourke was born and educated in Dublin, Ireland, and came to the U.S. in 1850. He founded two architectural firms in Newark that carried his name and made his reputation designing Catholic churches and schools. He had a hand in designing the Basilica of the Sacred Heart in Newark, New York's Church of St. Paul the Apostle and the main building of what was then Seton Hall College. In 1893, O'Rourke was appointed supervising architect of the U.S. Treasury. There, he designed federal buildings, including post offices, in Buffalo; Duluth, MN; Kansas City, MO; Washington, DC, and elsewhere.

LIVED: 49 Adams St.; 152 Plane St.; 17 & 45 Burnet St.

Shaquille O'Neal

⌒ William Hamilton Osborne: writer & copyright lawyer ⌒
Jan. 7, 1873 - Dec. 25, 1942

Born and educated in Newark, Osborne practiced law in the 1890s, at one point representing the Authors League of America and Dramatists Guild of America. He turned to writing around 1902 and wrote short stories for many of the leading magazines of the day, such as *The Saturday Evening Post*. Besides hundreds of stories, Osborne wrote screenplays, essays and novels, many of them crime stories. Among his better known books were *The Red Mouse*; *Catspaw*; *Blue Buckle* and *The Running Fight*, which was made into a film. Osborne's *Neal of the Navy* was made into a motion picture serial.

LIVED: 118 Fifth Ave.; 213 Highland Ave.

⌒ Franklin Pangborn: comedic character actor ⌒
Jan. 23, 1889 - July 20, 1958

Pangborn started out on stage and later appeared in dozens of short features and full-length comedies and musicals from the silent film era through the 1940s. He worked for Preston Sturges, Mack Sennett and Hal Roach in supporting roles, often as a foil to great comedians. He was in the W.C. Fields' classics *The Bank Dick* and *Never Give a Sucker an Even Break*. Pangborn grew up in Newark, attended local schools and served in World War I. He also appeared on Red Skelton's TV show, with Jack Benny on the radio and TV and was the announcer on Jack Paar's late-night network TV show.

LIVED: 89 Pacific St.; 22 Vernon Ave.; 64 Millington Ave.; 10 Kearny Ave.

⌒ Cortlandt Parker: lawyer & prosecutor ⌒
June 27, 1818 - July 29, 1907

Parker was born in Perth Amboy, graduated first in his 1836 Rutgers College class and studied for the law with the noted Theodore Frelinghuysen. He was admitted to the bar in 1839 and, as a lawyer practicing in Newark, wasted no time getting involved in local politics. He campaigned for the Whig ticket of Henry Clay and Frelinghuysen in 1844, later turning Republican. Parker was Essex County prosecutor from 1857-67, the only public job he ever held. He turned down judgeships and ambassador posts to Vienna and Russia. He was president of the American, New Jersey and Essex County bar associations.

LIVED: 1 Park Pl.; 161, 566 & 568 Broad; 21 Washington St.; 7 Lombardy

✎ Maj. Gen. James "Galloping Jim" Parker: war hero ✎
Feb. 20, 1854 - June 2, 1934

A son of Cortlandt, Parker enjoyed a long and distinguished Army career after graduating from Rutgers and West Point. He began his service with campaigns against the Indians in the West — one of his missions was to track down Geronimo — and ended with the advent of World War I. In between, he led troops in the Mexican border clashes, Spanish-American War and the Philippine Insurrection, where he earned the Medal of Honor. Parker wrote several books and numerous articles about his military exploits. One of his brothers was a congressman, and another was a N.J. Supreme Court justice.

LIVED: 161 Broad St.

✎ Dr. Aaron E. Parsonnet: heart specialist & bookbinder ✎
Oct. 14, 1888 - Aug. 20, 1950

Parsonnet began practicing medicine in Newark after getting his degree from Loyola University Medical School in Chicago. He was a family doctor and specialist in heart disease, as well as chief of medicine at Newark Beth Israel Hospital. He wrote extensively on heart health and problems and was one of the founders of the American College of Cardiology. Parsonnet's hobbies included playing the cello and collecting rare books and Russian antiques. He was also a noted bookbinder. His re-bound books, some with embossed gold lettering, can be found in medical libraries and The Newark Museum.

LIVED: 131 W. Kinney St.; 95 Avon Ave.; 3 Madison Ave.

✎ Marion R. Parsonnet: writer, producer & director ✎
Feb. 21, 1905 - Dec. 7, 1960

Parsonnet graduated from Newark Academy, Harvard and NYU Law School before devoting himself to writing. He's best known for the screenplay of the 1946 movie *Gilda* that turned Rita Hayworth into a sex symbol. His other movie projects included *Cover Girl* and *I'll Be Seeing You*. Parsonnet was the dramatic director of the Columbia Broadcasting Co. He also wrote and produced radio shows, including one for Mary Pickford, as well as early TV shows, including *The Doctor* and *Steve Randall*. He later wrote for TV's *Bonanza*; *Maverick*; *Zane Grey Theater* and *Tombstone Territory*.

LIVED: 25 Stengel Ave.; 24 Hillside Ave.; 134 W. Kinney St.

Dr. Victor Parsonnet: pioneering cardiologist & surgeon

Aug. 29, 1924 -

Parsonnet is a cardiovascular surgeon with a long list of operating-room firsts in New Jersey, including first bypass surgery, first heart and kidney transplants, first stents and first pacemakers. He graduated from Cornell and NYU Medical School and trained at the top cardiac centers. Parsonnet has been chief of surgery at Beth Israel Medical Center in Newark, a hospital his grandfathers founded. He is a founding member of the N.J. chapter of the American College of Cardiology and co-founded the Heart Rhythm Society. He has written extensively and also served as chairman of the New Jersey Symphony.

LIVED: 777 High St.; 18 Keer Ave.

Donald M. Payne Sr.: New Jersey's first black congressman

July 16, 1934 - March 6, 2012

Payne was born in Newark and graduated from Barringer H.S, then Seton Hall. He was a teacher and executive at the Prudential Insurance Co. before entering politics. He joined the Newark YMCA in 1957 and in 1970 was elected the first black president of the group's national council. Payne was first elected an Essex County freeholder in 1972 and later served as board president. In 1982, he was elected to the city council from the South Ward and served until elected to the House of Representatives in 1988. He died in his twelfth term in office. He also chaired the Congressional Black Caucus.

LIVED: 52 High St.; 24 Hunterdon St.; 94 Peabody Place; 14 Bock Ave.

Lute Pease: Pulitzer Prize-winning cartoonist

March 27, 1869 - Aug. 16, 1963

Lucius Curtis Pease was born in Nevada and raised in Vermont. He lived a varied and adventurous life in the West, including mining for gold in Alaska, before coming east in 1912 and working for the *Newark Evening News*. He had previously worked for *The Oregonian* in Portland and was editor of the *Pacific Monthly*. Pease worked at *The News* for 40 years, winning a Pulitzer Prize in 1949 at the age of 80 for a cartoon of labor leader John L. Lewis. He created a comic strip for the paper as well, called the *Adventures of Powder Pete*. Pease was also a painter and published at least one book of his work.

LIVED: 31 Franklin St.; 38 Spruce St.

Dr. Victor Parsonnet

⤙ William T. Pecora: geologist and U.S. government official ⤚
Feb. 1, 1913 - July 19, 1972

Pecora was a world-renowned geologist who became undersecretary of the U.S. Interior Department. He graduated from Barringer H.S. and Princeton and took a doctorate from Harvard. He was a fencing champion in college and an Olympian. Pecora was director of the U.S. Geological Survey and led many field expeditions in the U.S. and abroad. The mineral *pecoraite* was named for him. He promoted the early uses of satellite technology to assess the earth's resources and dangers from earthquakes. He was elected to the National Academy of Science and American Academy of Arts and Sciences.

LIVED: 360 Bloomfield Ave.

⤙ Thomas B. Peddie: businessman, politician & philanthropist ⤚
Feb. 12, 1808 - Feb. 16, 1889

Peddie came to the U.S. from Scotland and set up shop in Newark after scouting several cities. He apprenticed as a leather worker before starting his own business making trunks and traveling bags. When he died, his factory covered a city block and employed hundreds. Peddie served as mayor, an assemblyman and congressman. He was also a bank president, an insurance company director and a member of charitable and civic groups. A religious man who believed in giving back to the community, he endowed the Peddie School in Hightstown and Peddie Memorial Baptist Church in Newark.

LIVED: 382 & 393 Broad; 1 Fair; 4, 16 & 49 Harrison; 14 Camfield; 33 Park Place

⤙ Joseph F. "Joe" Pesci: actor & musician ⤚
Feb. 9, 1943 -

Pesci was born to working-class parents in Newark and raised in Belleville. He began performing on stage at age 5 and on a TV variety show at 10. His first film was *The Death Collector* in 1975, a role that opened the door to a part in *Raging Bull* and a number of other movies. In 1990, Pesci won an Oscar for best supporting actor in *Goodfellas*. His other movies include *Casino*; *My Cousin Vinny*; *Home Alone* and the *Lethal Weapon* series. In 1999, he announced his retirement from acting to pursue music. He was a producer of the Broadway musical *Jersey Boys* and is portrayed in the play.

LIVED: 625 N. 7th St.

Home of Joe Pesci
625 N. 7th St.

William Pennington: U.S. House speaker & governor
May 4, 1796 - Feb. 16, 1862

A descendant of Newark's first settlers, Pennington was born in Newark and graduated from Princeton. His father, William S., had been governor and a judge. He studied law and was licensed in 1817, then served as a court clerk. He was elected to the state Assembly in 1828 and elected governor annually from 1837 to 1843. Pennington then returned to Newark to practice law and turned down an appointment to be territorial governor of Minnesota. He was elected to Congress in 1858 and served as speaker of the House in 1859 in his only term. After leaving office, he resumed his law practice in Newark.

LIVED: 228 Broad St., corner of Cedar; 129 High St.

Rev. Abraham Pierson: pastor & Yale University founder
1645 - March 5, 1707

Pierson's father was a minister who came to America on the Mayflower and was one of Newark's founders. The younger Pierson was born on Long Island and graduated Harvard in 1668. He was then ordained and studied with his father in Newark, becoming pastor of the First Congregational Church with his father's death in 1678. After the church turned Presbyterian, Pierson moved to Connecticut to continue his life as a clergyman and was the first rector (1701-1707) and a founder of the Collegiate School, later Yale University, in New Haven. There is a bronze statue of him at Yale.

LIVED: Market Street, between High & Washington streets

Addison B. Poland: educator
March 26, 1851 - Sept. 15, 1917

Poland was born in Massachusetts and educated at Wesleyan University in Connecticut. He was a Massachusetts high school principal before becoming a school principal and then superintendent in Jersey City. He was assistant school superintendent in New York City, superintendent in Paterson and New Jersey state school superintendent before being named Newark school superintendent in 1901. Poland held that position for 15 years and, in 1912, introduced a year-round school program in Newark that lasted for 19 years. It is often considered the most successful program of its kind in the country.

LIVED: 60 Abington Ave.; 258 Montclair Ave.

ᐅ Marquis D. "Bo" Porter: baseball player & manager ᐊ
July 5, 1972 -

Porter was a star in three sports at Weequahic H.S. and then excelled in football and baseball at the University of Iowa. He was drafted by the Chicago Cubs in 1993 and made his big league debut in 1999. He also played for the Texas Rangers and Oakland A's before turning to coaching and managing, first in the minor leagues. Porter later served as third-base coach for the Florida Marlins, Arizona Diamondbacks and Washington Nationals. At the end of the 2012 season, he was named manager of the Houston Astros, the first Newarker to manage a Major League ball club.

LIVED: 793 S. 14th St.

ᐅ Napolean W. "Teddy" Powell: concert promoter ᐊ
Feb. 1, 1921 - July 18, 1990

Powell was a native of North Carolina but, from a base in Newark, became one of the most prominent black promoters in the country. He promoted most of the top African-American performers of the day at venues in and around Newark, performers such as Nat "King" Cole, Billy Eckstine, B.B. King, Ray Charles, Whitney Houston, Count Basie, Sarah Vaughan, Billie Holiday, Miles Davis, James Brown, Muddy Waters and Aretha Franklin. Powell also owned a couple of nightclubs in Newark and was one of the forces behind the Randall's Island Jazz Festival in New York in the 1960s.

LIVED: 337 Belmont Ave.

ᐅ Clement A. Price: professor & historian ᐊ
Oct. 13, 1945 - Nov. 5, 2014

Price earned a Ph.D. in history from Rutgers and began teaching history at Essex County College in 1968. He joined the Rutgers faculty in 1975 and, in time, became one of Newark's most respected and recognized scholars. Price received many prestigious awards, wrote extensively, was a consultant and lecturer, got numerous project grants and served on the boards of many civic and educational organizations, including the N.J. State Council on the Arts. He was a member of President Obama's transition team in 2008 and served as vice chair of the National Advisory Council on Historic Preservation.

LIVED: 55 Lincoln Park

⚮ Rabbi Joachim Prinz: Jewish leader & civil rights advocate ⚮
May 10, 1902 - Sept. 30, 1988

Prinz grew up in rural Germany and was ordained a rabbi in 1925 after receiving a Ph.D. in philosophy. He spoke out against the dangers of Hitler's rising power early on and left Germany for the U.S. in 1937, after serving as a rabbi in Berlin. Two years later, he was named rabbi at the Temple B'nai Abraham in Newark. Prinz was president of the American Jewish Congress and chairman of a conference that represented a majority of American Jews. He retired in 1977 but continued preaching. He was an ardent supporter of civil rights causes and helped organize the 1963 March on Washington, DC.

LIVED: 49 Shanley Ave.; 826 S. 11th St.

⚮ Ike Quebec: jazz saxophonist ⚮
Aug. 17, 1918 - Jan. 16, 1963

Ike Quebec Abrams was a dancer and pianist, but he began his professional career playing tenor sax with the Newark-based Barons of Rhythm in the 1940s. He recorded for Savoy and Blue Note as a sideman and a leader. Quebec recorded and performed with Hot Lips Page, Roy Eldridge, Ella Fitzgerald, Benny Carter, Coleman Hawkins and Cab Calloway. He was also a talent scout for Blue Note, helping bring Thelonius Monk and Bud Powell to the label. Quebec had his highs and lows. In the '50s, while he performed regularly, he recorded only sporadically. He was also a feared pool player.

LIVED: 179 Morris Ave.

⚮ Queen Latifah: singer, actress & show host ⚮
March 18, 1970 -

"Queen Latifah," Dana Elaine Owens, was born and lived her early years in Newark, attending a Catholic grammar school. She released her first hip-hop single in 1988. With a keen eye for business, she quickly branched out into record production, TV, film, movie production and product endorsements. She also turned to singing jazz and soul. Owens has won Grammy, Golden Globe and Screen Actors Guild awards. She has also been nominated for an Emmy, and an Oscar for her role in the adaptation of the musical *Chicago*. She has a star on the Hollywood Walk of Fame and her own TV talk show.

LIVED: 79 Broad St.

Queen Latifah

✌ Bernard Rabin: art restorer & gallery owner ✌
Nov. 1, 1916 - March 24, 2003

Rabin was born in the Bronx but was in Newark by his teens and attended Newark State College. He later studied with Brooklyn Museum conservators and became one of the world's most respected and innovative art restoration experts. Rabin led a team that restored art at the Uffizi Gallery in Florence after floods in 1966, as well as artwork at the White House, U.S. Capitol, Library of Congress, Metropolitan Museum of Art and Museum of Modern Art. He and his partner Nathan Krueger owned two landmark art galleries in Newark. He also taught conservation and restoration at Princeton University.

LIVED: 290 Wainwright St.; 32 Pennington St.

✌ Ralph Rainger: pianist & Oscar-winning composer ✌
Oct. 7, 1901 - Oct. 23, 1942

Rainger was born "Ralph Reichenthal" in New York City and moved with his family as a boy to Newark, where his father had a carpet business. He graduated from Barringer H.S. and became a lawyer, though his first love was music. Rainger barely practiced law before devoting himself entirely to playing the piano and composing. He began his music career in New York and later moved to the West Coast, writing songs for film. He had many hits, including Jack Benny's theme song and Bob Hope's *Thanks for the Memory*, which won an Academy Award in 1939. He died in a freak plane accident.

LIVED: 329 Broad St.; 510 Summer Ave.; 175 Keer Ave.

✌ Oliver Randolph: lawyer & civil rights advocate ✌
Oct. 31, 1877 - Sept. 2, 1951

Born in Mississippi, Randolph went to college in Texas and graduated from Howard Law School. In 1914, he was the first black admitted to the state bar. He was also the first black assistant U.S. Attorney in New Jersey and only black delegate at the state's 1947 Constitutional Convention, where he successfully argued for a ban on segregation in public schools and militia. Randolph was a Republican assemblyman from Essex County and a national convention delegate. He practiced law in Newark and was a deputy attorney general. The Garden State Bar Association gives an award in his honor.

LIVED: 230 Bank St.; 69 Plane St; 123 S. 13th St.

Home of Ralph Rainger
510 Summer Ave.

⌁ Richard H. Ranger: radio engineer & inventor ⌁
June 13, 1889 - Jan. 10, 1962

Ranger graduated from MIT, served in World War I and later joined RCA as an engineer, where he invented a forerunner of the fax machine. His other inventions included the pipeless electronic organ and electronic chimes. He helped develop radar, airborne radio relays and magnetic recording. Ranger won an Oscar in 1956 for inventing a machine that synchronized film and sound. He left RCA in 1930 to form his own company, Rangertone, and to offer his services as a radio, acoustic and electronics consultant. During World II, he was a lieutenant colonel assigned to technical intelligence work.

LIVED: 574 Parker St.

⌁ Edward S. Rankin: renowned sewer expert & author ⌁
March 6, 1861 - March 8, 1945

Rankin took a civil engineering degree from Princeton and, a few years later, became Newark's assistant surveyor. In 1903, he was put in charge of the city's sewer system and then named division engineer. He was a consultant on sewer issues and designed sewer systems for other municipalities. Rankin was president of the American Society of Municipal Engineers in 1922 and received its medal of honor. He also wrote books on early Newark that were used in the schools, edited the N.J. Historical Society's quarterly magazine and compiled a historical map of Newark for the city's 250th anniversary.

LIVED: 751 High St.; 245 Grafton Ave.; 104 13th Ave.; 88 Abington Ave.

⌁ Willie Ratner: sportswriter ⌁
June 10, 1895 - April 3, 1980

Ratner started out at the *Newark Evening News* as a copyboy in 1912 and didn't leave until the paper closed in August 1972. He began his writing career covering bicycle racing before moving on to boxing during World War I and also thoroughbred racing. He covered Jack Dempsey before Dempsey won the heavyweight title and was friends with Dempsey for years. Over time, Ratner gained a national reputation for his fight coverage and column, "Punching the Bag." He also hosted a sports radio call-in show and was inducted into the N.J. Boxing Hall of Fame in the year that he died.

LIVED: 98 Quitman St.; 301 Goldsmith Ave.; 2 Custer Ave.

⤙ Thomas L. Raymond: mayor ⤚
April 26, 1875 - Oct. 4, 1928

Raymond was born in East Orange to a father who was a banker in New York. He studied at Newark Academy and NYU Law School, passing the bar in 1896. He held a variety of public jobs in his life, including judge and Essex County prosecutor. He was married to the daughter of the chief justice of the N.J. Supreme Court. Raymond served two terms as mayor, 1915-17 and 1925-28. Work on Port Newark began in his first term. He had his eye on higher office but was defeated in his bid for state Senate in 1908 and in the 1920 gubernatorial primary. He was a delegate to two GOP conventions.

LIVED: 16 E. Kinney St.

⤙ Richard J. "The Cat" Regan: basketball player, coach & AD ⤚
Nov. 30, 1930 - Dec. 24, 2002

Regan was an all-state basketball player at West Side H.S. who later starred at Seton Hall. His 1953 team won the NIT championship and was ranked the No. 2 team in the country. Regan was MVP of the East-West college all-star game after the season. He was a first-round pick of the NBA's Rochester Royals in the 1953 and played in the pros for three seasons after spending two years in the Marines. He was an NBA all-star his final year. He later served as Seton Hall's basketball coach, athletic director, head of its athletic fundraising arm and an assistant to the vice president of university affairs.

LIVED: 438 Central Ave.; 388 W. Market St.; 35 S. 7th St.

⤙ William C. "Billy" Reick: New York newspaper owner ⤚
Sept. 29, 1864 - Dec. 7, 1924

Reick began his newspaper career in Philadelphia but, before he was done, had become owner of *The New York Sun* and a part owner of *The New York Times*. Harvard-educated, he made his name with *The New York Herald* as a reporter in Newark starting in 1888, later as head of its Paris and London editions and finally as its city editor, publisher and president in Manhattan. Reick spent four years with *The Times* before buying *The Sun*, one of the most influential papers in America in its day. After selling *The Sun*, he took control of the *New York Journal of Commerce* before he retired in 1923.

LIVED: 577 Broad St.

﹥ Louis A. Reilly: banker & public official ﹤
Dec. 26, 1893 - Jan. 1, 1972

Reilly began his banking career as a messenger for the Federal Trust Co., staying more than 25 years and eventually becoming treasurer. A Democrat, he was allied with Jersey City's powerful mayor, Frank Hague, and was named commissioner of the N.J. State Banking and Insurance Department in 1938. Reilly later served as first chairman of the N.J. Racing Commission when it was formed in 1940. He ended his career as Newark's postmaster, a job he held from 1943 until he retired in 1962. He was a member of nearly three dozen civic, charitable and financial groups, often in an executive role.

LIVED: 97 Pennington St.; 77 Weequahic Ave.; 16 Park Place

﹥ Jehudah Reinharz: Brandeis University president ﹤
Aug. 1, 1944 -

Born in Israel, Reinharz immigrated to the U.S. from Germany and attended Weequahic H.S. He has a Ph.D. in modern Jewish history from Brandeis, where he began teaching in 1982 and then held a series of academic and administrative posts. He served as president of Brandeis from 1994 until 2011. Reinharz has written many articles and books, including a standard college text on modern Jewish history. He's been the recipient of numerous awards and honors, the President of Israel Prize among them. He also served on the Presidential Advisory Commission on Holocaust Assets in the U.S.

LIVED: 25 Bragaw Ave.

﹥ Adrian Riker: attorney ﹤
Aug. 16, 1858 - Sept. 27, 1926

Riker was one of New Jersey's most highly regarded attorneys around the turn of the twentieth century, specializing in corporate law. He was educated at Newark Academy and Princeton and took his law degree from Columbia. He was a classmate of Woodrow Wilson at Princeton. Riker was admitted to the bar in 1882 and practiced law in New Jersey for more than 40 years. He was president of the Essex County Bar Association in 1904. The firm of Riker & Riker that he founded with his brother Chandler continues to this day. Riker was also the president, chairman or director of several banks.

LIVED: 169 Clinton Ave.; 19 Penn. Ave. 325 Ridge St.; 222 Ballantine Parkway

⌒ Louis G. "Luigi" Rist: artist ⌒
1888 - Nov. 25, 1959

Rist studied at the Newark Technical School and at an art school in New York. His early work as a painter didn't amount to much. It wasn't until he was introduced to Japanese woodcut prints around 1930 that he found his medium and made his name. Largely self-taught and using tools he made himself, Rist combined traditional Japanese painting, woodcarving and print techniques with his own artistry and painstaking attention to detail to make exquisite color prints, mostly of vegetables, fruits and flowers. He won a number of prizes and his work has been collected by many major museums.

LIVED: 207 Sussex Ave.; 203 & 222 N. 6th St.; 47 Hecker Ave.

⌒ Ritz Brothers: comedy team ⌒

The Ritz Brothers — Al, Harry and Jimmy Joachim — were a popular stage and screen act that lasted from the 1920s to the 1960s. Born in Newark six years apart, they began as dancers and added comedy to their routine. By the early 1930s, they were headliners. Their first movie was in 1934, leading 20th Century Fox to sign them to do full-length musicals. One was Irving Berlin's *On the Avenue*. Their last movie together was in 1943. They returned to performing live, and then on TV, and were a top draw in Las Vegas. Jimmy and Harry continued on after Al died in 1965. They died in the mid-1980s.

LIVED: 501 Springfield Ave.

⌒ Rev. Lawrence C. Roberts: minister & gospel producer ⌒
Aug. 12, 1936 - July 14, 2008

Roberts was a driving force behind Newark's thriving post-World War II gospel scene. He not only sang, he led, recorded and toured with his own groups, including The Angelic Choir. He also worked with many gospel greats for the Newark-based Savoy label, the Rev. James Cleveland among them. Roberts is credited with being the first black gospel producer for a major American record company. He won two Grammys, was given the keys to several cities and was inducted into the N.J. Gospel Hall of Fame. A Newark native, he was a church pastor in Nutley for more than 30 years.

LIVED: 42 Boyd St.; 31 Seymour Ave.

⟩⟩⟩ Peter W. Rodino Jr.: congressman ⟨⟨⟨
June 7, 1909 - May 7, 2005

Born in Newark with the first name of "Pellegrino," Rodino graduated from Barringer H.S., the University of Newark and the Newark Law School. After World War II military service, he won a congressional seat in 1948 on his second try, serving in the House of Representatives for 40 years and retiring in 1989. Rodino sponsored a bill making Columbus Day a national holiday but is best known for serving as chairman of the House Judiciary Committee during televised hearings into the impeachment of President Nixon in 1974. After retiring, he taught and lectured at Seton Hall University Law School.

LIVED: 61 Clifton Ave.; 205 Grafton Ave.

⟩⟩⟩ Narciso Rodriguez: fashion designer ⟨⟨⟨
Jan. 27, 1961 -

The son of Cuban immigrants, Rodriguez grew up in Newark and studied at the Parsons School of Design in New York. After working freelance in the city's garment industry, he took jobs designing women's clothes for Anne Klein under Donna Karan and then Calvin Klein. Rodriguez started his own line in 1997 and rose to fame after designing a wedding dress for the late Carolyn Bessette Kennedy. Michelle Obama also wore one of his dresses the night her husband first won the presidency. He was the first American to win the Council of Fashion Designers of America's top award two years in a row.

LIVED: 105 McWhorter St.

⟩⟩⟩ Philip M. Roth: novelist ⟨⟨⟨
March 19, 1933 -

Roth grew up in Newark and graduated from Weequahic H.S. After studying at Bucknell and the University of Chicago, he began writing short fiction and criticism for magazines. His first novel, *Goodbye Columbus*, won the first of his three National Book Awards in 1960. Roth has won just about every award in literature, including the Pulitzer Prize, PEN/Faulkner Award and National Book Critics Circle Award. Four of his works have been turned into movies. He also has taught at several colleges and received an honorary doctorate from Harvard. Newark has been the setting for much of his fiction.

LIVED: 385 Leslie St.; 81 Summit Ave.

Home of Peter W. Rodino Jr.
205 Grafton Ave.

✎ Theodore Runyon: mayor, diplomat & Civil War general ✎
Oct. 29, 1822 - Jan. 27, 1896

Runyon graduated from Yale, studied law in Newark and was admitted to the bar in 1846. He practiced law in Newark before serving as city attorney, city counselor and then mayor from 1864-66. He was also chancellor of New Jersey, a job he held for 14 years and that made him wealthy. Runyon was appointed a brigadier general in 1857 and the major general in charge of the New Jersey National Guard soon thereafter. During the Civil War, he was in charge of the New Jersey brigade of volunteers. He lost the governor's race to Marcus Ward in 1865 and ended his career as ambassador to Germany.

LIVED: 153 Plane St.; 1 Bruen Place; 15 Hill; 745 High St.; 1 Park; 76 Wash. St.

✎ Eva Marie Saint: Academy Award-winning actress ✎
July 4, 1924 -

Born in Newark, Saint appeared on early TV before her Oscar-winning performance in the popular film *On the Waterfront* with Marlon Brando got her career rolling. She has acted in two dozen movies, Alfred Hitchcock's *North by Northwest*, *A Hatful of Rain* and *Exodus* were three others, in many TV shows or made-for-TV films and on Broadway. She has been nominated for five Emmys and won once, for the TV miniseries *People Like Us*. Saint went to high school in upstate New York and graduated in 1946 from Bowling Green, where a campus theater was named in her honor.

LIVED: 51 Fabyan Place

✎ Isadore "Dore" Schary: playwright & movie producer ✎
Aug. 31, 1905 - July 7, 1980

Schary was born in Newark to a family that ran a kosher catering business. He graduated from Central H.S. and was a reporter, drama coach and actor before turning to writing. In 1938, he won an Oscar for the *Boys Town* screenplay. Schary was producer or executive producer at M-G-M and RKO, producing or supervising dozens of films, including *An American in Paris* and *The Blackboard Jungle*. He wrote books, more than 40 screenplays and also Broadway's *Sunrise at Campobello*. He fought blacklisting, supported Jewish causes and served as New York's first cultural affairs commissioner.

LIVED: 132 Court St.; 584 & 604 High St.; 104 Clinton Ave.

Eva Marie Saint

ᴥ John Scher: concert promoter, producer & manager ᴥ
June 11, 1950 -

More than any other promoter, Scher helped the world realize New Jersey was an entertainment market unto itself. He has put on shows all over New Jersey (in other states, too), most notably at Passaic's Capitol Theater and The Meadowlands in East Rutherford. He's promoted as many as 300 events a year, featuring most of the modern era's top acts, including Frank Sinatra, Bruce Springsteen, The Who, CSNY, Prince, The Rolling Stones and James Brown. Scher won a Tony award for his work with Liza Minelli during the 2008-09 Broadway season and was chosen promoter of the year three times.

LIVED: 10 Custer Place

ᴥ Frederick R. "Ted" Schroeder: tennis champion ᴥ
July 20, 1921 - May 26, 2006

A Newark native, Schroeder was one of the outstanding tennis players of his era, winning the men's singles title at Wimbledon in 1949 and U.S. National Championships in 1942, the year he was ranked No. 1 in the world. He also won doubles titles at those tournaments, along with four Davis Cups. One of his doubles partners was the famed Jack Kramer. Schroeder retired from the game in 1951 without ever turning pro, which may have hurt his legacy. But he was inducted into the International Tennis Hall of Fame in 1966. During World War II, he served three years on destroyers and as a fighter pilot.

LIVED: 15 Bellair Place; 211 Summer Ave.

ᴥ Dutch Schultz: gangster ᴥ
Aug. 6, 1901 - Oct. 24, 1935

Schultz was born "Arthur Flegenheimer" in the Bronx. After his father abandoned the family when Schultz was a teen, Schultz quit school to work, eventually turning to a life of crime. Notorious for his quick temper and murderous ways, he rose through the mob's ranks and became rich as a bootlegger during Prohibition and from a successful numbers operation. Schultz set up shop in Newark when authorities in New York set their sights on him after his acquittal on federal tax evasion charges. The mob ordered him killed when he threatened Thomas Dewey, U.S. Attorney for New York.

LIVED: Robert Treat Hotel, 50 Park Place

Frederick R. "Ted" Schroeder

﹏ H. Norman Schwarzkopf Sr.: lawman ﹏
1895 - Nov. 26, 1958

Schwarzkopf was only 26 when he was chosen to organize the N.J. State Police, serving as its first superintendent and gaining fame heading the investigation into the kidnapping of the Lindbergh baby. A graduate of West Point, he served in World Wars I and II. Later, he was called on by President Franklin D. Roosevelt to train Iran's national police force. Afterward, he returned to the military and served in Europe, attaining the rank of brigadier general. Before retiring in 1956, he commanded a unit of the Army Reserve Corps and was a director in the New Jersey Department of Law and Public Safety.

LIVED: 80 W. Kinney St.; 1034 Broad St.

﹏ James V. "Little Jimmy" Scott: jazz singer ﹏
July 17, 1925 - June 12, 2014

Scott was born in Cleveland but considered Newark his second home. He began singing as a boy and rose to prominence in the late 1940s with Lionel Hampton's band. He disappeared from music in the 1960s, only to resurface in 1985 at a comeback show in Newark. His 1992 album, *All the Way,* was nominated for a Grammy and another in 1998 was named the year's top jazz album in Japan. Scott received an NEA Jazz Master Award in 2007, and the Kennedy Center gave him a living legend award. He performed with Charlie Parker, Lester Young and Ray Charles, among many other great musicians.

LIVED: 59 Court; 79 Sherman Ave.; Georgia King & Stephen Crane villages

﹏ Louise Scott: beauty salon & hotel owner ﹏
c1903 - April 21, 1983

Scott was from South Carolina and came to New York for a domestic's job at 30. She went to night school and became a beautician, moving to Newark in 1938. She opened a beauty shop in Newark and expanded it into a chain of salons, later adding a beauty college, restaurant and hotel to her holdings. Scott was active in civic affairs, organizing voter drives and establishing two churches and a community-minded foundation. In the 1950s, she purchased the former High Street mansion of beer baron Gottfried Krueger. Scott lived upstairs and used other areas for her school and to host community events.

LIVED: 58 & 155 Barclay St.; 601 High St.

➤ Wallace M. Scudder: newspaper founder & publisher ➤
Dec. 26, 1853 - Feb. 24, 1931

Scudder and several associates started the *Newark Evening News* in 1883, believing the city was in need of a progressive, independent newspaper. But in the face of stiff competition, the others dropped out and he went it alone, eventually building *The News* into the largest and most prominent paper in the state. Scudder was a descendant of early Colonial settlers, had a degree in engineering from Lehigh and, with a Harvard law degree, practiced law before turning to newspapers. He was a nationally respected figure and also an ardent supporter of many civic groups, especially The Newark Museum.

LIVED: 10 Washington Place; 510 Parker St.

➤ Bernard M. Shanley: lawyer & politician ➤
Aug. 3, 1904 - Feb. 25, 1992

A member of a prominent family, Shanley was born in Newark and went to St. Benedict's, Columbia University and Fordham Law School. After serving in World War II, he began his political career in the late 1940s as counsel to the New Jersey Republican State Committee. He joined the presidential campaign of Dwight D. Eisenhower in 1952 and served as Ike's special counsel, appointments secretary and deputy chief of staff in the White House for five years. Twice he lost bids to become a U.S. senator from New Jersey. He co-founded the Shanley & Fisher law firm and was its senior partner.

LIVED: 993 Broad St.

➤ Woody Herman Shaw Jr.: jazz trumpeter & composer ➤
Dec. 24, 1944 - May 10, 1989

Shaw was born in North Carolina and moved with his family to Newark when he was 1. He attended local public schools, including Arts H.S., and picked up the trumpet at 11. He got his start playing in local youth bands and sitting in at the clubs in Newark. Shaw first recorded in 1963 and was a sideman in the bands of many legendary jazz figures — Eric Dolphy, Max Roach, Joe Henderson, Dexter Gordon, Art Blakey and Horace Silver among them. But he also led and recorded with his own groups. He is especially remembered for the five albums he made for Columbia starting in 1977.

LIVED: 125 Bergen St.; 18 Speedway Ave.

⤳ Burton "Burt" Shevelove: writer, director & producer ⤨
Sept. 19, 1915 - April 8, 1982

Shevelove wrote, directed and produced for Broadway, the movies and TV, winning Emmy, Peabody and Tony awards in the process. His biggest hit was *A Funny Thing Happened on the Way to the Forum*, a 1962 play he co-wrote that won six Tonys. With a graduate degree in theater from Yale, he began his Broadway career in 1948 and continued on until 1980. *No, No, Nanette* and *Hallelujah, Baby!* were among his other popular productions. Shevelove also wrote screenplays and TV shows, working with the likes of Judy Garland and Jack Paar. He was an ambulance driver in World War II.

LIVED: 54 Schuyler Ave.; 121 Bigelow St.

⤳ Wayne Shorter: saxophonist & composer ⤨
Aug. 25, 1933 -

Shorter was born in Newark and graduated from Arts H.S. He credits seeing Lester Young at a Newark concert with stimulating his interest in jazz. As a young musician, he was active on the local jazz scene and worked his way through NYU playing with the Nat Phipps Orchestra. He later played with the Jazz Messengers and Miles Davis before co-founding Weather Report. Shorter led his own groups after 1986. He has released more than 20 albums for Vee-Jay, Blue Note, Verve and Columbia records, winning 10 Grammys. He is considered one of the great composers and improvisers in all of jazz.

LIVED: 106 South St.

⤳ Paul Simon: singer-songwriter ⤨
Oct. 13, 1941 -

Simon was born in Newark, but his family moved to Queens when he was a boy. He met Art Garfunkel in school there, and they began performing together as teens. They formed a group in 1964 and became one of the most successful teams in music history before Simon went solo. He got a degree from Queens College and thought about a legal career before settling on music. He's won a dozen Grammys, including a Lifetime Achievement Award, written for Broadway and is in the Rock and Roll Hall of Fame. In 2007, he won the first Library of Congress Gershwin Prize for Popular Song.

LIVED: 163 Huntington Terrace

Wayne Shorter

ᐳᐸ Naomi Sims: first African-American supermodel ᐳᐸ
March 30, 1948 - Aug. 1, 2009

Sims was born in Mississippi, grew up in Pittsburgh and studied at the Fashion Institute of Technology in New York. She tried modeling while still in her teens at a time when blacks weren't in demand, but persisted. Her first break was appearing on the cover of a *New York Times* fashion supplement in 1967; her big break, getting featured in an AT&T national TV campaign. She later modeled for top designers and appeared on many magazine covers, including *Life* and *Ladies Home Journal*. Sims left modeling in 1973 to start her own wig business that was expanded into a health and beauty empire.

LIVED: 90 Tiffany Blvd.

ᐳᐸ Carrie Louise Smith: singer ᐳᐸ
Aug. 25, 1925 - May 20, 2012

Smith performed at venues as famous as the Newport Jazz Festival and Carnegie Hall and as modest as the Baptist churches and clubs in and around Newark. She was born in Georgia and came to Newark with her mother as a girl. Her career began in the 1960s, first as a singer with a variety of bands and later as a soloist. Equally adept singing jazz, gospel, blues or pop, Smith was as popular in Europe as she was in the U.S., maybe more so. But she found an American audience when she appeared on Broadway in *Black and Blue*, a tribute to black jazz and blues artists that ran from 1989 to 1991.

LIVED: 531 Bergen St.; 24 Stratford Place; 2 Hillside Ave.; 29 Bedford St.

ᐳᐸ Willie "The Lion" Smith: jazz pianist & composer ᐳᐸ
Nov. 23, 1893 - April 18, 1973

William Henry Joseph Bonaparte Betholoff Smith was born in Goshen, NY, but spent the first part of his life in Newark, where he attended school, picked up the piano and regularly performed. He began recording in the 1920s and made his name in Harlem. Along with Fats Waller and James P. Johnson, Smith developed a distinct playing style known as "stride." Duke Ellington cited him as a major influence. Smith's music became popular in the 1940s and, for several decades, he toured the U.S. and Europe. He saw combat action during World War I and got his nickname for his bravery.

LIVED: 76 Academy St.; 90 Broome St.

Willie "The Lion" Smith

✎ Frank H. Sommer: sheriff, lawyer & law school dean ✎
Sept. 3, 1872 - Aug. 18, 1957

Sommer was so good as a witness in a case involving his employer that he was soon offered his first job in the law, later studying for the bar at night and becoming a leading attorney of his day. He was the first president of the state's Public Utilities Commission and also president of the Newark Board of Education. He was elected Essex County sheriff in 1906 and, as chairman of the judiciary committee at the Constitutional Convention in 1947, helped streamline the state's judicial process. Sommer also spent 42 years at NYU's Law School, the last 27 as dean. His portrait hangs in Trenton's Statehouse.

LIVED: 467 Springfield Ave.; 11 Baldwin St.; 246 6th Ave.; 156 Heller Pkwy.

✎ Albert E. Sonn: spy-tracker & radio pioneer ✎
Oct. 13, 1892 - May 22, 1968

Sonn helped develop a portable radio receiver during World War I that was said to locate German spies by tracking down submarine transmissions. He was also the longtime radio editor of the *Newark Sunday Call*, got the first government license for a car radio and appeared on early TV in the 1930s. But Sonn was best known for his commercial radio work on WOR and WJZ, lecturing on ways to build home radios and reading children's stories as *The Man in the Moon*. It was one of the first children's shows in the U.S. and, when it ended after three years, he got 43,000 letters from young listeners.

LIVED: 282 Parker St.; 150 2nd Ave.

✎ George C. Sonn: teacher, meteorologist ✎
Jan. 1, 1859 - May 10, 1906

Sonn graduated with an honors from Yale before becoming an associate of Thomas Edison, helping Edison perfect the phonograph. While in his early 20s, he began teaching in Newark, first as an instructor of Latin and the classics before turning his attention to science. He is credited with offering the first physical science course in the country at Newark High School. Sonn also played a key role in setting up a weather bureau in Newark, using his own money to buy equipment as the station gained in prominence. He was often called as an expert to testify about weather conditions in court cases.

LIVED: 96 S. Prospect St.; 71 & 285 Belleville Ave.; 29 Clark St.

Angelique Marie "Lilly" Martin Spencer: painter

Nov. 26, 1822 - May 22, 1902

Spencer was a well-known and popular artist of the 19th century who struggled to make ends meet in a male-dominated field. Her themes often involved female subjects and family life. She was born in England to French parents and came to the U.S. in 1830. Spencer was schooled at home and studied art but was mostly self-taught. She and her husband (they had 13 children) came to Newark in 1858, living off the land to keep the family going. They stayed 20 years before moving to upstate New York, where she worked until the day she died. She also illustrated books and magazines.

LIVED: 294 & 461 High St.

Dick Stabile: orchestra leader

May 29, 1909 - Sept. 18, 1980

The son of a musician, Stabile became one of the leading saxophonists of the Big Band Era. He began playing in Broadway shows in his teens and struck out on his own in the 1930s, recording and forming his own orchestra. The band's popularity took off after it appeared at the New York World's Fair in 1939-40. Following military service during World War II, Stabile settled in Los Angeles and resumed his career. For years, his band backed the comedy team of Jerry Lewis and Dean Martin, and he remained the musical director for both after they split. Stabile continued leading an orchestra until he died.

LIVED: 219 Academy St.; 279 Parker St.

Rodney S. "Rod" Steiger: Academy-Award winning actor

April 14, 1925 - July 9, 2002

One of America's great character actors, Steiger won an Oscar for his role as Sheriff Bill Gillespie in the 1967 movie *In the Heat of the Night*. He was also nominated for two others. His parents were in show business, and he moved with his mother to Newark from New York after they divorced. He dropped out of West Side H.S. to serve in the Navy during World War II. Steiger began his career on stage and on early live TV and then appeared in more than 100 films, including *On the Waterfront, Doctor Zhivago* and *The Pawnbroker*. He also had many TV roles and acted right up until his death.

LIVED: 718 S. 18th St.

～ W. Paul Stillman: banker & insurance executive ～
Sept. 17, 1897 - April 30, 1989

Stillman was a high school graduate who was later awarded six honorary college degrees. He began his career in banking as a messenger and was later a U.S. Treasury Department examiner. He eventually rose to serve simultaneously as CEO and chairman of the First National State Bank and Mutual Benefit Life Insurance Co. In the mid-20th century, Stillman led the effort to keep businesses in downtown Newark. A World War I veteran, he was an ardent Republican and a party fundraiser. He also helped raise funds for the W. Paul Stillman School of Business Administration at Seton Hall.

LIVED: 51 1/2 9th Ave.

～ Horace C. Stoneham: owner, New York & S.F. Giants ～
April 27, 1903 - Jan. 7, 1990

Stoneham took over as owner of the Giants in 1936 with the death of his father, who'd bought the team 17 years earlier with money he had made as broker of dubious distinction in New York. The younger Stoneham was familiar with the operation from working a series of jobs in the organization. With Willie Mays their most prominent player, his teams won five pennants and the World Series in 1954 in his 40 years as owner. At the end of the 1957 season, Stoneham moved the Giants from New York to San Francisco, a move that coincided with the move of the Dodgers from Brooklyn to Los Angeles.

LIVED: 549 High St.

～ George "Mule" Suttles: Negro Leagues player & manager ～
March 31, 1900 - July 5, 1966

Suttles was from Louisiana but grew up in Alabama. He began playing baseball before the Negro Leagues got under way and continued until after Jackie Robinson broke baseball's color line. A power-hitting first baseman and outfielder, he played for more than a half-dozen teams in his career, including the Newark Eagles, where he was a part of the "Million Dollar Infield." He later managed the Eagles. Suttles led the league in home runs, played in five all-star games and won the 1935 all-star game with an extra-inning home run. He was elected to the National Baseball Hall of Fame in 2006.

LIVED: 17 Richmond St.

Horace C. Stoneham with Willie Mays, (on left)

⤙ Lt. Gen. Joseph M. Swing: leader of Japan occupation ⤚
Feb. 28, 1894 - Dec. 9, 1984

Swing graduated from Barringer H.S. before becoming a member of the famous West Point Class of 1915 that included Dwight Eisenhower and Omar Bradley. He spent almost 50 years in the U.S. Army, serving as a commander in both world wars and commandant of the Army War College. During World War II, Swing commanded the 11th Airborne Division in the Pacific that sent the first air-transported troops to occupy Japan following its surrender. He was later awarded the Distinguished Service Cross. Swing ended his career in public service as head of the U.S. Immigration Service.

LIVED: 125 & 127 Montclair Ave.

⤙ J. Wesley Tann II: designer & etiquette expert ⤚
July 17, 1928 - Nov. 23, 2012

Tann was born in rural North Carolina but spent six years in Washington, DC, living at the home of Rep. Adam Clayton Powell Jr. after his father died. He attended Hartford Art School of Fashion before moving to New York to become a fashion designer. His clothes were worn by the likes of Jackie Kennedy and opera singer Leontyne Price, and New York's best stores sold his designs. His popularity peaked in the 1950s and '60s. Tann also designed the interiors of private homes and office buildings and later taught the finer points of dining and social etiquette to Newark children.

LIVED: 50 & 52 Osborne Terrace

⤙ Herbert H. Tate Sr.: judge, diplomat & civil rights leader ⤚
Dec. 24, 1908 - May 1, 1988

Tate went to college and law school in Newark and later argued the case in which the state Supreme Court overturned the "separate but equal" doctrine. He was vice president of the Newark Board of Education, counsel to the state NAACP and the first black American diplomat assigned to Asia when he served as the U.S. cultural affairs attache to Pakistan in 1951. As a state legislator, Tate was the Assembly's first black assistant minority leader. He was appointed to the bench in 1969 and, after retiring, was one of a dozen judges who traveled overseas to review China's juvenile justice system.

LIVED: 126 Court St.; 477 Lake St.

⤞ George Tice: photographer ⤝
Oct. 13, 1938 -

Tice is a native of Newark who briefly studied photography in school and continued his picture-taking interest while in the Navy. Self-trained, he was a portrait photographer before turning to fine art photography, moving from small camera to a large camera format. His work has been collected by many of the world's major museums, and he has exhibited widely, including a one-man show at the Metropolitan Museum in 1972. Tice has published more than a dozen photography books, and his subjects have ranged from the Amish and Shaker communities to Maine fishermen and the city of Paterson.

LIVED: 68 Court St.; 608 S. 12th St.; 16 Camp St.

⤞ Andre Tippett: NFL Hall of Fame linebacker ⤝
Dec. 27, 1959 -

A native of Alabama, Tippett was a star football player at Barringer H.S. before going off to college in Iowa. At the University of Iowa, he was team captain and an All-American defensive end who played in the Rose Bowl. He was picked in the second round of the 1982 NFL draft and spent his entire 12-year pro career as a linebacker with the New England Patriots. Tippett was a member of three playoff teams, including the 1985 AFC champions. He was elected to the NFL Hall of Fame in 2008. After his playing days ended, he stayed on with the Patriots in a front-office position.

LIVED: 325 W. Market St.; 454 S. 10th St.; 416 13th Ave.

⤞ David Toma: detective & motivational speaker ⤝
March 1933 -

Toma is probably Newark's best-known police officer. He joined the Newark police force after a stint in the Marines and a couple of years in minor league baseball. His use of disguise in his undercover work was instrumental in helping him make 9,000 arrests, many of them in drug, gambling and vice cases, he wrote in 1973. Toma's life as a cop was dramatized in two TV crime series that aired in the 1970s: *Toma* and *Barretta*, starring Tony Musante and Robert Blake. He's written several books and also became a sought-after motivational speaker, particularly on the dangers of illicit drugs.

LIVED: 204 Littleton Ave.

✺ George Oakley Totten Jr.: architect ✺
Dec. 5, 1866 - 1939

The son of a Newark real estate executive, Totten earned a doctorate at Columbia and later went to Washington, DC, becoming one of the best-known architects in the world. He designed homes in DC, along with a dozen or so embassies. In Newark, he designed the federal courthouse and post office building. Franklin Roosevelt appointed Totten secretary-general of the Congresses of Architects, one of the many architectural groups with which he served. He was also an expert on Mayan architecture. The Tottenville section of Staten Island was named in honor of his family.

LIVED: 62 N. 11th St.

✺ Robert Treat: city founder ✺
Feb. 23, 1662 - July 12, 1710

No name is more synonymous with the founding of Newark in 1666 than Robert Treat. Born in England, he came to the New World with his family as a teen and later settled in Connecticut, becoming a leader of the New Haven Colony. When a dispute over settlers' rights prompted some members of the colony to seek a new home, Treat led a Puritan group to Newark, where they bought land from the Indians and were joined by some other dissidents from Connecticut. Treat returned to Connecticut in 1672 to spend the rest of his life, leading the militia and serving as the colony's governor for many years.

LIVED: Broad & Market, southeast corner

✺ Irvine I. Turner: Newark's first black city councilman ✺
1914 - Sept. 9, 1974

Turner was a Newark native who was active on the local political scene for more than 20 years. He studied for the ministry but then turned to journalism as a career. He was a member of the *New Jersey Guardian* staff and later helped establish the *New Jersey Record*, serving as co-editor and publisher. Turner twice ran for city commissioner and lost but was elected Newark's first black councilman in 1954 after the change of government. He was re-elected three times. He tried for the Democratic nomination for Congress in 1960, but lost to Hugh Addonizio. A street in Newark was named for him.

LIVED: 613 High St.

Frank J. Urquhart: newspaperman, historian & author
May 1865 - Feb. 25, 1921

Born in Canada, Urquhart was an editor at *The Sunday Call* who wrote pamphlets on the city's history in 1904 and 1906 after the city librarian found there wasn't much on his shelves about Newark's founding and its early years. They were later made part of the public school curriculum. In 1908, Urquhart wrote the book *A Short History of Newark*. He was a member of the committee that planned the elaborate celebration of Newark's 250th anniversary in 1916. He was also a driving force behind the effort to put plaques on historic sites, a project undertaken by the Schoolmen's Club.

LIVED: 275, 343 Belleville Ave.; 337, 357 Summer Ave; 333, 342 Clifton Ave.

Frankie Valli: singer
May 3, 1934 -

Born "Frank Castelluccio" in Newark, Valli is best known as the lead singer of The Four Seasons, a group that had more than two dozen Top 40 hits and is in the Rock and Roll Hall of Fame. Their story inspired a hit Broadway play and a movie. Valli began his career in 1951, cutting his first single two years later. His first hit was "Sherry," recorded with The Four Seasons in 1962. He also had a solo career while with the group and continued it after the group broke up. Valli has toured extensively as a headliner and has appeared in acting roles on TV and in film, most notably on HBO's *The Sopranos*.

LIVED: 9 High St.; 35 Pine Lane N, Stephen Crane Village

Arthur T. Vanderbilt: N.J. Supreme Court chief justice
July 7, 1888 - June 16, 1957

Vanderbilt was born in Newark and went to Newark H.S. A graduate of Columbia Law School, he practiced law in Newark before serving as chief justice of the N.J. Supreme Court from 1948-57. Vanderbilt was the first chief justice after the state court system was revised and the Supreme Court became New Jersey's highest court. Many of his reforms were incorporated into the changes, including creation of the first state administrative office of the courts in the U.S. He served as ABA president and dean of the NYU Law School, wrote books and articles and received many honorary degrees.

LIVED: 14 N. 9th St.; 76 N. 9th St.

✂ Wynant D. Vanderpool: banker & golfer ✂
Aug. 15, 1875 - Aug. 20, 1944

Vanderpool was born in Newark and graduated from Princeton, then Harvard Law School. He was admitted to the bar in 1903. He was an avid golfer and helped introduce the sport to Princeton, where he played on the school's first team and won an intercollegiate championship. He was a member of the U.S. Golf Association's advisory board and served as group president in 1924-25. Vanderpool was a member of the world's oldest golf course in St. Andrews, Scotland. Though trained in the law, he spent most of his career in banking, serving as president of the Howard Savings Bank.

LIVED: 22 Washington Place

✂ Mina C. Van Winkle: pioneering policewoman & suffragist ✂
March 26, 1875 - Jan. 16, 1933

Van Winkle brought a long and distinguished career as a social worker that began in Newark to police work when she organized and became chief of the women's bureau in the Washington, DC, police force in 1919. She gained a national reputation as a law enforcement official interested in the protection of girls and women and was chosen head of the International Association of Policewomen. In Newark, Van Winkle spearheaded a number of charitable and social causes, including one to give women the right to vote. She left to direct the speakers' bureau of the U.S. Food Administration in Washington.

LIVED: 35 Lincoln Park

✂ Sarah L. Vaughan: jazz vocalist ✂
March 27, 1924 - April 3, 1990

Vaughan was born and raised in Newark, attending local schools. She began playing the piano and singing in a church choir as a girl before frequenting Newark's lively nightclub scene as a teen. Winning an amateur contest at the Apollo Theater helped her start her professional career. Vaughan sang with the Earl Hines and Billy Eckstine bands before setting off on a solo career. She had songs on the charts from the 1940s into the 1980s, won Grammy and Emmy awards, performed at the world's top venues and was designated an NEA Jazz Master. She is a member of the American Jazz Hall of Fame.

LIVED: 72 Brunswick St.; 21 Avon Ave.; 455 Elizabeth Ave.; 28 Weequahic Ave.

Sarah Vaughan

⤞ Edward M. Waldron Sr.: builder, city official ⤝
Nov. 1, 1864 - Jan. 31, 1942

Waldron came to the U.S. as a teenager from Ireland. After working as a weaver and brick mason, he started his own construction business in Newark that put up buildings throughout the East and Midwest. In Newark, the company built City Hall, the Basilica of the Sacred Heart and the city's first 10-story building. Waldron was a member of the Board of Education, a director of several banks and insurance companies and was elected a city alderman, serving as its president. "Miss Newark," a boat he gave a college boat club in Dublin, won a race in England's Henley Royal Regatta in 1929.

LIVED: 208 Mt. Pleasant Ave.; 317 Roseville Ave.; 814 Mount Prospect Ave.

⤞ Henry Wellington Wack: lawyer, editor & outdoorsman ⤝
Dec. 21, 1867 - Dec. 18, 1954

A native of Maryland, Wack was the founder and first editor of *Field and Stream* magazine, as well as the author of a number of books on wildlife and living in the outdoors. He was also a lawyer who was editor of a medical-legal journal, partner in a law firm in New York and a legal advisor in the controversy between Robert Peary and Frederick Cook over who had been the first to reach the North Pole in the early 20th century. Wack served as the executive advisor to the group that planned Newark's 250th anniversary in 1916 and also for a time was chairman of Newark's Little Theater Guild.

LIVED: 324 Parker St.

⤞ Marcus L. Ward: governor, congressman & friend to vets ⤝
Nov. 9, 1812 - April 25, 1884

Ward was the descendant of a founder of Newark who joined his father's prosperous soap and candle factory and was involved in many civic activities. He entered politics at age 44 and was elected governor on his second try, serving from 1866-69. He also served one term in Congress, was a delegate to the 1860 Republican National Convention and was chairman of the Republican National Committee. During the Civil War, Ward looked out for the medical and financial needs of Union soldiers and visited battlefields. He also established a soldiers' home in Newark for wounded war veterans.

LIVED: 27 & 51 Washington St.; 27 Smith St.; 12 New St.

Home of Marcus L. Ward
Washington Street

⇜ Samuel A. Ward: organist and composer ⇝
Dec. 28, 1848 - Sept. 28, 1903

The son of a shoemaker, Ward began playing musical instruments as a boy and, by 16, was a church organist. Later, he owned a music store in Newark, gave lessons and, around 1880, began playing organ at the Grace Episcopal Church on Broad Street. Within a couple of years, he'd written the hymn-tune *Materna* on a boat ride home to Newark after a trip to Coney Island. The melody took 10 years to be published and, after Ward died, was paired with a poem by Katherine Lee Bates to become *America, The Beautiful*. He was inducted into the Songwriters Hall of Fame in 1970.

LIVED: 42 Academy St.; 26 Franklin St.; 5 Linden St.; 1130 Broad St.

⇜ Rev. William Hayes Ward: editor & clergyman ⇝
June 25, 1835 - Aug. 28, 1916

Ward graduated from Amherst and the seminary before serving as pastor of a church in Kansas and teaching Latin at a college in Wisconsin. In 1868, he joined the staff of *The Independent*, a New York publication that began as an abolitionist paper, and later was its editor-in-chief for 17 years. An ardent supporter of rights for blacks, Ward opened the conference in New York City in which the NAACP was established. He was also interested in Eastern studies and led an expedition to Babylonia to inspect archeological sites in 1884. He was twice elected president of the American Oriental Society.

LIVED: 54 Abington Ave.

⇜ Jack Warden: actor ⇝
Sept. 18, 1920 - July 19, 2006

Warden was born "John Lebzelter" in Newark and attended local schools but did not graduate high school. He boxed and held a variety of odd jobs before trying his hand at acting after serving in the U.S. Merchant Marines and in the Army during World War II. Warden appeared on TV from its early years almost until his death, performed on Broadway and had roles in some great films, including *From Here to Eternity*, *Twelve Angry Men* and *All the President's Men*. He won an Emmy for the 1971 TV movie *Brian's Song* and was twice nominated for an Oscar in the best-supporting-actor category.

LIVED: 774 Bergen St.; 709 & 803 Hunterdon St.; 43 Norwood St.

Grace Church (church of Samuel A. Ward)
Broad St.

✎ Reuben W. Warner: pharmacist & pioneering crimefighter ✎
March 12, 1879 - Feb. 14, 1951

Warner was a registered pharmacist who, as Newark's city chemist, devised a variety of scientific methods of detecting crime. He was so good that he testified in many trials and FBI Director J. Edgar Hoover sent federal agents to Newark for his training. A native of Russia, Warner came to the U.S. as a teen, attended Newark schools and received a doctorate in pharmacy in 1904. He was a drugstore owner and chemist before turning his attention to police work. His lab developed innovative ways of examining blood, liquor, narcotics, fuels, explosives and money and identifying bodies and criminals.

LIVED: 9 Hillside Ave.; 12 Leo Place

✎ Rev. John P. Washington: World War II hero ✎
July 18, 1908 - Feb. 3, 1943

In the winter of 1943, Washington, a Catholic priest, and three other Army chaplains from other faiths were on board the U.S.A.T. Dorchester heading from Newfoundland to Greenland when it was sunk by a German sub. The chaplains first offered aid and comfort to the 902 servicemen, seamen and civilians aboard and later gave up their life preservers so others could live. Arms linked, the four drowned together. They were posthumously awarded the Distinguished Service Cross, Purple Heart and the one and only Special Medal for Heroism. A chapel in Pennsylvania was named in their honor.

LIVED: 103 1/2 & 107 S. 12th St.

✎ Leonard I. Weinglass: champion of activist causes ✎
Aug. 27, 1933 - March 23, 2011

Weinglass was a Yale-educated lawyer who set up a one-man practice in Newark after serving with the JAG Corps in the Air Force. In the 1960s, he represented the Newark Community Union Project of the Students for a Democratic Society. He was later an attorney at the Chicago 7 trial for SDS founder Tom Hayden. Weinglass spent a half-century involved in highly publicized and controversial legal matters. One was the Pentagon Papers case. Among his clients were Angela Davis, Amy Carter, Jane Fonda, AIM organizers and Mumia Abu-Jamal. He also taught law at Rutgers-Newark.

LIVED: 43 Bleeker St.

⌒ Joseph Weintraub: judge ⌒
March 5, 1908 - Feb. 6, 1977

Weintraub grew up in Newark and was in the same class at Barringer H.S. as U.S. Supreme Court Justice William J. Brennan. He took his undergraduate and law degrees from Cornell. He practiced in Newark, served as a special attorney general and was in the JAG Corps during World War II. Weintraub was appointed to the Superior Court and then the N.J. Supreme Court after backing Democrat Robert Meyner's successful bid for governor in 1953. He was chief justice from 1957 to 1973 before retiring. He was unanimously confirmed for the position by the Republican-controlled state Senate.

LIVED: 827 S.19th St.

⌒ Nathan "Nat" Weiss: Kean College president ⌒
Dec. 25, 1922 - April 9, 2013

With a Ph.D. from NYU and military service behind him, Weiss began teaching in Newark State College's department of history and social sciences in 1961. He became a full professor in 1967 and college president in 1969, serving for 20 years. He continued teaching until 1999. During his tenure as president, the school changed its name to Kean College, acquired the Pingry School property, expanded educational opportunities and upgraded its programs. Weiss was also an author and a frequent guest speaker, and he served a term as president of the New Jersey Public Administrators Association.

LIVED: 112 Watson Ave.; 185 Jelliff Ave.

⌒ Peter Westbrook: Olympic fencer ⌒
April 16, 1952 -

Westbrook was a member of five Olympic teams and won a bronze medal in the 1984 Olympics in Los Angeles, the first American fencer in 24 years to win a medal. He also competed in six Pan-American Games, winning two gold medals, captured 13 national titles and appeared in 10 world championships. Westbrook picked up fencing in Newark, where he attended grade school and high school. He continued his education and fencing career at NYU. After retiring from the sport, he set up a club and a foundation that has given fencing instruction to thousands of students and disadvantaged youth.

LIVED: 88 Boyd, 5B Hayes Homes

✙ Edward Weston: inventor ✙
May 9, 1850 - Aug. 20, 1936

Weston was born and educated in England, showing an early interest in power generation. He studied medicine first but, after moving to the U.S. in 1870, focused on the application of science and technology to industry, starting with electro-plating. He obtained more than 300 patents and set up cutting edge companies in Newark — one for lighting, the other for precision measuring instruments. Weston was president of the American Institute of Electrical Engineers, received honorary degrees from Stevens Institute and Princeton and was a founding board member of what has become NJIT.

LIVED: 645 High St.; 187 Ballantine Parkway

✙ Charles L. Whigham: funeral home owner & banker ✙
Feb. 27, 1921 - Nov. 7, 1993

Whigham was born in Georgia but spent most of his life in Newark. He graduated from South Side H.S. and the Renouard School of Embalming in New York City. He founded his funeral business in 1946 across the street from where it stands today. In 1973, Whigham raised the capital to start City National Bank, the state's first black-owned bank, serving as president and CEO before retiring in 1990. He was affiliated with many business, civic and professional groups and was a UMDNJ trustee. A city corner was named for him in 1992, and a day for him was held in Newark on three occasions.

LIVED: 580 & 581 Martin Luther King Blvd.; 44 Montgomery St.

✙ William A. Whitehead: historian, civic leader & writer ✙
Feb. 10, 1810 - Aug. 8, 1889

A native Newarker, Whitehead was fully engaged in the city's civic life. He was president of the library association and board of education; he was a founder of the New Jersey Historical Society and edited the first eight editions of *The New Jersey Archives*; he wrote hundreds of newspaper articles and was board president of what is now The College of New Jersey. He worked as a stockbroker, railroad executive and bank president. For Newark's 200th anniversary, Whitehead wrote about the city's first settlement. Earlier, he had surveyed and mapped the city of Key West, FL, and served as its mayor.

LIVED: 5 & 12 Lombardy St.; 21 Washington St.

Edward Weston

✍ C.K. Williams: poet ✍
Nov. 2, 1936 - Sept. 20, 2015

Charles Kenneth Williams was born and raised in Newark but attended high school in Maplewood. He graduated from the University of Pennsylvania and began a college teaching career after working as a psychotherapist and in some editing and writing jobs. He wrote his first book of poetry in 1969 and then became one of the country's most acclaimed poets. Williams won a National Book Award (2003), Pulitzer Prize (2000) and a National Book Critics Circle Award (1997), along with the Ruth Lilly Poetry Prize. He lived near Princeton and taught at Princeton University for many years.

LIVED: 104 Mount Vernon Place; 259 Eastern Parkway

✍ Hubert Williams: police official ✍
Aug. 19, 1939 -

Williams graduated from Central H.S. and thought about becoming an electrician before deciding on a law enforcement career. He took his B.S. degree from John Jay College of Criminal Justice in New York and his law degree from Rutgers-Newark. Williams worked his way up the department ranks and, at age 34, was appointed Newark police director by Mayor Ken Gibson in 1974. In 1985, he was named director of the Police Foundation, a national nonprofit think tank established by the Ford Foundation to come up with innovative ways of improving policing. He retired from there in 2012.

LIVED: 39 Charlton St.; 180 Ridgewood; 21 Goodwin Ave.; 520 Highland Ave.

✍ Beatrice Winser: librarian & museum director ✍
March 11, 1869 - Sept. 14, 1947

Winser was born in Newark to a father who'd covered the Civil War for *The New York Times*. She studied library science at Columbia and served on the Newark library staff for more than 50 years. In 1929, she was named chief librarian, succeeding founder John Cotton Dana. For much of the same time, Winser was also Newark Museum director, a job she kept after retiring from the library in 1942. She got both institutions through the Depression, with the museum expanding its reach throughout the state. It also exhibited the commercial products of craftsmen as art, a move that generated controversy.

LIVED: 14 Mt. Prospect Pl.; 330 Mount Prospect Ave.; 666 Highland Ave.; 189 Broad

⌒ Jacob Wiss: cutler & businessman ⌒
Dec. 1, 1817 - June 25, 1880

Wiss came to the U.S. from Switzerland in 1847, planning to settle in Texas. He chose Newark instead and worked for a company that made shears and cutlery. He soon opened his own shop, using a dog on a treadmill to power his grindstone. As it grew, J. Wiss made its name producing high quality scissors, shears, surgical instruments, table knives and razors. Two sons joined the firm in the 1870s, and J. Wiss & Sons became the world's largest producer of fine shears and scissors. Jewelry and real estate were later added to the business, which was acquired by Cooper Industries in 1976.

LIVED: 7, 8, 13, 26 & 28 Bank St.

⌒ Constance "Connie" Woodruff: journalist, women's advocate ⌒
Oct. 23, 1921 - Oct. 18, 1996

Woodruff served 16 years as chairwoman of the N.J. Commission on the Status of Women, two terms as president of the National Association of Commissions on Women and was also a Democratic state committeewoman. She graduated from South Side H.S. and Empire State College and took a master's in labor studies from Rutgers. She was with the ILGWU for 20 years and also taught at Rutgers-Newark and Essex County College. Earlier in her career, she had been city editor of the *Herald News*, a black-owned weekly in Newark, and later wrote a political column for the *City News*.

LIVED: 50 & 64 Waverly Ave.; 10 Ludlow St.

⌒ Admiral Jerauld Wright: NATO commander & diplomat ⌒
June 4, 1898 - April 27, 1995

Wright graduated from Annapolis in 1917 and made the Navy his career, serving in both world wars in a variety of positions, including commanding battleships. After World War I, he served as an aide to Presidents Coolidge and Hoover, and he helped plan the invasion of North Africa during World War II as a member of Gen. Eisenhower's staff. During the Cold War, he led American naval forces in the Atlantic and also served as NATO's Supreme Allied Commander. After he retired from active duty in 1960, Wright was tapped by President Kennedy to serve as ambassador to Nationalist China.

LIVED: 24 Park Place

ᗢ Lawrence "Lonnie" Wright: pro athlete ᗢ
Jan. 23, 1945 - March 23, 2012

Wright was one of only a few athletes to play both pro football and pro basketball, and he did so in the same year. He was a star in four sports at South Side H.S., leading his team to a state basketball championship in 1962, before excelling at Colorado State. With football and basketball his primary sports, Wright played five seasons in the ABA with the Denver Rockets and Floridians and two years in the AFL with the Denver Broncos. He later returned to Newark and began a decades-long career at UMDNJ, recruiting and mentoring minority and underprivileged medical students.

LIVED: 142 Brunswick St.; 784 High St.

ᗢ Marion Thompson Wright: educator & historian ᗢ
Sept. 13, 1902 - Oct. 26, 1962

Wright graduated from Barringer H.S. and continued her education, despite being married and divorced and having children, until she was able to earn two degrees from Howard and a doctorate from Columbia. Her dissertation is still considered a groundbreaking study on race relations in New Jersey. Wright was employed as a social worker in Newark but, with her doctor's degree, returned to Howard to teach and mentor students. She also continued publishing scholarly works, some of which were used in *Brown v. Board of Education,* the landmark U.S. Supreme Court case on school desegregation.

LIVED: 50 Thomas St.

ᗢ Larry Young Jr.: jazz organist ᗢ
Oct. 7, 1940 - March 30, 1978

Young got his start at the urging of his father, a Newark club owner. He played with a series of R&B bands in the 1950s and turned to straight-ahead jazz in the mid -'60s before joining some early fusion groups. He recorded as a leader for the Prestige, Blue Note and Arista labels. His best known work was the 1965 recording *Unity.* As a sideman, Young recorded with Grant Green, Tony Williams, John McLaughlin and Carlos Santana. He appeared on Miles Davis' *Bitches Brew* album and a posthumous Jimi Hendrix album, *Nine to the Universe.* He took the name "Khalid Yasin" in his later years.

LIVED: 26 Clinton Place; 846 S. 18th St.; 96 Shanley Ave.

Lawrence "Lonnie" Wright, (shooting jumpshot)

⚬ James R. Zazzali: N.J. Supreme Court chief justice ⚬
June 17, 1937 -

The son and grandson of prominent Newark residents, Zazzali attended Seton Hall Prep and Georgetown, where he took his undergraduate and law degrees. He practiced law in Newark and also had a series of public jobs. He worked for the Essex County Prosecutor's Office, was general counsel to the N.J. Sports Authority, chairman of the State Commission of Investigation and a special jail master. Zazzali was attorney general from 1981-82 and sat on the state's high court from June 2000 to June 2007, the last eight months as chief justice. He returned to private practice after retiring from the bench.

LIVED: 35 Eastern Parkway

⚬ Abner "Longy" Zwillman: mob boss ⚬
July 27, 1904 - Feb. 27, 1959

Zwillman was born in Newark, quit school to sell produce after his father died and quickly turned to a life of crime. From illegal numbers, he moved into bootlegging during Prohibition, using the proceeds to finance his gambling, prostitution and racketeering enterprises, as well as legitimate businesses. A wealthy man in his 20s, Zwillman was both feared and highly respected, sitting at the table with the major figures of organized crime's golden era. By controlling local cops and politicians, he was able to maintain his power, and he later expanded his influence to Hollywood and Las Vegas.

LIVED: 84 Charlton St.; Riviera Hotel, 169 Clinton Ave.

Abner "Longy" Zwillman

Armondo Fontoura

Harold Lockwood

James M. Baxter

John F. Dryden

Marcus Ward

George Clinton

Home of Paul Simon

163–169
HUNTINGTON TERRACE

10 Lehigh Ave.

Home of Jerry Lewis

Home of Donald Payne

Home of Joseph DiVincenzo

Home of Philip Roth

Home of Savion Glover

The Kearny Homestead

Residence of Washington Irving

OTHER
NOTABLES

✤ **Janet Abu-Lughod: urban sociologist**
(Aug. 3, 1928 - Dec. 14, 2013)
LIVED: 296 Meeker Ave.

✤ **Platt Adams: Olympic champion & state boxing official**
(March 23, 1885 - Feb. 27, 1961)
LIVED: 378 Summer Ave.; 186 Lincoln Ave.

✤ **Stephen N. "Steve" Adubato Jr.: TV host, author & motivational speaker**
(Oct. 7, 1957 -   )
LIVED: 130 2nd Ave.

✤ **Thomas S. "Tommy Attabat" Adubato: mob-fighting Newark cop**
(Oct. 17, 1871 - Aug. 17, 1918)
LIVED: 237 Eighth Ave.; 314 N. 6th St.

✤ **Rev. George W. Ahr: Catholic bishop, Diocese of Trenton**
(June 23, 1904 - May 5, 1993)
LIVED: 658 Springfield Ave.; 83 Plane St.; 74 James St.

✤ **Dr. Edwin H. Albano: NJ's first state medical examiner**
(July 19, 1906 - Sept. 4, 1986)
LIVED: 242 Clifton Ave.

✤ **Hughes Allison: author, journalist & playwright**
(March 29, 1908 - Aug. 26, 1974)
LIVED: 611 Hunterdon St.; 15 Wallace Place; 214 Market St.

✤ **Augusto Amador: first Portuguese-American city council member**
(Jan. 1, 1949 -   )
LIVED: 380 Lafayette St.

✤ **Phillip "Sonny" Amster: bagel king**
(Jan. 11, 1929 - July 19, 2008)
LIVED: 325 Belmont Ave.; 857 S. 16th St.

✤ **John Angelo: "Singin' in the Rain" dancer & actor**
(1923 -   )
LIVED: 243 & 252B Clifton Ave.

✤ **Diego C. Asencio: U.S. ambassador to Brazil & Colombia**
(July 15, 1931 -   )
LIVED: 166 Elm St.

✢ **Frank Askin: ACLU attorney & Rutgers law professor**
(Jan. 8, 1932 -   )
LIVED: The Colonnade, 51 Clifton Ave.

✢ **Lily Auchincloss: journalist & philanthropist**
(April 5, 1922 - June 6, 1996)
LIVED: 110 Hillside Ave.

✢ **Paul Bacon: book jacket & album cover designer**
(Dec. 25, 1923 - June 8, 2015)
LIVED: 616 High St.

✢ **Angelo "Andy" Baglivo: reporter & Gov. Cahill communications chief**
(June 18, 1927 -   )
LIVED: 474 S. 13th St.

✢ **Mildred Baker: arts administrator & State Council on the Arts member**
(Aug. 14, 1905 - Dec. 9, 1998)
LIVED: 569 Mount Prospect Ave.

✢ **Walter Bakum: basketball player, teacher & coach**
(Dec. 29, 1914 - Jan. 29, 1985)
LIVED: 49 Quitman St.; 32 Morton St.

✢ **Anna E. Ballantine: Rutgers trustee, civic leader & philanthropist**
(Aug. 12, 1838 - Nov. 12, 1926)
LIVED: 37 Washington St.

✢ **Col. Lewis B. Ballantyne: National Guard commander & assemblyman**
(Oct. 31, 1886 - Sept. 29, 1947)
LIVED: 235 Delavan Ave.

✢ **Robert Banks: keyboardist, composer & music educator**
(Feb. 3, 1930 -   )
LIVED: 6 Prospect St.; 508 Bergen St.; 31 Boyd St.; 16 Montrose St.

✢ **Manuel Barrueco: classical guitarist**
(Dec. 16, 1952 -   )
LIVED: 6 N. 9th St.

✢ **Joseph Basile: band leader**
(Sept. 13, 1889 - June 22, 1961)
LIVED: 376 6th Ave.; 65 N. 14th St.; 285 Seymour Ave.

✦ **Madeline Bell: singer**
(July 23, 1942 -   )
LIVED: 97 Sherman Ave.

✦ **James Warner Bellah: novelist**
(Sept. 14, 1899 - Sept. 22, 1976)
LIVED: 256 6th Ave.; 2 S. 8th St.

✦ **Drayton G. Bembry Jr.: Central H.S. basketball player**
(Jan. 23, 1945 - July 8, 1970)
LIVED: 22 Demarest St.

✦ **Henry "Heinie" Benkert: Rutgers All-American & NY Giants halfback**
(July 6, 1901 - July 15, 1972)
LIVED: 275 Renner Ave.

✦ **Clyde E.B. Bernhardt: jazz trombonist**
(July 11, 1905 - May 20, 1986)
LIVED: 32 Barclay St.

✦ **Seymour Bernstein: concert pianist, composer & educator**
(April 24, 1927 -   )
LIVED: 350 Keer Ave.; 192 & 251 Osborne Terrace

✦ **James O. Betelle: architect**
(April 1, 1879 - June 3, 1934)
LIVED: 50 Park Place

✦ **Andrew W. "Andy" Bey: jazz singer & pianist**
(Oct. 28, 1939 -   )
LIVED: 32 Chester Ave.

✦ **Dr. Angelo R. Bianchi: obstetrician & Columbus Day parade founder**
(March 27, 1873 - Dec. 4, 1966)
LIVED: 104 7th Ave.; 184 Hunterdon St.; 154 Elwood Ave.

✦ **Moses Bigelow: mayor**
(Jan. 12, 1800 - Jan. 10, 1874)
LIVED: 29 Park Place; 463 & 1020 Broad St.; 19 & 29 Smith St.

✦ **Charles E. Blaney: playwright, producer & theater owner**
(1871 - Oct. 21, 1944)
LIVED: 58 Court St.

✤ **Nathan G. "Nat" Bodian: journalist & historian**
(Feb. 12, 1921 - May 1, 2010)
LIVED: 29 Montgomery St.

✤ **Marion A. Bolden: Newark school superintendent**
(April 28, 1946 -   )
LIVED: 127 Ridgewood Ave.

✤ **Jerome P. & Marylou (Tibaldo) Bongiorno: filmmakers**
(Dec. 5, 1961 & Aug. 17, 1962 -   )
LIVED: 43 Tiffany Boulevard

✤ **Rev. Paul G. Bootkoski: Catholic bishop, Diocese of Metuchen**
(July 4, 1940 -   )
LIVED: 89 Ridge St.

✤ **Cephas Bowles: WBGO-Jazz 88.3 president & CEO**
(April 20, 1952 - Feb. 21, 2015)
LIVED: 1897 McCarter Highway

✤ **Alex Bradford: award-winning stage & gospel singer, composer**
(Jan. 23, 1927 - Feb. 15, 1978)
LIVED: 103 Lyons Ave.; 19 Stratford Place

✤ **Doryce Bradley: Swing Era exotic dancer**
(Sept. 18, 1914 - Sept. 24, 1996)
LIVED: 266 Vassar Ave.

✤ **Dr. Fredric Brandt: celebrity dermatologist**
(1949 - April 5, 2015)
LIVED: 844 S. 16th St.

✤ **George Breitman: editor, "The Militant"**
(Feb. 28, 1916 - April 19, 1986)
LIVED: 185 Spruce St.; 73 Stratford Pl.; 57 Rose St.

✤ **Robert E. Brennan: penny stock financier & racing stable owner**
(Feb. 6, 1944 -   )
LIVED: 755 S. 17th St.

✤ **Carl "Tiny Prince" Brinson: chronicler of Newark nightlife**
(May 12, 1918 - Aug. 19, 2015)
LIVED: 10 E. Runyon St.

⚜ **L. Russell Brown: songwriter**
(June 29, 1940 -   )
LIVED: 103 Center Terrace; 126 Schley St.

⚜ **Oliver W. Brown: newspaper editor & Newark Eagles PR director**
(Jan. 9, 1900 - Nov. 7, 1966)
LIVED: 94 Barclay St.; 188 Belmont Ave.; 107 Somerset St.

⚜ **Walter E. Brown: Prohibition agent**
(Oct. 17, 1890 - May 27, 1963)
LIVED: 40-42 Orleans St.; 80 Roseville Ave.

⚜ **Lewis Browne: rabbi, writer & lecturer**
(1897- Jan. 4, 1949)
LIVED: 41 Lincoln Park; 281 Mount Prospect Ave.

⚜ **Mabel Brownell: actress & wife of Louis Aronson**
(Dec. 19, 1888 - Jan. 23, 1972)
LIVED: 32 W. Kinney St.

⚜ **Curtis E. Burnett: freeholder, hospital chairman & exposition chairman**
(Oct. 5, 1870 - Dec. 22, 1942)
LIVED: 815 Clifton Ave.

⚜ **J. Mercer Burrell: "Trenton Six" lawyer & early black assemblyman**
(Nov. 11, 1894 - June 15, 1969)
LIVED: 561 High St.; 23 Howard St.

⚜ **Oscar "Ozzie" Cadena: record producer & label owner**
(Sept. 26, 1924 - April 9, 2008)
LIVED: 68 Congress St.; 257 Lafayette St.; 98 Malvern St.

⚜ **Archie Callahan Jr.: U.S. Navy Pearl Harbor victim**
(c1922 - Dec. 7, 1941)
LIVED: 84 Winans Ave.; 141 Boyd St.; 75 Somerset St.

⚜ **Tisha Campbell-Martin: actress & singer**
(Oct. 13, 1968 -   )
LIVED: 115 N. 17th St.

⚜ **Manuel Carballo: state and federal health & human services official**
(June 29, 1941 - Jan. 27, 1984)
LIVED: 555 N. 7th St.

⚜ **Peter A. "Pete" Carlesimo: coach & athletic administrator**
(Sept. 12, 1915 - June 23, 2003)
LIVED: 386 Market St.; 85 Longfellow Ave.; 73 River St.

⚜ **Leo P. Carlin: mayor**
(Aug. 12, 1908 - Dec. 17, 1999)
LIVED: 194 Eastern Parkway; 78 Richelieu Place

⚜ **Owen T. "Ownie" Carroll: Major League pitcher & Seton Hall coach**
(Nov. 11, 1902 - June 8, 1975)
LIVED: 47 Tuxedo Parkway

⚜ **Sally G. Carroll: NAACP national board member**
(Sept. 30, 1920 -   )
LIVED: 138 S. 13th St.

⚜ **John Catlin: Newark's first schoolmaster**
(???? - Feb. 29, 1704)
LIVED: 744 Broad St., site of National Newark Bldg.

⚜ **John P. Caufield: state senator, city fire director & fire safety expert**
(Sept. 21, 1918 - Aug. 24, 1986)
LIVED: 84 Brookdale Ave.; 105 Montrose St.

⚜ **Peter A. Cavicchia II: Secret Service agent & head of agents' assoc.**
(August 1944 -   )
LIVED: 71 Congress St.; 279 Parker St.

⚜ **Cyrus Durand Chapman: artist, photographer & architect**
(Sept. 23, 1856 - April 3, 1918)
LIVED: 889 Broad St.

⚜ **George D. Chapman: national champion motor-paced cyclist**
(June 22, 1898 - July 19, 1974)
LIVED: 57 & 121 Underwood St.; 95 Melrose Ave.

⚜ **Gladys Churchman: family & children's advocate**
(Oct. 28, 1902 - Jan. 14, 1974)
LIVED: 16 Frelinghuysen Ave.; 17 & 152 Somerset St.; 28 & 84 Barclay St.

⚜ **Ronald J. "Ron Carey" Cicenia: comic actor**
(Dec. 11, 1935 - Jan. 16, 2007)
LIVED: 251 Clifton Ave.

✤ **Huldah Clark: Cold War foreign exchange student**
(March 10, 1947 -   )
LIVED: Columbus Homes, 64 Seventh Ave.

✤ **William Clark: federal judge ruled Prohibition unconstitutional**
(Feb. 1, 1891 - Oct. 10, 1957)
LIVED: 346 Mount Prospect Ave.

✤ **Dr. Henry Leber Coit: public health & pediatric pioneer**
(March 11, 1854 - March 12, 1917)
LIVED: 108 Warren St.; 51 Halsey St.; 63 New St.; 277 Mount Prospect

✤ **Barbara Bell Coleman: foundation president & civic leader**
(Aug. 19, 1950 -   )
LIVED: 649 Lake St.

✤ **Cynthia "Ann Cole" Coleman: R&B & gospel singer**
(Jan. 29, 1934 - Nov. 1986)
LIVED: 267 Livingston St.

✤ **Warren Coleman: singer & actor**
(1901 - Jan. 13, 1968)
LIVED: 95 Pennington St.

✤ **Sheila Coley: city's first female police chief & police director**
(Sept. 5,1962 -   )
LIVED: 106 S. Devine St.

✤ **Rev. Bismark J. Coltorti: pastor & labor relations expert**
(May 1, 1879 - April 4, 1948)
LIVED: 192 Hunterdon St.; 77 Oakland Terrace

✤ **Juanita Grubbs Coltrane: jazz legend's wife**
(Jan. 2, 1926 - 1996)
LIVED: 217 W. Market St.

✤ **Vincent J. Commisa: New Jersey's first chief U.S. bankruptcy judge**
(Nov. 1, 1921 - March 5, 1990)
LIVED: 21 Mount Prospect Ave.; 233 N. 11th St.

✤ **Fillmore Condit: inventor, politician, oil executive & philanthropist**
(Sept. 4, 1855 - Jan. 6, 1939)
LIVED: 28 Marshall; 452 Washington St.

✤ **Silas Condit: sheriff, congressman & banker**
(Aug. 18, 1778 - Nov. 29, 1861)
LIVED: 3 Park Place

✤ **Jerome T. Congleton: corporation counsel & Depression-era mayor**
(Aug. 25, 1876 - Dec. 10, 1936)
LIVED: 488 Highland Ave.; 257 Roseville Ave.; 197 N. 11th St.

✤ **James F. Connelly: city clerk & Japanese consul**
(c1849 - Feb. 2, 1917)
LIVED: 556 High; 15 Hedden Terr.; 133 Monmouth; 10 & 28 Hill; 1139 Broad

✤ **Sydney A. "Morgan Conway" Conway: Hollywood's "Dick Tracy"**
(March 16, 1900 - Nov. 16, 1981)
LIVED: 425 Mount Prospect Ave.; 125 Polk St.; 27 13th Ave.

✤ **Sophie L. Cooper: first city councilwoman**
(Aug. 18, 1912 - Aug. 20, 1971)
LIVED: 374 Badger Ave.; 298 Goldsmith Ave.; 100 Keer Ave.

✤ **Margaret Coult: Barringer H.S. English teacher & author**
(c1861 - June 21, 1930)
LIVED: 58 Mount Pleasant Ave.

✤ **Jay Everett Crane: chairman, Federal Reserve Bank of New York**
(Sept. 13, 1891 - April 11, 1973)
LIVED: 202 Summer Ave.

✤ **"Major" Albert J. Criqui: midget actor**
(July 23, 1878 - June 2, 1945)
LIVED: 78 Howard St.; 50 South Orange Ave.

✤ **Timothy J. Crist: historian, library advocate & Prudential executive**
(June 8, 1951 -   )
LIVED: 288 & 551 Clifton Ave.

✤ **Michael Critchley: criminal defense lawyer**
(Nov. 5, 1944 -   )
LIVED: 221 Sussex Ave.; 351 7th Ave.

✤ **David Cronheim: real estate mogul**
(Dec. 23, 1891 - Oct. 20, 1960)
LIVED: 219 Delavan; 796 Parker; 828 DeGraw; 375 Mount Prospect Ave.

⚜ **Dolores E. Cross: Chicago State University president**
(Aug. 29, 1938 -   )
LIVED: 57 Fairview Ave.; 200 Baxter Terrace, 3A; Seth Boyden Homes

⚜ **Samuel H. Crothers: Broadway & Hollywood producer**
(c1938 - April 13, 2013)
LIVED: 442 S. 13th St.

⚜ **Mildred Crump: first black councilwoman & female council president**
(Nov. 15, 1938 -   )
LIVED: 88 Hansbury Ave.

⚜ **Mark Crumpton: Bloomberg TV program host**
(Jan. 8, 1960 -   )
LIVED: 180 Ballantine Parkway; 54 James St.

⚜ **John F. Cryan: Essex County sheriff & state assemblyman**
(May 6, 1929 - Feb. 6, 2005)
LIVED: 18 Noll Place; 544 Sanford Ave.

⚜ **Clive S. Cummis: lawyer**
(Nov. 21, 1928 - Feb. 9, 2010)
LIVED: 820 S. 19th St.

⚜ **George O. Cureton: teacher & founder of innovative reading program**
(March 8, 1930 - Dec. 11, 1995)
LIVED: 63 Quitman St.; 203 Howard St.

⚜ **James A. Curtis: lawyer & Essex County's first black freeholder**
(Dec. 2, 1909 - April 1980)
LIVED: 381 New St.; 325 N. 11th St.

⚜ **Dr. Max Danzis: surgeon & Beth Israel Hospital co-founder**
(Feb. 12, 1874 - Oct. 20, 1953)
LIVED: 46 Mercer St.; 66 Morton St.; 608 High St.

⚜ **Ben J. D'Avella: pharmacist, radio broadcaster & publisher**
(1909 - May 22, 1994)
LIVED: 167 Parker St.; 424 Clifton Ave.

⚜ **Coningsby W. Dawson: novelist, journalist & soldier**
(Feb. 26, 1883 - Aug. 9, 1959)
LIVED: 1028 Broad St.; 533 Mount Prospect Ave.

✤ **Raymond Del Tufo: U.S. Attorney for N.J. & judge**
(July 31, 1919 - March 18, 1970)
LIVED: 315 Park Ave.; 216 Elwood Ave.; 197 Ballantine Parkway

✤ **Kathleen "Kat" DeLuna: singer-songwriter**
(Nov. 17, 1987 -   )
LIVED: 439-441 N. Third Ave., #2

✤ **August "Gus" Desch: NCAA & AAU champion hurdler, Olympian**
(Dec. 12, 1898 - Jan. 1, 1964)
LIVED: 284 Hunterdon St.

✤ **John J. Dios: NJ's first Hispanic state judge**
(c1923 - April 21, 2004)
LIVED: 181 Walnut St.; 151 Union St.

✤ **John C. Dolph: pioneering varnish manufacturer**
(c1866 - Feb. 6, 1937)
LIVED: 569 Mount Prospect Ave.; 50 Milford; 83 Pomona; 78 Court St.

✤ **Li'za Donnell: pro basketball player**
(Oct. 4, 1967 -   )
LIVED: 46 Goldsmith Ave.

✤ **Henry M. Doremus: mayor**
(May 23, 1851 - Jan. 16, 1921)
LIVED: 173 & 294 Mount Prospect Ave.

✤ **Sidney "Sid" Dorfman: sportswriter**
(Feb. 9, 1920 - February 15, 2014)
LIVED: 347 Clinton Place; 283 Lehigh Ave.

✤ **Robert E.A. Dorr: newspaper editor & publisher**
(June 8, 1854 - Nov. 27, 1900)
LIVED: 26 Center St.; 192 Roseville Ave.

✤ **Nathaniel Dorsky: avant-garde filmmaker**
(July 28, 1943 -   )
LIVED: 1 Mapes Ave.

✤ **Amanda Minnie Douglas: novelist, poet & short story writer**
(July 14, 1831 - July 18, 1916)
LIVED: 375, 380 Summer Ave.

⚜ **Robert J. "Bob" Dunn Jr.: nationally syndicated cartoonist**
(March 5, 1908 - Jan. 31, 1989)
LIVED: 158 Washington Ave.; 168 Bloomfield Ave.; 93 N. 9th St.

⚜ **"Princess White" Durrah: blues singer**
(Jan. 14, 1881 - March 21, 1976)
LIVED: 387 S. 18th St.

⚜ **Donald T. Dust: newspaperman, city official & preservationist**
(1937 - Aug. 19, 1992)
LIVED: 21 James St.

⚜ **Edward J. "Eddie" Dwyer: Dwyer's Elbow Room proprietor**
(1900 - February 1979)
LIVED: 239 Montclair Ave.; 454 Broad St.

⚜ **Dr. Wells P. Eagleton: brain surgeon & medical author**
(Sept. 18, 1865 - Sept. 11, 1946)
LIVED: 15 Lombardy St.; 212 Elwood Ave.

⚜ **Frederick L. Eberhardt: machine tool manufacturer**
(Feb. 27, 1868 - July 18, 1946)
LIVED: 17 Hillside Ave.; 97 Congress St.

⚜ **Oliver Tarbell Eddy: painter & inventor**
(Nov. 14, 1799 - Oct. 8, 1868)
LIVED: Washington Street, near Kinney; 8 Clinton St.

⚜ **Martin Edelston: publisher & direct marketing pioneer**
(Feb. 14, 1929 - Oct. 2, 2013)
LIVED: 418-20 Belmont Ave.; 153 Aldine St.

⚜ **Dr. Emma Cornelia Edwards: pioneering female physician**
(June 5, 1845 - March 28, 1896)
LIVED: 11 Washington St.

⚜ **Meyer C. Ellenstein: Jewish mayor**
(Oct. 15, 1886 - Feb. 11, 1967)
LIVED: 594 High St; 583 Parker St.; 19 Lyons Ave.

⚜ **Linda Epps: college dean & N.J. Historical Society president**
(Jan. 10, 1951 -   )
LIVED: 55b James St.

✤ **Kenneth Faried: college & pro basketball player**
(Nov. 19, 1989 -   )
LIVED: Zion Towers, 515 Elizabeth Ave.

✤ **Vincent DePaul Farrell: Olympic basketball ref & recreation official**
(Jan. 3, 1908 - July 30, 1989)
LIVED: 27 Leo Place

✤ **Harvey L. Fassett: high school math teacher & principal**
(October 1868 - Oct. 16, 1941)
LIVED: 254 Parker St.; 554 Highland Ave.

✤ **Sarah A. Fawcett: art educator**
(1846 - Nov. 17, 1899)
LIVED: 243 Mount Pleasant Ave.; 11 John; 27 Clark; 2 & 39 Lombardy Place

✤ **Rev. Joseph Fewsmith: Second Presbyterian Church pastor**
(Jan. 7, 1816 - 1888/89)
LIVED: 15 Washington St.

✤ **Dr. Joseph Fewsmith Jr.: physician**
(1851 - April 8, 1921)
LIVED: 12 Lombardy; 47 Central Ave.; 72 Washington St.; 12 Bridge St.

✤ **William H.F. Fiedler: mayor, congressman, assemblyman & postmaster**
(July 25, 1847 - Jan. 1, 1919)
LIVED: 488 High St.; 21 West; 35 South Orange Ave.; 171 Littleton Ave.

✤ **William J. Fielding: author, editor & sex scholar**
(1886-1974)
LIVED: 13 S. 12th St.

✤ **Roy G. Fitzsimmons: geophysicist & polar explorer**
(1916 - May 5, 1945)
LIVED: 50 Leslie St.

✤ **Tino Fiumara: reputed Genovese crime family boss**
(Aug. 11, 1941 - Sept. 16, 2010)
LIVED: 190 Elm St.

✤ **Richard Florida: social & economic theorist**
(Nov. 26, 1957 -   )
LIVED: 212 Highland Ave.

✤ **John G. Forrest:** *New York Times* **financial editor**
(July 4, 1898 - Oct. 4, 1982)
LIVED: 730 S. 19th St.; 16 Jefferson St.

✤ **Rabbi Solomon Foster: Jewish elder, author & civic leader**
(Feb. 15, 1878 - June 15, 1966)
LIVED: 90 Treacy Ave.; 264 Clinton Ave.

✤ **Rev. William Hiram Foulkes: Old First Church pastor & radio minister**
(June 26, 1877 - Dec. 9, 1961)
LIVED: 371 Lake St.; 583 Mount Prospect Ave.

✤ **Geraldine "GiGi" Foushee: NJ's first black female jail warden**
(Aug. 14, 1947 - Jan. 27, 1997)
LIVED: Scudder Homes; 150 Lehigh Ave.

✤ **Muriel Fox: NOW co-founder**
(Feb. 3, 1928 -   )
LIVED: 386 Hawthorne Ave.

✤ **Marvin E. Frankel: federal judge, author & human rights advocate**
(July 25, 1920 - March 3, 2002)
LIVED: 71 Milford Ave.

✤ **Pearce R. Franklin: lawyer, city commissioner & state assemblyman**
(March 31, 1892 - Oct. 26, 1969)
LIVED: 18 Camp St.

✤ **Dr. Robert E. Fullilove: physician**
(July 10, 1910 - August 1986)
LIVED: 24 Waverly Ave.; 53 Lincoln Park

✤ **Charley Fusari: welterweight boxing contender**
(Aug. 20, 1924 - Nov. 1, 1985)
LIVED: 212 1/2 Camden St.; 296 Littleton Ave.; 207 Lake St.

✤ **Edward Garbely: painter**
(Aug. 15, 1908 - Jan. 26, 1999)
LIVED: 245 1/2 S. 19th St.

✤ **Rev. L. Hamilton Garner: clergyman, labor official & civic leader**
(Nov. 23, 1899 -????)
LIVED: 385 Highland; 815 S. 11th St.; 142 Pomona Ave.; 340 Parker St.

✤ **C. Albert Gasser: editor, safety official & disabled soldiers' home head**
(March 1872 - Aug. 15, 1927)
LIVED: 30 Brientnall Place; 18 Millington Ave.

✤ **Henry M. Gasser: painter**
(Oct. 31, 1909 - December 1981)
LIVED: 255 Florence Ave.; 398 Avon Ave.; 55 Lincoln Ave.; 502 Summer Ave.

✤ **Gustave "Gus" Getz: World Series infielder**
(Aug. 3, 1889 - May 28, 1969)
LIVED: 1 Avenue L

✤ **Baroness Gevers: partner in early international marriage**
(1822 - Oct. 13, 1908)
LIVED: 8 Park Place

✤ **Louis Ginsberg: poet, teacher & Allen's father**
(Oct. 1, 1895 - July 8, 1976)
LIVED: 322 15th Ave.; 114 Johnson Ave.; 163 Quitman St.

✤ **Anthony Giuliano: judge, assemblyman, councilman & federal prosecutor**
(Dec. 14, 1897 - Feb. 4, 1970)
LIVED: 364 Roseville Ave.

✤ **Edward C. "Eddie" Gladden: jazz drummer**
(Dec. 6, 1937 - Aug. 25, 2003)
LIVED: 73 Crane St.; 195 Livingston St.

✤ **Edward Lees Glew: artist, author & newspaper founder**
(March 3, 1817 - Oct. 7, 1870)
LIVED: corner of Elm & Adams streets

✤ **Arthur M. Goldberg: trucking executive & casino CEO**
(Dec. 30, 1941 - Oct. 19, 2000)
LIVED: 604 Hawthorne Ave.

✤ **Lorraine Stein Gordon: Village Vanguard owner**
(Oct. 15, 1922 -   )
LIVED: 85 Johnson Ave.; 266 & 429 Peshine Ave.

✤ **Frank Grad: architect**
(1882 - Jan. 19, 1968)
LIVED: 134 Johnson Ave.; 885 S. 13th St.; 218 South Orange Ave.; 45 Quitman

✤ **DeMingo Graham: NFL lineman**
(Sept. 10, 1973 -   )
LIVED: 506 Bergen St.; 12 Oriental St.

✤ **Glenn A. Grant: judge & state court administrator**
(Aug. 29, 1952 -   )
LIVED: 111 Mulberry St., 4T

✤ **Gwendolyn Goldsby Grant: psychologist & author**
(Dec. 15, 1935 -   )
LIVED: 29 Wilbur Ave.

✤ **Edward W. Gray: congressman, newspaperman & insurance executive**
(Aug. 18, 1870 - June 10, 1942)
LIVED: 131 Elizabeth Ave.; 903 S. 14th St.; 94 Alpine; 141 Wakeman Ave.

✤ **Werner Groshans: realistic painter**
(1913 - July 31, 1986)
LIVED: 30 Wainwright St.; 90 Schley St.

✤ **Sanford "Sandy" Grossman: TV sports director**
(June 12, 1935 - April 2, 2014)
LIVED: 643 Belmont Ave.

✤ **Warren Grover: author & historian**
(Sept. 1, 1938 -   )
LIVED: 199 Renner Ave.; 60 Hansbury Ave.

✤ **Col. Lawrence N. "Larry" Guarino: fighter pilot & Vietnam War POW**
(April 16, 1922 - Aug. 18, 2014)
LIVED: 151 Parker St.

✤ **Charles P. Gulick: founder & chairman, chemical products company**
(May 21, 1885 - Sept. 3, 1955)
LIVED: 47 Rector St.; 319 Clifton Ave.; 133 Heller Parkway

✤ **Gwen Guthrie: singer-songwriter**
(July 14, 1950 - Feb. 3, 1999)
LIVED: Baxter Terrace, 142 James St.

✤ **Thomas H. Guthrie: shoemaker for the rich & famous**
(February 1860 - June 6, 1937)
LIVED: 41 Mercer St.; 240 & 242 Halsey St.

✤ **Dan Gutman: children's book author**
(Oct. 19, 1955 -   )
LIVED: Ivy Hill Apts.; 176 Norman Rd.

✤ **Robert M. Haas: Hollywood set designer**
(Jan. 3, 1889 - Dec. 17, 1962)
LIVED: 67 Lang St.; 68 Ann St.

✤ **John Hagney: portrait & still life painter**
(1833 - 1876)
LIVED: 7 Liberty St.; 11 & 25 Orleans St.

✤ **Oliver S. "Pet" Halsted Jr.: confidante of Mary Todd Lincoln**
(1818 - July 2, 1871)
LIVED: 108 S. Broad St.; 1120 Broad St.

✤ **Lawrence "Larry" Hamm Jr.: social activist**
(Dec. 24, 1953 -   )
LIVED: 5 Ridgewood Ave.; 527 S. 12th St.; 74 Tremont Ave.

✤ **Alan B. Handler: N.J. Supreme Court justice**
(July 20, 1931 -   )
LIVED: 175 Pomona Ave.

✤ **J. Vreeland Haring: handwriting expert**
(March 13, 1868 - Oct. 1, 1954)
LIVED: 174 Summer Ave.; 114 Park Ave.; 881 Lake St.

✤ **Dr. James Hawk: state veterinarian & Animal Industry Bureau chief**
(1843 - Aug. 29, 1906)
LIVED: 133 Bank St.; 34a Clay St.; 20 Burnet St.

✤ **Thomas E. "Tom" Hayden: activist, Chicago 7 defendant & legislator**
(Dec. 11, 1939 -   )
LIVED: 227 Jelliff Ave.

✤ **Alice W. Hayes: city parks benefactor**
(Oct. 17, 1852 - March 22, 1914)
LIVED: 688 High St.; 28 Washington St.

✤ **Dr. William H. Hayling: 100 Black Men of America co-founder**
(Dec. 7, 1925 -   )
LIVED: 614 High St.

✤ **Joseph E. Haynes: Newark mayor & educator**
(July 31, 1827 - Dec. 6, 1897)
LIVED: 126 Mulberry St.; 264, 385 & 433 Plane St.

✤ **James L. Hays: state senator, postmaster & state board of ed. member**
(September 1835 - June 1, 1916)
LIVED: 137, 149 & 325 Washington St.; 102 & 104 Clinton Ave.

✤ **Harry J. Hazelwood Jr.: Newark's first black municipal judge**
(Oct. 8, 1921 - Sept. 20, 2007)
LIVED: 64 Miller St.; 804 S. 11th St.

✤ **Louis B. Heller: company president & evangelist**
(1844 - March 10, 1927)
LIVED: 95 Bruen St.

✤ **Alfred "Al" Henderson: photographer of African-American life**
(July 5, 1913 - Jan. 30, 1989)
LIVED: 701 Clinton Ave.

✤ **Dorland J. "DJ" Henderson: state engineer & famous home preserver**
(Feb. 4, 1898 - March 11, 1996)
LIVED: Sydenham House, 29 Old Road to Bloomfield

✤ **Gloria Hendry: James Bond girl & Blaxploitation film star**
(March 3, 1949 -   )
LIVED: 5 Hayes St.

✤ **Joseph Hensler: beer baron**
(Feb. 2, 1830 - March 29, 1902)
LIVED: 35 Hamburg Place; 83 Wilson Ave.

✤ **Hilda A. Hidalgo: educator & activist**
(Sept. 1, 1928 - Nov. 8, 2009)
LIVED: 218 Grafton Ave.

✤ **Thomas J. Higgins: four-sport athlete, NFL player & coach**
(Feb. 26, 1930 - Sept. 16, 2013)
LIVED: 9 Salem St.; 9 & 213 S. 6th St.; 141 Smith St.

✤ **Cleo Hill: pro basketball player & coach**
(April 24, 1938 - Aug. 10, 2015)
LIVED: 173 Irvine Turner Boulevard

✤ **Harry "The Great Inman" Hillman: circus clown & contortionist**
(c1873 - Aug. 14, 1949)
LIVED: 316 Van Buren St.; 21 Malvern St.; 183 Pacific St.; 97 Garden

✤ **Richard Himber: band leader & magician**
(Feb. 20, 1898 - Dec. 11, 1966)
LIVED: 318 & 320 N.J. Railroad Ave.; 25 Milford Ave.; 201 Broome St.

✤ **Harold Hodes: government chief of staff & lobbyist**
(Jan. 30, 1942 -   )
LIVED: 223 Chancellor Ave.; 303 Jelliff Ave.

✤ **Albert M. Holbrook: Newark City Directory publisher**
(April 27, 1824 - Sept. 5, 1891)
LIVED: 34 Park St.

✤ **Arthur C. Holden: daredevil diver & trick cyclist**
(c1877 - April 9, 1942)
LIVED: 69 Quitman St.; 186 Highland Ave.; 274 Parker St.

✤ **Col. Clinton G. Holden: hotel & club manager**
(July 22, 1872 - April 17, 1932)
LIVED: Newark Athletic Club, 16 Park Place

✤ **Dr. Edgar Holden: physician, larynx expert & insurance doctor**
(Nov. 3, 1838 - July 18, 1909)
LIVED: 13 Central Ave.; 105 Orange St.; 318 High St.

✤ **Michael Hollander: fur industry leader**
(Feb. 16, 1884 - Oct. 20, 1947)
LIVED: 293 Hunterdon St.; 299 Clinton Ave.; 34 Farley; 36 Prince St.

✤ **Danny Hope: drummer, orchestra leader, promoter & radio personality**
(May 15, 1902 - March 19, 1999)
LIVED: 137 Parker St.; 81 N. 10th St.; 515 Mount Prospect Ave.

✤ **J.K. Hoyt: newspaper editor & author**
(c1825 - Feb. 9, 1895)
LIVED: 285 Belleville Ave.; 22 Franklin St.

❦ **Sanford B. Hunt: newspaper editor & All-American football player**
(Jan. 2, 1881 - March 31, 1943)
LIVED: 63 Weequahic Ave.; 757 Parker St.

❦ **Clara Husserl: concert pianist & piano teacher**
(Aug. 3, 1877 - Sept. 20, 1952)
LIVED: 777 Clinton Ave.

❦ **Darrow Igus: actor**
(May 12, 1948 -   )
LIVED: Hayes Homes, 73 17th Ave.

❦ **Dr. Charles L. Ill: surgeon & hospital medical staff president**
(Dec. 25, 1864 - May 4, 1939)
LIVED: 441 Parker St.; 299 Clinton Ave.; 188 Clinton Ave.

❦ **Dr. Hutchins F. Inge: physician & NJ's first black state senator**
(April 16, 1900 - March 28, 2002)
LIVED: 205 & 221 South Orange Ave.

❦ **George Inness: landscape painter**
(May 1, 1825 - Aug. 3, 1894)
LIVED: 448 High St.; 4 Bleeker St.

❦ **Abraham J. Isserman: labor, civil rights & ACLU attorney**
(May 11, 1900 - April 22, 1988)
LIVED: 53 Poe St.; 322 & 680 Clinton Ave; 280 Goldsmith Ave.

❦ **Col. Huntington W. Jackson: Civil War officer & Chicago lawyer**
(Jan. 28, 1841 - Jan. 31, 1901)
LIVED: 145 High St.; 384 Broad St.

❦ **Mildred "Millie" Jackson: R&B & soul singer**
(July 15, 1944 -   )
LIVED: 40 Fairmount Ave.; 78 Osborne Terrace

❦ **Sanford Jaffe: Governor's Select Commission on Civil Disorder head**
(Feb. 2, 1932-   )
LIVED: 281 Hawthorne Ave.

❦ **Leonard Jeffries Jr.: black studies professor & activist**
(Jan. 19, 1937 -   )
LIVED: 1 Alpine St.

✤ **Katherine Johnson:** *Vogue* **editor & special writer for** *Look* **magazine**
(Feb. 9, 1896 - May 12, 1955)
LIVED: 11 Tichenor St.; 10 Chestnut St.; 90 2nd Ave.

✤ **Leo Johnson: jazz saxophonist**
(Oct. 19, 1939 -   )
LIVED: 55 Goodwin Ave.; 730 High St.; 525 Bergen St.; 347 Market St.

✤ **James F. "Chops" Jones: jazz trumpeter & bassist**
(Aug. 18, 1916 - Feb. 2, 2011)
LIVED: 543 Bergen St.; 2 Nevada St.; 1 Court St.

✤ **Jorgen Jorgensen: artist**
(Dec. 6, 1871 - 1954)
LIVED: 191 Avon Ave.; 685 S. 20th St.

✤ **Edward C. Jurist: TV writer & producer**
(April 8, 1916 - March 12, 1993)
LIVED: 125 Johnson Ave.; 400 South Orange Ave.; 356 Clinton Place

✤ **Mildred Kaiser: artist & art educator**
(1904 - May 13, 1991)
LIVED: 11 Court St.

✤ **Dr. Samuel W. Kalb: obstetrician & nutrition specialist**
(Nov. 12, 1897 - Nov. 1, 1992)
LIVED: 416 Clinton Place

✤ **Samuel Kalish: N.J. Supreme Court justice**
(April 18, 1851 - April 29, 1930)
LIVED: 988 Broad St.; 24 Johnson Ave.

✤ **Donald M. Karp: banker, lawyer & Newark memorabilia collector**
(Jan. 15, 1937 -   )
LIVED: 19 Lyons Ave.

✤ **William H. Kelly: N.J. banking commissioner & Democratic chairman**
(1886 - Oct. 3, 1961)
LIVED: Robert Treat Hotel; 375 Mount Prospect Ave.

✤ **Dr. John A. Kenney: pioneering African-American physician & surgeon**
(June 11, 1874 - Jan. 29, 1950)
LIVED: 134 Kinney St.

✤ **Bernard B. "Bernie" Kerik: NYC police commissioner**
(Sept. 4, 1955 -   )
LIVED: 27 Conklin Ave.

✤ **Howard L. Kern: attorney general & acting governor of Puerto Rico**
(Feb. 4, 1886 - May 13, 1947)
LIVED: 330 Mount Prospect Ave.; 530 Ridge St.

✤ **Edward L. Kerr: Newark's first black police director**
(Feb. 26, 1924 - Oct. 11, 2002)
LIVED: 96 Osborne Terrace

✤ **Raymond J. Kerrigan: U.S. Navy Pearl Harbor victim**
(June 6, 1915 - Dec. 7, 1941)
LIVED: 698 Hunterdon St.; 311 Florence Ave.

✤ **Samuel I. Kessler: lawyer, prosecutor & county Democratic chairman**
(Feb. 22, 1889 - Nov. 2, 1972)
LIVED: 359 S. 6th St.; 369 Parker St.

✤ **Irwin I. Kimmelman: attorney general, judge & state assemblyman**
(Sept. 10, 1930 -   )
LIVED: 183 Weequahic Ave.; 94 Wainwright St.

✤ **Sandra "Sandy" King: journalist & TV host**
(Sept. 18, 1948 -   )
LIVED: 358 Ridge St.

✤ **Isidore N. Klein: cartoonist & animator**
(Oct. 12, 1897 - 1986)
LIVED: 68 Monmouth St.; 36 Boyd St.

✤ **William "Willie" Klein: *Star-Ledger* sports editor**
(June 24, 1913 - Feb. 26, 2001)
LIVED: 141 Prince St.; 222 Waverly Ave.; 279 Lehigh Ave.; 345 Goldsmith

✤ **Dave Klurman: basketball player & recreation director**
(Oct. 19, 1937 -   )
LIVED: 146 West End Ave.

✤ **Melvin "Mel" Knight: Seton Hall basketball player**
(Oct. 1, 1949 -   )
LIVED: 308 W. Kinney St.

✤ **William W. Kolb: originator of the candy apple**
(Feb. 27, 1888 - June 6, 1964)
LIVED: 164 S. 11th St.; 63 S. 7th St.; 80 N. 11th St.

✤ **Rabbi Joseph Konvitz: national Orthodox rabbi leader**
(April 15, 1878 - June 6, 1944)
LIVED: 345 Belmont Ave.; 783 S. 10th St.

✤ **Milton R. Konvitz: lawyer, author & Cornell professor**
(March 12, 1908 - Sept. 5, 2003)
LIVED: 345 Belmont Ave.; 783 S. 10th St.

✤ **Rev. Carl Emil Ludwig Krepper: pastor & Nazi spy**
(May 11, 1884 - June 21, 1972)
LIVED: 140 Court St.; 68 James St.

✤ **Carl Kress: jazz guitarist, producer & club owner**
(Oct. 20, 1907 - June 10, 1965)
LIVED: 901 S. 18th St.

✤ **Otto Kretchmer: factory owner & Newark Housing Authority member**
(Nov. 8, 1886 - Oct. 12, 1950)
LIVED: 140 Lyons; 189 Osborne Terrace; 34 Millington Ave.; 9 Keer Ave.

✤ **Barbara Kruger: conceptual artist**
(Jan. 26, 1945 -   )
LIVED: 125 Osborne Terrace; 27 Grumman Ave.

✤ **Gabriel J. "Gabe" LaConte: N.J. Hall of Fame boxing promoter**
(Oct. 4, 1944 -   )
LIVED: 228 Hunterdon St.; 151 N. 6th St.

✤ **Donald Lambert: stride pianist**
(Feb. 12, 1904 - May 8, 1962)
LIVED: 189 Broome St.; 83 Wickliffe St.; 257 Mount Pleasant Ave.

✤ **Arthur C. "Art Landy" Landmesser: "Peter Pan" animator**
(May 18, 1904 - May 21, 1977)
LIVED: 44 Millington Ave.

✤ **Alfredo R. "Uncle Fred" Landolphi: educator**
(Aug. 16, 1908 - Aug. 6, 2001)
LIVED: 238 Renner Ave.

✤ **J.K. Lasser: tax expert & best-selling author**
(Oct. 7, 1896 - May 11, 1954)
LIVED: 74 South Orange Ave.

✤ **Charles Laufer: magazine founder & publisher**
(Sept. 13, 1923 - April 5, 2011)
LIVED: 168 Clinton Place; 43 Dewey St.; 12 Osborne Terrace

✤ **Howard C. Lawrence: insurance industry leader**
(Sept. 19, 1892 - June 10, 1946)
LIVED: 253 N. 7th; 181 Woodside Ave.; 573 Highland Ave.

✤ **Dennis "Mo" Layton: All-American & pro basketball player**
(Dec. 24, 1948 -   )
LIVED: 872 S.14th St.

✤ **Charles O. Lenz: engineer & expert on steam power**
(May 18, 1868 - April 8, 1955)
LIVED: 612 Clifton Ave.; 47 South St.

✤ **Harold A. Lett: civil rights leader**
(Jan. 8, 1896 - July 25, 1974)
LIVED: 120 Littleton Ave.; 87 Spruce St.

✤ **Dr. Philip Levine: medical researcher & discoverer of Rh factor**
(Aug. 10, 1900 - Oct. 18, 1987)
LIVED: 1133 Bergen St.

✤ **Albert Lewin: writer, producer & film director**
(Sept. 23, 1894 - May 9, 1968)
LIVED: 107 Littleton Ave.

✤ **Dr. Albert J. Lewis Jr.: minister & choir director**
(June 16, 1946 -   )
LIVED: 123 Lyons Ave.

✤ **Philip "Uncle Phil" Lindemann: Essex County freeholder 24 years**
(Nov. 2, 1860 - Aug. 26, 1952)
LIVED: 18 Vernon Ave.

✤ **Kenneth F. Lockwood: *Newark Evening News* outdoors writer**
(Dec. 2, 1881 - April 2, 1948)
LIVED: 92 Richelieu Terrace

❧ **Rembrandt Lockwood: painter**
(1815 - 1889)
LIVED: 76 East River; 461 High St.

❧ **Joseph P. Lordi: prosecutor & casino commission's first chairman**
(June 28, 1919 - Oct. 21, 1983)
LIVED: 268 Walnut St.; 11 Reynolds Place

❧ **Harry "David Lowe" Lowenthal: TV's "Harvest of Shame" producer**
(c1913 - Sept. 24, 1965)
LIVED: 22 & 66 Summit Ave.; 182 Chancellor Ave.

❧ **Frank Lucas: "American Gangster"**
(Sept. 9, 1930 -   )
LIVED: 15 Hill St.; 163 Dickerson St.

❧ **"Bernarr Macfadden": health advocate & magazine publisher**
(Aug. 16, 1868 - Oct. 12, 1955)
LIVED: Newark Athletic Club, 16 Park Place

❧ **Hubert Platt Main: composer of hymns & anthems**
(1839 - Oct. 7, 1925)
LIVED: 12 & 34 N. 9th St.

❧ **Robert E. "Bobby" Malkmus: Major League infielder & scout**
(July 4, 1931 -   )
LIVED: 20 Poinier St.

❧ **Themistocles Mancusi-Ungaro: judge & Italian-American advocate**
(Sept. 11, 1883 - Dec. 26, 1940)
LIVED: 25 Oakland Terrace

❧ **David M. Mandelbaum: developer, lawyer & NFL owner**
(Dec. 13, 1935 -   )
LIVED: 251 Osborne Terrace

❧ **Giorgi Manuilov: Russian-born painter & muralist**
(Oct. 14, 1897 - March 1972)
LIVED: 368 Mount Prospect Ave.

❧ **John S. March: Titanic postal clerk**
(Oct. 1861 - April 14, 1912)
(LIVED: 59 Emmet St.

✤ **Henry "Hank" Martinez: first Hispanic council member & president**
(Feb. 25, 1936 -   )
LIVED: 127 Van Buren St.; 13 Niagara St.; 41-51 Wilson Ave.

✤ **John A. Matthews: lawyer, assemblyman, & Catholic layman**
(Sept. 22, 1882 - April 21, 1960)
LIVED: 375 S. 11th St.

✤ **Kevin Maynor: opera singer**
(July 24, 1954 -   )
LIVED: 32 Howard Court

✤ **Dr. Ernest Mae McCarroll: City Hospital's first black physician**
(1898 - Feb. 20, 1990)
LIVED: 59 Hillside Place; 73 Hansbury; 96 Milford Ave.; Court Towers

✤ **Peter B. McCord: artist, newspaper cartoonist & author**
(1868- Nov. 9, 1908)
LIVED: 190 S. 9th St.

✤ **John A. McDougall: landscape & portrait painter**
(Aug. 30, 1811 - July 29, 1894)
LIVED: 446 High St.; 151 Kinney St.; 31 Market St.

✤ **Dr. O. Currier McEwen: NYU Medical School dean & Holocaust hero**
(April 1, 1902 - June 23, 2003)
LIVED: 299 Belleville Ave.; 56 Oriental St.

✤ **Frederick T. McGill Jr.: New Jersey Law School & Rutgers professor**
(May 6, 1904 - Sept. 17, 2002)
LIVED: 16 James St.

✤ **Joseph V. McKee: New York City mayor**
(Aug. 8, 1889 - Jan. 28, 1956)
LIVED: 378 Walnut St.; 134 Madison St.

✤ **Rev. Dr. Michael A. McManus: beloved rector**
(Sept. 29, 1849 - Nov. 16, 1909)
LIVED: 66 Bowery St.

✤ **Fred Means: Jersey City State dean & community activist**
(July 15, 1932 -   )
LIVED: 118 Ridgewood Ave.

✤ **Frank Merrill: gymnast, policeman & movie "Tarzan"**
(March 21, 1893 - Feb. 12, 1966)
LIVED: 142 West St.; 579 Bergen St.

✤ **Marie Mesmer: drama critic & Manson trial juror**
(Feb. 14, 1920 - Dec. 29, 1988)
LIVED: 655 S. 18th St.

✤ **Herbert "Taurean Blacque" Middleton Jr.: actor**
(May 10, 1941 -   )
LIVED: 97 S. 8th St.

✤ **Lucy Karr Milburn: teacher, activist & poet**
(May 21, 1895 - May 25, 1998)
LIVED: 822 DeGraw Ave.

✤ **Emily Miles: fashion designer, model & charm school founder**
(July 31, 1910 - June 11, 1999)
LIVED: 117 Wickliff St.

✤ **Rev. Stefanie R. Minatee: Jubilation Choir director, minister, educator**
(April 15, 1957 -   )
LIVED: 14 Edwin Place

✤ **Anthony F. Minisi: lawyer, assemblyman, city commissioner & judge**
(June 13, 1895 - April 1, 1958)
LIVED: 96 Garside Place; 147 & 336 Clifton Ave.; 570 Ridge St.

✤ **Harold "Hal" Mitchell Sr.: jazz trumpeter**
(Jan. 28, 1916 - Nov. 2, 1998)
LIVED: 129 Baldwin St.; 155 W. Kinney St.; 175 N. 9th St.

✤ **Grachan "Brother" Moncur II: jazz bassist**
(Sept. 2, 1915 - Oct. 31, 1996)
LIVED: 219 18th Ave.; 602 High St.

✤ **Grachan Moncur III: jazz trombonist**
(June 3, 1937 -   )
LIVED: 602 High St.; 569 N. 12th St.; 170 Howard St.

✤ **Antoinette Montague: singer & festival organizer**
(July 22, 1960 -   )
LIVED: 322 Hunterdon St., 9C; 52 S. 13th St.

⚜ **Amelia B. Moorfield: Press Club president, peace activist & suffragist**
(April 17, 1876 - Feb. 24, 1950)
LIVED: 35 Columbia St.

⚜ **Rev. Patrick Moran: Catholic priest & Newark Archdiocese vicar-general**
(c1798 - July 25, 1866)
LIVED: 16, 18 Mulberry St.

⚜ **Domenico Mortellito: muralist, painter & sculptor**
(Aug. 21, 1906 - July 31, 1994)
LIVED: 118 Walnut St.; 125, 150 & 152 Green St.

⚜ **Dr. Joseph L. Mosquera: internist &** *Consumer Reports* **medical adviser**
(Aug. 31, 1954 -   )
LIVED: 137 Prospect St.

⚜ **Gwen Moten: singer, educator, music director & cultural affairs official**
(June 16, 1951 -   )
LIVED: 362 Parker St.

⚜ **Murad Muhammad: boxing promoter & Muhammad Ali bodyguard**
(Oct. 14, 1949 -   )
LIVED: Dayton Street projects; 48 Fabyan Place

⚜ **Florence Mulford: opera singer**
(1876 - Sept. 8, 1962)
LIVED: 424 Parker St.

⚜ **Loren C. Murchison: champion sprinter & Olympic gold medalist**
(Dec. 17, 1898 - June 11, 1979)
LIVED: 719 High St.

⚜ **George J. Murdock: inventor**
(April 15, 1858 - July 25, 1942)
LIVED: 33 Wallace Place; 41 Kearny St.; 213 W. Market St.

⚜ **Stanley J. Myers: jazz historian, radio host & emcee**
(July 10, 1927 -   )
LIVED: 38 Scheerer Ave.

⚜ **Frank "Frankie" Negron: salsa singer**
(Jan, 21, 1977 -   )
LIVED: 324 Montclair Ave.

✤ **Reginald "Redman" Noble: rap artist & actor**
(April 17, 1970 -   )
LIVED: 324 S. 20th St.

✤ **Dr. Max M. Novich: sports medicine doctor**
(Dec. 9, 1914 - Nov. 18, 2000)
LIVED: 476 Bergen St.; 530 S. 19th St.; 262 Schley St.

✤ **Arthur W. Nugent: cartoonist & national tumbling champion**
(Feb. 20, 1891 - March 25, 1975)
LIVED: 12 Tuxedo Parkway; 12 Mercer Place; 15 Silver St.

✤ **Brendan A. "Dan" O'Flaherty: economist, professor & author**
(May 24, 1951 -   )
LIVED: 62 Roseville Ave.; Ivy Hill Apts.; 23 Reynolds Place

✤ **Sheila Y. Oliver: Assembly's first black female speaker**
(July 14, 1952 -   )
LIVED: 7 Bock Ave.; 244 Chadwick Ave.

✤ **Eamon J. O'Reilly: champion cross-country & distance runner**
(June 2, 1944 -   )
LIVED: 247 Myrtle Ave.

✤ **Ilo Orleans: lawyer & children's poet**
(Feb. 24, 1897 - Sept. 27, 1962)
LIVED: 134 Vassar Ave.

✤ **Arthur Ortenberg: Liz Claiborne co-founder**
(Aug. 13, 1926 - Feb. 3, 2014)
LIVED: 921 Bergen St.

✤ **Robert Ortner: Reagan administration economist**
(Oct. 19, 1927 -   )
LIVED: 373 Wainwright St.

✤ **Sherry Beth Ortner: anthropologist & MacArthur Foundation fellow**
(Sept. 19, 1941 -   )
LIVED: 109 Johnson Ave.; 290 Keer Ave.

✤ **Emil Oxfeld: attorney, ACLU-NJ founder & president**
(June 26, 1915 - July 20, 2003)
LIVED: 100 16th Ave.

✤ **Nell Irwin Painter: author, historian, college professor & artist**
(Aug. 2, 1942 -   )
LIVED: 577 Ridge St.

✤ **Robert B. Parker Jr.: foreign correspondent & author**
(June 14, 1906 - April 29, 1955)
LIVED: 694 Parker St.

✤ **Wilbur Parker: NJ's first black CPA & city budget director**
(June 15, 1926 - March 25, 2015)
LIVED: 515 Mount Prospect Ave.; 214 Sherman Ave.

✤ **Chester L. "Chet" Parlavecchio: NFL player & coach**
(Feb. 14, 1960 -   )
LIVED: 300 E. Kinney St.

✤ **Dr. Eugene Parsonnet: Beth Israel chief of surgery & Jewish leader**
(May 4, 1899 - March 1, 1986)
LIVED: 777 High St.; 18 Keer Ave.

✤ **Dr. Victor Parsonnet: surgeon & Beth Israel Hospital co-founder**
(Dec. 15, 1871 - July 20, 1920)
LIVED: 134 W. Kinney St.; 177 Court St.

✤ **Joseph D. Paterno: reputed crime boss**
(Aug. 5, 1923 - March 16, 1988)
LIVED: 422 N. 7th St.; 352 N. 6th St.

✤ **Francis F. Patterson Jr.: newspaperman, banker & congressman**
(July 30, 1867 - Nov. 30, 1935)
LIVED: 99 Spruce St.; 24 Walnut St.

✤ **Ira Pecznick: mob informant & federally protected witness**
(June 30, 1946 - ????)
LIVED: 108 Center Terrace

✤ **Joseph R. Perella: financier & CEO**
(Sept. 20, 1941 -   )
LIVED: 333 Parker St.; 122 Chester Ave.

✤ **Lewis B. Perkins: first black deputy mayor & AFL player**
(May 21, 1930 - Aug. 23, 1995)
LIVED: 168 South Orange Ave.

✤ **Bernard Perlin: painter**
(Nov. 21, 1918 - Jan. 14, 2014)
LIVED: 76 Treacy Ave.

✤ **Houston Person: jazz saxophonist**
(Nov. 10, 1934 -   )
LIVED: 160 Goldsmith Ave.

✤ **Mary Philbrook: N.J.'s first female attorney**
(Aug. 6, 1872 - Sept. 2, 1958)
LIVED: 375 Mount Prospect; 69 N. 7th St. and 69 N. 11th
St.;143a Monmouth; 81 Underwood

✤ **Robert C. "Bobby" Plater: jazz saxophonist**
(May 13, 1914 - Nov. 20, 1982)
LIVED: 66 Monmouth St.; 11 Bedford St.

✤ **Leopold S. Plaut: department store owner**
(Oct. 19, 1848 - April 26, 1886)
LIVED: 26 Fulton St.

✤ **Max Pollikoff: violinist, conductor & "Music in Our Times" organizer**
(March 30, 1904 - May 13, 1984)
LIVED: 169 Livingston St.; 129 Lillie St.

✤ **Jennie E. Precker: pioneering woman financier**
(Dec. 22, 1892 - March 1981)
(LIVED: 205 Court St.; 115 Park View; 139 Goldsmith; 130 Johnson Ave.

✤ **Carl E. Prince: historian, NYU professor & author**
(Dec. 8, 1934 -   )
LIVED: 39 Eckert Ave.

✤ **Leonard Pytlak: painter, lithographer & teacher**
(March 3, 1910 -1998)
LIVED: 15 Brookdale Ave.; 26 Montrose St.

❧ **Robert C. "Bob" Queen:** *New Jersey Afro-American* **editor**
(June 11, 1912 - Oct. 20, 1996)
LIVED: 404 S. 15th St.

❧ **Luis A. Quintana: first Hispanic mayor (acting)**
(Feb. 28, 1960 -   )
LIVED: 81 Bellair Place

❧ **John S. Ragin: actor**
(May 5, 1929 -   )
LIVED: 692 S. 20th St.

❧ **Henry B. Rathbone: NYU journalism department chairman**
(July 3, 1871 - June 13, 1945)
LIVED: 332 Montclair Ave.

❧ **Irving D. Ravetch: "Hud" & "Norma Rae" screenwriter**
(Nov. 14, 1920 - Sept. 19, 2010)
LIVED: 152 Prince St.; 564 S. 19th St.

❧ **Harry S. Reichenstein: "Mr. City Clerk"**
(Feb. 8, 1896 - Oct. 16, 1977)
LIVED: 10 Lehigh Ave.; 852 S. 11th St.; Military Park Hotel

❧ **A. Gordon Reid: manager of theaters in Newark & New York**
(c1875 - April 10, 1948)
LIVED: 12 Pennsylvania Ave.; 39 Lincoln Park

❧ **Walter W. Reid Jr.: Charms Candy Co. founder**
(August 1881 - March 2, 1960)
LIVED: 1108 Broad St.; 106 Clinton Ave.; 228 Mulberry St.; 2 Stratford Place

❧ **Hugh V. Reilly: Timmy's dad on TV's "Lassie"**
(Oct. 30, 1915 - July 17, 1998)
LIVED: 368 Seymour Ave.; 438 Jelliff Ave.

❧ **Joseph H. Reinfeld: bootlegger turned liquor baron**
(c1891 - Dec. 29, 1958)
LIVED: 309 Avon Ave.; 63 Vassar Ave.

❧ **Ronald L. Rice: city councilman, deputy mayor & state senator**
(Dec. 18, 1945 -   )
LIVED: 61 Brookdale Ave.; 34 Sanford Place

✤ **Herbert "Herb" Rich: All-SEC & all-pro defensive safety, lawyer**
(Oct. 7, 1928 - March 28, 2008)
LIVED: 280 Goldsmith Ave.; 262 Keer Ave.

✤ **George Richardson: social activist & state assemblyman**
(Feb. 19, 1931 -   )
LIVED: 172 & 174 Chestnut St.

✤ **Robert Rickel: home improvement store chain founder**
(July 13, 1923 - March 9, 2014)
LIVED: 69 Goodwin Ave.

✤ **Julius S. Rippel: financier & N.J. Bankers Association president**
(Sept. 21, 1868 - Dec. 9, 1950)
LIVED: 67 Johnson Ave.

✤ **Marteese Robinson: NCAA batting champ & Major League scout**
(April 17, 1966 -   )
LIVED: 711 Springfield Ave.; 55 & 65 Manor Dr.; 225 Meeker Ave.

✤ **Eugene G. Rochow: inorganic chemist**
(Oct. 4, 1909 - March 21, 2002)
LIVED: 102 Madison St.

✤ **Beatriz E. Rodriguez: principal dancer, Joffrey Ballet**
(April 25, 1951 -   )
LIVED: 627 18th Ave.; 94 Spruce St.

✤ **Russell "Russ" Rogers: champion hurdler & Olympic track coach**
(Jan. 9, 1939 -   )
LIVED: 330 18th Ave.; 59 S. 9th St.; 103 Chancellor Ave.; 14 Ivy St.

✤ **George Gates Ross: portrait painter**
(April 10, 1815 - Aug. 17, 1856)
LIVED: 51 Commerce St.; 42 Smith; 60 Washington St.; 31 Academy St.

✤ **Solomon "Dean Collins" Ruddosky: dancer & choreographer**
(May 29, 1917 – June 1, 1984)
LIVED: 209 Prince St.; 14 Wolcott Terrace

✤ **M. Teresa Ruiz: NJ's first Hispanic state senator**
(June 28, 1974 -   )
LIVED: 366 Clifton Ave.; 420 Clifton Ave.

✤ **Lucius T. Russell:** *Newark Ledger* **founder & publisher**
(1875 - June 20, 1948)
LIVED: 197 Ballantine Parkway; 16 Park Place

✤ **Antonio "Little Pussy" Russo: "Boss of the Jersey Shore"**
(July 13, 1916 - April 26, 1979)
LIVED: 15 Sheffield St.

✤ **Giovanni P. "Big Pussy" Russo: Richie Boiardo's right-hand man**
(Jan. 4, 1909 - Dec. 2, 1978)
LIVED: 19 Drift St.; 15 Sheffield St.; 209 Garside St.

✤ **James "Niggy" Rutkin: Depression-era bootlegger**
(March 25, 1899 - April 19, 1956)
LIVED: 45 Osborne Terrace; 201 Midland Ave.; Hotel Park Lane

✤ **William Q. Sanchez: Emmy-winning producer & director**
(April 13, 1951 -   )
LIVED: 54 Bleeker St.; 15 New St.; 92 Seventh Ave.

✤ **Seymour B. Sarason: pioneering social psychologist**
(Jan. 12, 1919 - Jan. 28, 2010)
LIVED: 212 Chadwick Ave.; 179 Schuyler Ave.

✤ **Frank Sauchelli: football player**
(Aug. 28, 1927 - July 22, 2011)
LIVED: 203 Lafayette St.

✤ **Dr. Edward O. Schaaf: physician & composer**
(Aug. 7, 1869 - June 26, 1939)
LIVED: 217 South Orange Ave.

✤ **Herman Schalk: brewer, public official & city financial savior**
(May 3, 1830 - May 2, 1908)
LIVED: 136 Quitman St.; 83 Hamburg Place

✤ **Richard Schechner: avant-garde theater director**
(Aug. 23, 1934 -   )
LIVED: 18 Renner Ave.

✤ **Max Scheck: director, theatrical agent & choreographer**
(May 16, 1883 - ????)
LIVED: 167 Broome St.; 75 Stratford Place; 58 Hillside Place; 50 Treacy Ave.

✤ **Carl A. Schleusing: German court painter & art instructor**
(Nov. 21, 1865 - March 11, 1953)
LIVED: 92 Hawthorne Ave.

✤ **William F. Schnitzler: AFL-CIO secretary-treasurer**
(Jan. 21, 1904 - June 17, 1983)
LIVED: 26 Bragaw Ave.

✤ **H. August Schwabe: stained glass designer**
(Feb. 2, 1843 - Feb. 8, 1916)
LIVED: 220 Fairmount; 32 Osborne Terr.; 797 S. 11th; 449 Belmont Ave.

✤ **Antoinette Q. Scudder: author & Paper Mill Playhouse co-founder**
(Sept. 10, 1898 - Jan. 27, 1958)
LIVED: 49 Manchester; 10 Washington Place; 212 Montclair Ave.; 510 Parker

✤ **Richard B. Scudder: newspaper publisher**
(1913 - July 11, 2012)
LIVED: 234 Ballantine Parkway

✤ **David Shapiro: poet, literary critic & art historian**
(Jan. 2, 1947 -   )
LIVED: 146 Goldsmith Ave.; 69 Parkview Terrace

✤ **Robert Sherman Sharp: chief U.S. postal inspector**
(Nov. 5, 1869 - March 9, 1932)
LIVED: 311 Mount Prospect Ave.

✤ **Michael J. "Mike" Sheppard Sr.: Seton Hall baseball coach**
(April 13, 1936 -   )
LIVED: 94 Tuxedo Parkway; 25 Marion Ave.

✤ **Herman E. Shumlin: theatrical director & producer**
(Dec. 6, 1898 – June 4, 1979)
LIVED: 444 Orange St.; 504 Washington St.

✤ **Rabbi Julius Silberfield: Jewish spiritual leader**
(March 5, 1876 - Dec. 2, 1957)
LIVED: 825 S. 10th St.; 148 Hunterdon St.; 31 13th Ave.; 32 Ingraham Place

✤ **Daniel "Danny Stiles" Silberg: radio personality**
(Dec. 2, 1923 - March 11, 2011)
LIVED: 513 S. 14th St.; 218 Waverly Ave.

✦ **Edwin S. "Piggy" Simandl: Newark NFL owner**
(Sept. 17, 1899 - Sept. 21, 1975)
LIVED: 801 N. 6th St.

✦ **Harry M. Simeone: composer, "The Little Drummer Boy"**
(May 9, 1911 - Feb. 22, 2005)
LIVED: 338 S. 12th St.; 256 Fairmount Ave.; 56 Wallace Place

✦ **Lucy Elliott "Lu Elliott" Sims: jazz singer**
(Aug. 3, 1924 - March 5, 1987)
LIVED: 404 S. 15th St.

✦ **Winfield Scott Sims: ordnance inventor**
(April 6, 1844 - Jan. 7, 1918)
LIVED: 163 Mount Prospect Ave.

✦ **Cladys "Jabbo" Smith: jazz trumpeter**
(Dec. 24, 1908 - Jan. 16, 1991)
LIVED: 63 Monmouth St.

✦ **James Smith Jr.: U.S. senator, newspaper owner & leather maker**
(June 12, 1851 - April 1, 1927)
LIVED: 569 Mount Prospect; 63 Crane; 57 Washington St.; 81 Lincoln Park

✦ **Albert H. Sonn: painter & author**
(Feb. 7, 1867 - Sept. 23, 1936)
LIVED: 282 Parker St.

✦ **Herbert Sonn: "Yosemite's Birdman"**
(Aug. 9, 1880 - Aug. 7, 1944)
LIVED: 71 Belleville Ave.; 282 Parker St.

✦ **Joseph "Doc Rosen" Stacher: Zwillman underboss & casino owner**
(1901 - ???)
LIVED: 55 W. Runyon St.

✦ **Mother Alberta Stango: African missionary**
(March 1, 1924 - June 2, 1983)
LIVED: 262 8th Ave.

✦ **Michael A. Stavitsky: real estate executive & national Jewish leader**
(Jan. 8, 1895 - Feb. 17, 1967)
LIVED: 485 Hunterdon St.; 345 Hillside Ave.; 193 Goldsmith Ave.

✤ **Rev. Dr. William H. Steele: missionary**
(Feb. 18, 1818 - Aug. 11, 1905)
LIVED: 16 E. Park St.

✤ **William A. Stickel: Essex County engineer & bridge namesake**
(March 10, 1893 - May 4, 1944)
LIVED: 63 Hudson St.; 1035 Hunterdon St.

✤ **Otto A. Stiefel: lawyer & Steuben Society of America national chairman**
(Feb. 10, 1876 - April 9, 1943)
LIVED: 148 Roseville Ave.

✤ **Allie Stoltz: professional prizefighter**
(Sept. 1, 1918 - Sept. 4, 2000)
LIVED: 72 Mapes Ave.

✤ **Lewis Straus: leather maker, hospital chairman & philanthropist**
(April 6, 1869 - Dec. 18, 1935)
LIVED: 19 Tichenor St.; 1086 Broad St.; 79 Lincoln Park

✤ **Morton A. "Morton Stevens" Suckno: "Hawaii Five-0" composer**
(Jan. 30, 1929 - Nov. 11, 1991)
LIVED: 138 Dewey St.; 297 Hawthorne Ave.; 138 Schuyler; 59 Stecher

✤ **Lawrence "Larry" Sutton: Brooklyn Dodgers scout**
(July 31, 1858 - June 22, 1944)
LIVED: 159 Elizabeth Ave.; 207 Camden St.; 104 Orchard St; 47 Tichenor

✤ **Alice H. Swanson: dancer, dance critic & dance instructor**
(Sept. 13, 1908 - ????)
LIVED: 32 S. 10th St.; 22 Camp St.; 897 & 919 S. 18th St; 157 Seymour

✤ **Albert C. Sweet: bandleader & composer**
(July 7, 1876 - May 10, 1945)
LIVED: 177 Clinton Ave.

✤ **Margery Ann Tabankin: VISTA director & social justice advocate**
(Dec. 10, 1947 -   )
LIVED: 70 Shephard Ave.; 65 Hansbury Ave.

✤ **Malcolm Talbott: Rutgers law professor & VP of Newark campus**
(March 25, 1920 - July 8, 1980)
LIVED: 352 Mount Prospect Ave.

✤ **Michelle "Mikki" Taylor: ESSENCE editor**
(1954 -   )
LIVED: 26 Avon Ave.

✤ **Ralph Tedeschi: NCAA fencing champion**
(Nov. 20, 1927 -   )
LIVED: 324 Parker St.

✤ **Albert P. Terhune: author & dog breeder**
(Dec. 21, 1872 - Feb. 18, 1942)
LIVED: 476 High St.

✤ **Edlin "Buddy" Terry: jazz saxophonist**
(Jan. 30, 1941 -   )
LIVED: 9 Avon Place; 165 James St. 1B; 86 Rose St.; 564 Hunterdon St.

✤ **Michael Tree: classical violinist**
(1934 -   )
LIVED: 45 Ingraham Place

✤ **Donald Tucker: Newark councilman & assemblyman**
(March 18, 1938 - Oct. 17, 2005)
LIVED: 84 Hansbury Ave.

✤ **Jean-Rae Turner: reporter, historian & author**
(Aug. 6, 1920 - Jan. 22, 2006)
LIVED: 69 Hansbury Ave.

✤ **Esther K. Untermann: first Essex female judge & philanthropist**
(Feb. 5, 1896 - Feb. 13, 1989)
LIVED: 38 Elizabeth Ave.; 1050 Broad St.

✤ **Beach Vanderpool: mayor, banker, railroad & gas company president**
(Oct. 25, 1808 - March 12, 1883)
LIVED: 22 Washington Place; 69 Broad St.

✤ **Harrison Van Duyne: Assembly speaker & board of education member**
(Dec. 25, 1845 - May 3, 1914)
LIVED: 350 Summer Ave.; 440 High St.; 16 Rankin Place

✤ **Amos H. Van Horn: merchant & philanthropist**
(Nov. 26, 1840 - Dec. 26, 1908)
LIVED: 261 Academy St.; 572 Warren St.; 88 N. 6th St.

✤ **Anthony J. "Tony" Verducci: Seton Hall Prep coach**
(May 9, 1924 - May 10, 1988)
LIVED: 221 Lake St.

✤ **Fortuna "Frank" Verducci: Barringer H.S. football coach**
(1934 -)
LIVED: 221 Lake St.

✤ **Ralph A. Villani: Italian-American mayor**
(Sept. 11, 1901 - Feb. 28, 1974)
LIVED: 52 Madison St.; 586 Parker St.

✤ **Marie L. Villani: first female at-large city council member**
(Sept. 6, 1925 -)
LIVED: 586 Parker St.; 380 Mount Prospect Ave.

✤ **Charles Wagenheim: actor**
(Feb. 21, 1896 - March 6, 1979)
LIVED: 131 Watson Ave.; 412 Peshine Ave.; 215 Broome St.

✤ **George M. Wallhauser: congressman & state highway official**
(Feb. 10, 1900 - Aug. 4, 1993)
LIVED: 27 Academy St.; 1007 Broad St.; 170 Roseville Ave.; 47 New St.

✤ **Dominic Walsh: architectural sculptor**
(c1867 - Feb. 24, 1943)
LIVED: 630 Summer Ave.; 181 Parker St.; 21 Heller Parkway; 35 Woodside

✤ **Frank R. Walsh: lawyer, FCC official & law school dean**
(Jan. 1, 1924 - March 27, 2005)
LIVED: 77 Dover St.

✤ **Tyrone Washington: jazz saxophonist**
(1944 -)
LIVED: 73 17th Ave.

✤ **Vanessa Watson: basketball coach**
(Oct. 2, 1958 -)
LIVED: 33 Synott Place; 2 Krueger Ct.; 23 Netherwood Place

✤ **Reid H. Weingarten: criminal defense attorney**
(March 9, 1950 -)
LIVED: 317 Peshine Ave.

⚜ **John Welsher: athlete & running shoe pioneer**
(Oct. 8, 1842 - Aug. 15, 1910)
LIVED: 74 Warren St.; 181 Newton St.; 513 & 936 South Orange Ave.

⚜ **Richard Wesley: playwright, screenwriter & NYU professor**
(July 11, 1945 -   )
LIVED: 100 Chapel St.; 96 Congress St.

⚜ **Calvin D. West: city councilman & political adviser**
(Nov. 15, 1932 -   )
LIVED: 91 Stratford Place; 9 Somerset St.; 86 Richmond St.

⚜ **Benjamin S. Whitehead: printer & manufacturer of novelty items**
(Jan. 24, 1858 - April 16, 1940)
LIVED: 375 & 379 Mount Prospect; 255 Ballantine Parkway; 34 13th Ave.

⚜ **William Wiener: city's official meteorologist & school principal**
(Jan. 19, 1867 - Aug. 1, 1948)
LIVED: 62 1/2 Nelson Place; 476 Ridge St.

⚜ **Eric Williams: NBA player**
(July 17, 1972 -   )
LIVED: Hayes Homes, bldg. #88

⚜ **Junius W. Williams: lawyer, community advocate & educator**
(Dec. 23, 1943 -   )
LIVED: 406 Parker St.

⚜ **James D. Winans: community leader**
(March 15, 1902 - Jan. 27, 1994)
LIVED: 368 & 406 Highland Ave.; 44 Spruce St.

⚜ **Stanley B. Winters: historian & civil rights advocate**
(June 5, 1904 - Jan. 28, 2011)
LIVED: 26 Shanley Ave.

⚜ **Karol D. "Karl" Witkowski: portrait painter**
(Aug. 16, 1860 - May 17, 1910)
LIVED: 65 Kenmore Ave.; 685 S. 17th St.

⚜ **Stanley "Tony" Woods: NFL linebacker & defensive end**
(Oct. 11, 1965 -   )
LIVED: 69 Stengel Ave.

✣ **Stella W. Wright: social worker**
(1882 - Aug. 18, 1932)
LIVED: 768 High St.

✣ **William T. "Willie" Wright: community activist**
(c1928 - March 3, 1987)
LIVED: 179 Newton St.; 402 S. 6th St.

✣ **Edward A. Wurth: architect**
(Jan. 13, 1857 - June 27, 1942)
LIVED: 861 & 863 S. 11th St.

✣ **Abbott James Zilliox: first American-born abbot**
(Oct. 14, 1847 - Dec. 31, 1890)
LIVED: 150 & 162 William St.

REFLECTIONS

WILLIAM A. ASHBY
By Walter D. Chambers

I first met Bill Ashby in the 1950s when we were both members of the service club, Frontiers of America. We also shared the same alma mater, Lincoln University in Pennsylvania.

In the last quarter-century of his life, Bill and I enjoyed a father-son relationship, and in his very last years, I spent weekends visiting him at the Brookhaven Nursing Home in East Orange, NJ. A man of style and grace, he dressed in a shirt and tie even during his nursing home days.

Bill was known as a civil rights leader who fought for the advancement of all people through his work in the Urban League, but he was also a passionate writer. He wrote in longhand, on yellow legal pads. He also kept journals, where he chronicled his thoughts, ranging from letters to the editor to a review of his favorite folk music group — Peter, Paul and Mary. If something made his journal, that meant he felt passionately about it. I remember one entry, on the occasion of his 75th wedding anniversary, where he wrote that he and his wife, Mary, had been married 75 years, three months and two hours. To me, that was incredible.

I read a lot of his journals. He wrote letters to everyone, and very often he made copies of the letters and put them in the journal. Some were comical, like the time he tried to cancel a subscription to a magazine but still had copies showing up in his mailbox. So he kept writing, getting more and more agitated with each letter. They were all in the journal. It was funny to me he would do that.

Bill was a voracious reader and a believer in the daily newspaper. In a sense, it was his bible, especially *The New York Times* on Sunday. The modest, one-bedroom apartment he shared with his wife on West Market Street in Newark was filled with literature. It annoyed him — and he found it very frustrating — when he began losing his sight and then could no longer read. I used to read to him quite a bit in the nursing home.

Bill and Mary Ashby loved dining out with friends at two of his favorite restaurants — Thomm's on Park Avenue in Newark, and The Manor in West Orange. He smoked one cigarette a day, after dinner. He'd go outside and light up a Pall Mall and just puff on it, but never inhaling. He did that even in the nursing home.

After Bill died, his niece invited me and Newark librarian Charles Cummings over to her South Orange home to view his journals and other writings, which she had all laid out in front of us. She asked us what we would like to have. I was interested in two things — at least one of the journals, as well as his 1911 diploma from Lincoln. At the time of his death, Bill was the school's oldest living graduate. The diploma was made of sheepskin and in pristine condition, and my hope was to deliver it to Lincoln. But before I could get a word out, Charles claimed it all for the library and that ended that. I understood he had a higher calling and let it go.

In 1986, Bill and I returned to Lincoln to celebrate his 75th class reunion. He was honored with the Outstanding Alumnus Award and five years later, the President's Medal.

I will always remember Bill's determination and his commitment to life. I recall him telling me when he was in his 80s, "Walt, I will live to see 100 years." He lived to be 101. ❑

Walter D. Chambers was born and raised in Newark. He is a 1952 graduate of Lincoln University. He worked in Newark City Hall as assistant executive director of the Mayor's Commission on Group Relations and later was an executive at New Jersey Bell and Bell Atlantic.

AMIRI BARAKA
By Celeste Bateman

For the last 10 years of his life, I had the privilege of representing Amiri Baraka, first as his publicist and then as his exclusive booking agent. We got along well and, while there were some challenges along the way, I'll look back upon those years and our relationship with great pride and personal satisfaction.

Amiri and I first crossed paths in the 1980s when he was a member of the transition team for arts and culture after Sharpe James was elected mayor of Newark. At the time, I was program coordinator at The Newark Museum and, though I was selected to serve as the city's cultural affairs supervisor under James, I don't know if I was Baraka's choice. What I do know is he felt strongly the job should be a cabinet-level position with the full weight and authority of the city's nine other departments, something that sadly never materialized. It was then I realized that Amiri was as much a cultural activist as he was a political activist.

I began working for Amiri in 2003, handling publicity for his local appearances and booking him for poetry readings, writers' conferences, book signings, jazz concerts, talk-backs after productions of his plays and an occasional prose reading. I signed on during the backlash that ensued after Baraka read his provocative poem "Somebody Blew Up America" at the Geraldine R. Dodge Foundation's biennial poetry festival in Stanhope in 2002, a backlash that included him being stripped of his title as Poet Laureate of New Jersey. Those were dark days indeed — getting publicity during that time was nearly impossible.

Amiri averaged around 50 bookings a year, most of them in the U.S. and in European countries such as Italy, Ireland, Scotland, France, Norway and England. More likely than not, if a date was on the U.S. Eastern seaboard, Baraka would take a train. He had no trepidations about flying except that he preferred, post 9/11, to travel under his birth name, "Everett L. Jones," since the name "Amiri Baraka" seemed to raise red flags!

When Baraka left Newark for an engagement, he never wanted to be away for more than a few days. He was always anxious to get back home to his family. Yes, Baraka was a family man. Amiri preferred staying in private rooms in hotels when he was on the road, and he had no special requests of his hosts when he read or performed. But I took it upon myself to make sure there'd be a chair with arms for him to sit in if he was going to talk for any length of time because I didn't like him sitting on stools. For overseas engagements, he traveled by himself, but in recent years when he flew within the U.S., he would be accompanied by his son Ahi, who handled book sales and oversaw his signings.

Amiri knew people all around the world, and it was not unusual for one or more of them (or his event hosts) to have him over for dinner if he happened to be in their neighborhood during his travels. He enjoyed talking literature, arts, culture and other topics with them. It's no surprise he especially enjoyed performing for his own people, and he'd be flexible with his fees for African-American groups facing budgetary problems. Baraka was also always willing to meet with students or young people during his visits.

Amiri accepted almost every booking he was offered. He had a hard time saying no, though occasionally he'd turn one down if there was unrest in a particular part of the world and his gut told him to stay away. I remember him turning down trips to Germany and Turkey based on sheer instinct.

Amiri had a couple of bookings canceled because of his politics, but he was well received everywhere he went once his bookings were confirmed. At least I never got any reports that people booed or walked out on him or demonstrated at any of his appearances. I do regret, however, booking him once for an appearance on Bill O'Reilly's TV show that turned contentious.

In the last months of his life, Baraka chose to keep it private that he was not feeling well. I do remember he began slowing down after he fell in October 2013 while on a short tour of Massachusetts that included stops at Harvard University's Poetry Room, UMass-Lowell and the Cape Ann Museum in Gloucester. After that, he started asking for wheelchairs at airports, particularly for getting to connecting flights. He happily got involved in the campaign of his son Ras for mayor of Newark, and put his engagements on the back burner for that.

Thankfully, Baraka appeared at The Newark Museum in November 2013 for a reading and jazz performance celebrating the fiftieth anniversary of his book *Blues People: Negro Music in White America*, a hybrid of music history and social commentary. For me, it was only fitting that one of his final appearances before he went into the hospital in December was in his hometown with the focus on his seminal work. When I learned on January 9, 2014, that Amiri had died, I cried a river. Not only had I lost a wonderful client, I'd also lost a mentor and a friend. ❏

Celeste Bateman has over 25 years of experience as a publicist and arts administrator. She is the founder of the Nia Network, a roster of artists and speakers who address topics and present art forms relative to the African Diaspora. She lives and works in Newark and is the mother of two adult children who are also in the arts/entertainment business.

CHARLES F. CUMMINGS

By Timothy J. Crist

Charles Cummings often said he was "a Newarker by choice," but to his many friends it was not really clear whether he had chosen Newark or whether Newark had chosen him. By the time of his death in 2005, after 42 years at The Newark Public Library and 17 years as city historian, what was clear was that Charles Cummings had become one of the most admired and beloved citizens of Newark.

He was an unlikely Newarker. Raised in the South and trained as an historian at Vanderbilt University, he came to Newark for the first time in 1963 to interview for a position at The Newark Public Library. He got the job, but he never gave up his Southern courtliness, his delight in high church Episcopal liturgy, or his bow ties. He worked first for Miriam Studley (in the library's New Jersey Room), from whom he learned how to curate collections and guide users to the most pertinent archival and reference material. Along the way, he started to build his encyclopedic knowledge of Newark's history. In that pre-digital age, one of his first tasks was to compile an index to the Records of the Town of Newark, dating back to the founding of Newark in 1666. He later took on indexing articles that appeared daily in *The Star-Ledger*; he worked on that each night at home for 25 years. He built the library's collection of photographs from 30,000 to over two million by helping to rescue the photo morgue and clippings files of the *Newark Evening News*. From 1996 until his death, he prepared weekly columns on Newark's history for *The Star-Ledger*, each one written longhand and then typed on a typewriter, on topics ranging from the beer industry to 19th century ethnic riots to food (his final series). The city of Newark recognized his singular knowledge and skill at engaging people of all backgrounds by making him the first official city historian in 1988.

Perhaps no one benefited more from Charles Cummings' knowledge of Newark than the great American novelist, Philip Roth. When Roth needed a glove factory for *American Pastoral*, the two of them walked up Central Avenue past the empty car showrooms until Roth spotted the factory building that he could then populate with his characters. So it went: Cummings tracked down the photograph that enabled Roth to describe the buttons on a policeman's jacket in *The Plot Against America*. He also accompanied Roth to France in 1999 and proudly staffed an exhibit about Newark during a major literary conference in Aix-en-Provence honoring Roth. Roth considered him a "devoted friend" and "the most generous of men."

Charles rarely said no when asked to give a tour, assist a community group, or aid a scholar. His calendar was nearly always full, and his speaking fees went to support his beloved Newark Public Library. He served on the boards of Mount Pleasant Cemetery and the Newark Preservation and Landmarks Committee, among others, and on the vestry of Grace Church. In 2002, he joined with Warren Grover and me to found the Newark History Society, and he contributed greatly to the society's immediate success.

As 2005 drew to a close, Charles was planning to retire from the library, although not from his Newark research. He needed a change of pace, but it was not to be. On December 14, following a holiday dinner with library trustees, he suffered a massive heart attack at home and was rushed to St. Michael's Hospital for surgery. I visited him at St. Michael's on December 20, the night before he died, just after he had received communion from Father Holland of Grace Church. We talked at length about his work, and I recalled his old Vanderbilt professor's comment that he had contributed more to the study of history than any of his other students. Charles smiled slyly and happily at that; he said the difference was focusing on local history. "You have to get local history right."

Charles Cummings got Newark right. ❑

Timothy J. Crist is a business executive in Newark and serves as president of the trustees of both The Newark Public Library and the Newark History Society. Trained as a historian, he earned his Ph.D. at Cambridge University in England.

JOHN COTTON DANA
By Ulysses Grant Dietz

Although legendary in the library field, John Cotton Dana, New Hampshire native son and descendant of old-line Boston Puritan Richard Dana, was even more important in the museum world. It was in Newark that he made his mark nationally in museological history.

A Dartmouth graduate trained as a lawyer, Dana became the head of the Newark Free Public Library in 1902. In that same year, a museum committee was established to oversee displays of both art and natural history specimens in two large fourth-floor galleries in the library. By the time the museum was formally established in 1909, Mr. Dana's vision had already begun to guide the newborn institution's direction.

The Newark Museum was founded to exhibit the "art of today." The founding collection was thousands of Japanese objects from the Edo and Meiji periods, acquired from a Newark pharmacist, George Rockwell. Dana was particularly interested in Japanese things because they represented daily life in Japan and could be exhibited as "art," even though many of them were functional objects.

Within the first few years of the museum's establishment, Mr. Dana began collecting modern European and American pottery, African objects, Native American objects, antiquities from the ancient Mediterranean, and contemporary American painting and sculpture. His vision for his museum was to exhibit and collect what other art museums of the day did not. He wanted the art in his museum to be approachable and to illuminate the way people lived all over the world. His attitude towards collections was anthropological: objects of art reflect people's lives and are influenced by the way people live.

Dana's most radical precept was in seeking out the kind of audience that would not normally visit a museum. He saw the large urban museums that had been appearing in America's cities as clubs for industrialist collectors: places where they could show off the rare and valuable treasures that they valued. Newark's museum would be a place where useful objects, beautifully designed and finely crafted (and this included painting and sculpture), could be shown to pique the public's curiosity and thus promote learning. Mr. Dana wanted the suburban matron and the urban factory worker to come to his museum and to experience art together.

This same approach influenced the museum's collecting of fine art. Museums in the New York metropolitan area did not take kindly to modern art in 1909 — there was no MoMA, no Whitney. In offering the modern artist Max Weber a one-man show at the museum in 1913, Newark became the first American museum to do so for a living artist in the twentieth century. Likewise, the "Modern German Applied Arts" exhibition of 1912-1913 was the first modern design exhibition in an American art museum. In 1915, "The Clay Products of New Jersey" became the first art museum exhibition in the nation to focus on the products of a single regional industry.

The most unusual exhibitions held at the museum, not long before Mr. Dana's death in 1929, were a series of displays based on the premise that "beauty has no relation to age, rarity or cost." Sending his staff to department stores in Newark and New York City, Mr. Dana assembled a huge exhibition of objects that cost anywhere from ten cents to no more than one dollar. In that same year he mounted an exhibition called "Modern American Design in Metal" that offered high-style modern home furnishings and objects designed by the leading modernists of the day.

John Cotton Dana's leadership in innovative museum practice is legendary within the museum world, even today. Much of what every museum takes for granted today was first envisioned and put into practice by him. Newark should be proud of the fact that the modern American art museum was born here. ❏

Ulysses Grant Dietz has been the decorative arts curator at The Newark Museum since 1980 and chief curator since 2012. He received his BA in French from Yale University and his MA in American Material Culture from the University of Delaware's Winterthur Program.

⤛ THOMAS EDISON ⤜
By Leonard DeGraaf

Thomas Edison spent his formative years as an inventor in Newark, where he operated shops that designed and manufactured new technologies for the telegraph industry. Edison's Menlo Park and West Orange laboratories, famous for introducing the phonograph, incandescent electric light and motion picture camera, get more attention from historians, but the five years Edison worked in Newark — from 1870 to 1875 — helped shape his approach to developing new technologies. Edison learned how to be an inventor in Newark.

A native of Ohio, Edison was a telegraph operator in the Midwest during the 1860s before moving to Boston in 1868. In January 1869, he became a full-time inventor who devoted his time to inventing instruments to help telegraph companies meet the growing demand for faster, more efficient communications systems in the years following the Civil War.

By the spring of 1869, Edison had patented his first important invention, a printing telegraph, a machine that transmitted financial information from stock exchanges to bankers and brokers. He moved to New York City to be closer to the managers of Western Union, a leader in the telegraph industry and, by the fall of 1869, had opened a small machine shop in Jersey City.

Edison depended on the support of the telegraph companies, which provided him with money for research and experiments and purchased the equipment produced in his shops. In February 1870, Edison signed a contract with the Gold and Stock Telegraph Co. that gave him $10,000 to invent an improved stock printer. Edison used the money to open his first major shop, the Newark Telegraph Works at 15 New Jersey Railroad Ave. Edison operated up to five different shops in Newark during the early 1870s, including ones at 24 Mechanic St., 4-6 Ward St., 115 New Jersey Railroad Ave. and a small shop along the Morris Canal.

Newark, a bustling industrial city that manufactured machine tools, jewelry, carriages, hats and chemicals, was an attractive environment for Edison. The shops and factories of Newark's diverse economy employed skilled mechanics and machinists, giving Edison access to a pool of talented workers. Edison pioneered collaborative industrial research, bringing together in one place scientific and technical knowledge, the best tools and equipment and experienced workers to turn ideas into marketable products. Edison refined this approach to innovation at Menlo Park and West Orange, but it emerged at his Newark shops in the early 1870s.

Most of Edison's work in Newark focused on the telegraph. Along with improved stock tickers, Edison and his team developed automatic telegraph systems, which recorded and transmitted the dots and dashes of Morse code without the need for human operators. They also invented duplex telegraph systems, which simultaneously transmitted two messages along a single wire in different directions. Another important Edison invention during the Newark years, the quadruplex telegraph, enabled telegraph companies to send four messages on a single wire, two in each direction, at the same time.

In the spring of 1875, Edison invented the electric pen, a battery-powered reciprocating needle that allowed office workers to produce stencils of hand-written documents. Insurance companies, railroads, law firms and other large organizations used the electric pen to make multiple copies of forms and circulars.

Over the course of his long career, Edison organized numerous companies to manufacture and market his inventions. One of the first, the News Reporting Telegraph Co., was established in Newark in October 1871. This company transmitted news via printing telegraphs from a central office to home subscribers. Anticipating twenty-four hour news cycles by more than 100 years, the company promised customers "all general news of the world – financial, commercial, domestic and foreign – the moment such news is received in the main Telegraph Office." The company placed printers in homes or offices without cost, but charged $3 a week for the service.

The News Reporting Telegraph Co. failed within three months but, before it closed, Edison noticed a female employee: 16-year-old Mary Stilwell. One day Edison approached Mary and asked her to marry him. "Don't be in a rush, though," he told her. 'Think it over; talk to your mother about it and then let me know as soon as convenient. Say Tuesday." After talking to her mother, Mary accepted the proposal and they were married on December 25, 1871. Before his marriage, Edison boarded in a house at 854 Broad St. In December 1871, he purchased a home at 53 Wright St. Thomas and Mary lived in this house until the end of 1874, when his need for money during an economic depression forced Edison to sell it and move his family to an apartment in Newark's downtown commercial district.

At the end of 1875, Edison bought land in Menlo Park to build a new laboratory. The move was motivated in part by a rent dispute with a Newark landlord. Edison had rented space in a padlock factory on a monthly basis. When he no longer needed the space, he gave notice and returned the keys at the end of the month. The landlord sued Edison under a city ordinance that made monthly renters responsible for a full year's rent. Outraged at the injustice of this law, Edison felt it was time to leave Newark.

Menlo Park was a small village on the Pennsylvania Railroad, approximately twenty-five miles south of Newark. Menlo Park's isolation allowed Edison and his team to avoid the distraction and noise of cities, while the new laboratory's proximity to the railroad gave them easy access to New York, Newark and Philadelphia. When a reporter asked Edison why he moved to Menlo Park, he said "I couldn't get peace and quiet and was run down by visitors . . . I like it first rate out here in the green country and can study, work and think."

Edison's sojourn in Newark was brief, but it was an important stop on his path towards becoming the pre-eminent inventor of his time. In his Newark shops, Edison learned how to manage and motivate the teams of workers who helped him introduce ground-breaking new technologies. He also learned how to organize shops to manufacture his inventions and cultivated his first relationships with the corporate managers and investors who provided him with the resources to innovate new ideas. ❏

Leonard DeGraaf is an archivist at Thomas Edison National Historical Park in West Orange, NJ. This essay is adapted from his book, "Edison and the Rise of Innovation," Sterling Publishing, 2013.

MARIA JERITZA
By Michael Redmond

Her fame faded over time, like the bouquets her legions of fans would bring to her, but the legend of Maria Jeritza endures in opera lore and history and is likely to endure as long as audiences keep turning out for *Tosca, Der Rosenkavalier, Turandot, Salome* and the other operas for which she was renowned.

Jeritza was a mysterious and glamorous figure, always richly dressed, wearing dark glasses and elaborate hats, who long fascinated residents of Newark's North Ward, where she spent the last 40 years of her life in a mansion on Elwood Avenue in Forest Hill. She would sometimes describe the residence as "my villa outside of New York." It wasn't a villa by any stretch of the imagination, but a stately walled and gated compound unusual even for Newark's most posh neighborhood.

As time went on, fewer and fewer Newarkers knew Jeritza's story or even how to pronounce her name. Urban legend spread. Neighborhood youngsters were certain she was a princess, which wasn't far off the mark, as she had been an Austrian baroness by marriage and a favorite of the Habsburg court. Some people claimed Jeritza never left the house, which was a complete fiction; she maintained an active social schedule through the late 1970s, including Wednesdays and Saturdays at the Metropolitan Opera and Sunday mass at St. Patrick's Cathedral. She was addressed everywhere as "Madame."

Jeritza's singing career spanned nearly four decades and 70 roles. She was the golden girl of opera's golden age. She sang just about anywhere she pleased, for top dollar. Leading composers such as Puccini and Richard Strauss wrote for her. In 1921, the year the Metropolitan Opera lost Enrico Caruso to an untimely death, the company brought in Jeritza from Vienna to keep its box office humming. She was one of the first distinctly modern opera singers, combining beauty and charisma, a brilliant voice, a powerful, naturalistic acting style and a knack for publicity. All these made her an international celebrity in a new age of mass readership, as hungry for news about opera stars as today's public is for news about pop singers, Hollywood personalities and star athletes. So big was the buzz about the "the thunderbolt from Moravia" (her birthplace, a region now part of the Czech Republic) that she made the cover of *Time* magazine in 1928.

For Vienna, the city she loved best, she had been "the prima donna of the century...It is very difficult," wrote Marcel Prawy in *The Vienna Opera* (1970), "to describe what Jeritza was like to a generation that never saw her in her great days with her tremendously erotic aura and her positively volcanic voice."

Jeritza's third marriage, to industrialist Irving P. Seery, brought her to Newark in 1948. The couple lived happily together until Seery's death in 1966. Jeritza had no children, but lived in Forest Hill with family members she had brought over from Europe following World War II, and with Liesl Hilfreich, her secretary and lady-in-waiting, who had accompanied the singer to the U.S. in the 1920s. Prior to her marriage to Seery, Jeritza was the widow of Winfield R. Sheehan, a Hollywood film producer she met in 1935 while singing in California. She had tried to break into the movies, without success, although she did star in a German operetta film in 1933. (The couple lived lavishly in Beverly Hills, where the dining room had seating for more than 150 guests.)

During her heyday in Newark, Jeritza was famed for her glittering formal parties and garden parties, which frequently included performances in a 200-seat theater in the basement of her house. No invitation was as prized as the one for her Viennese New Year's Eve. She told the press she would bring New York City society to Newark, and she did. But her presence in Forest Hill had a more approachable side, too. On Halloween, trick-or-treaters would line up at her home in droves, with their parents, for a glimpse of Jeritza and to receive a shiny new dime, which was quite a treat at the time. For Christmas, the house and grounds were extravagantly decorated. Forest Hill old-timers sometimes reminisce about the year that Jeritza turned on the Christmas lights and the entire neighborhood lost power.

Maria Jeritza sang her last *Salome* in Vienna in 1951. She was 64. She sang her last *Tosca* at Newark's Mosque Theatre in the 1960s. It was a private performance that she produced herself for an invitation-only audience. More than 2,000 people attended, some having flown in from Europe. She was in her mid-70s.

The Jeritza story isn't all *Sunlight and Song* (the title of her autobiography, published in 1924). Following World War II, Jeritza was indefatigable in performing and fundraising for the rebuilding of Vienna's opera house and cathedral and for postwar relief efforts. She was credited with having used her connections during the war to assist Moravian Jews and other victims of the Nazis. A devout Catholic, she was a generous supporter of the church, especially parishes and convents in then-communist Czechoslovakia and Hungary.

By the time Jeritza had reached her final years, the world she'd known was gone, and the grand New Year's Eve parties had given way to small gatherings. She disliked the loud pop music of the day, so the television's sound had been turned off, replaced by a recording of Strauss waltzes, as she and her company watched the ball drop in Times Square. Madame's hearing was no longer the best, and she thought the music was coming from the TV. Delighted, she said, "Listen, here in America, they are playing 'unser Strauss' (our Strauss)!" Even then, "Vienna, City of My Dreams" was the song she had never stopped singing. ❏

Michael Redmond is a native Newarker and former Forest Hill resident who served as The Star-Ledger's classical music critic from 1974 to 1998. He never imagined Maria Jeritza would be following stories in the local press until she happened to mention to him at an arts reception at Morven that she enjoyed his writing.

❧ AMELIA MOORFIELD ❧
By Warren Grover

Amelia Berndt Moorfield was an outstanding leader in Newark in the first half of the twentieth century. Promoting women's rights, civil rights and world peace and fighting Fascism and Nazism were her primary causes.

Amelia was born in 1876 into a middle-class family in Newport, KY, with strong social and philanthropic values. Early on, she displayed an interest in the less fortunate, collecting shoes and clothing for the poor and reading to the illiterate. She aspired to a career in teaching or social work.

Her parents moved the family to Newark after Amelia graduated from high school. Shortly after arriving, she realized her dream of becoming a social worker. In 1909, Amelia married Frank Moorfield, a wealthy Newark inventor and manufacturer, and the marriage allowed her to pursue her interest in volunteering. With her concern for the needy, an outgoing personality and a comfortable financial status, she became a force in Newark's women's groups.

Amelia first came to the public's attention with her work on behalf of the Newark branch of the Women's Political Union, a national women's suffrage group. She quickly became the union's state financial secretary and its leading fundraiser, traveling throughout New Jersey to solicit funds and sign up new members. She also became an expert on the technical and legal aspects of a proposed constitutional amendment giving women the right to vote. From 1915 until 1920, when the Nineteenth Amendment was passed, she frequently took part in public debates against men opposed to the amendment's adoption.

In 1923, Amelia's husband died, leaving her with a substantial inheritance. It was then she turned her attention to the world peace movement, joining the Women's International League for Peace and Freedom (WILPF) in 1925 and helping set up a branch in New Jersey. A year later, she became president of the branch. Her first accomplishment was organizing New Jersey's chapters by congressional district. When Japan invaded China in 1932, in violation of the Kellogg Briand Pact, Amelia's slogan "Do not give way to pessimism!" became the peace movement's national rallying cry.

During her presidency of the Contemporary, Newark's most active and prestigious women's club, Amelia established a monthly interracial Sunday, and she frequently denounced discrimination against blacks while a board member of the Newark Urban League.

Amelia was perhaps the only woman in Newark to raise her voice against Fascism and Nazism. She spoke at a packed rally denouncing domestic and foreign Nazism at the Newark YMHA in May 1935, the lone woman among six speakers. At a WILPF New Jersey convention, she introduced a resolution against the persecution of Jews in Germany. After the Italian invasion of Ethiopia, the Italian government sent recruiters to Newark's Italian-American community, prompting Amelia to lead a group of WILPF members to picket the Italian Consulate in downtown Newark.

Amelia also became active in the American League Against War and Fascism. Her denunciations of the Nazi treatment of Jews stirred the group's large membership, which was more than half Jewish. She was also active in the Newark branch of the Non-Sectarian Anti-Nazi League that picketed stores selling German goods.

Yet, despite her hatred of Nazism and Fascism, Amelia always had peace as her top priority. In May 1940, she spoke to a capacity crowd during a Mothers' Peace Day Rally at Newark City Hall. She also helped collect signatures on a mothers' petition that was submitted to Congress expressing opposition to any American participation in the war.

Amelia Moorfield remained active in many of Newark women's group until her death in 1950. Hers was a life dedicated to caring for those less fortunate and fighting tyranny. ❏

Warren Grover, author of "Nazis in Newark," is co-founder of the Newark History Society and a board member of the New Jersey Historical Society and the Jewish Historical Society of New Jersey. He is a past president of the JHSNJ.

W. PAUL STILLMAN
By Andre Briod

W. Paul Stillman, Newark's pre-eminent twentieth century business and financial figure, was sometimes described by major news organizations as New Jersey's most powerful man, or at least the most powerful in its private sector. However power is measured, he certainly was the city's private sector leader for nearly a half century, from the late 1930s to the 1980s.

Paul Stillman derived his power from his positions of leadership at two dominating financial industry organizations — First National State Bank of New Jersey (later First Fidelity Bancorporation) and Mutual Benefit Life Insurance Company, a nationally prominent insurance industry leader. Neither would survive to the 21st century as viable independent entities, an outcome that would have seemed inconceivable during Stillman's lifetime.

New Jersey historian John T. Cunningham, who knew Stillman personally, said of him, "If you wanted something important done in New Jersey, his office was your first stop."

Born in Newark, Stillman was in his early teens when he moved with his family to Monmouth County, outside of Red Bank. After graduating from Red Bank High School and serving a short stint as a submarine crewman during World War I, he entered the banking industry, first as a messenger with a New York bank and then in New Jersey through the developing bank regulation agencies of that era. He was so successful as an examiner that in early 1931 he accepted an officer's position at Newark's Fidelity Union Bank, and later that year as president of Newark's National State Bank. It was the latter that Stillman would build into the institution that would be formidable in the state, first as First National State and then as First Fidelity, as he was fading from the scene in the mid-1980s.

It was a merger of a big Philadelphia bank company into First Fidelity in 1988, founded on that city's Fidelity Bank, that led to the downfall of First Fidelity. By the time of the merger Stillman was retired, though he was still seen as First Fidelity's symbolic leader. He would die less than a year after the merger that undermined what he had built.

At Mutual Benefit, Stillman was the longtime controlling chairman. He utilized the firm's influence and financial muscle in the 1950s and 1960s to revitalize the area surrounding Newark's Washington Park. By his decisions, Mutual Benefit built its then-impressive 18-story headquarters towering over the park, and financing was provided for numerous other buildings there, including what opened in 1970 at 550 Broad St. as the First National State Building. First National State's home, and Mutual Benefit's, long flanked the prominent New Jersey Bell building at 540 Broad St. They all looked across the park, with its George Washington statue, at Newark's museum and its public library.

Stillman's influence and control over finances also brought other important development to the park area, as well as the launching of the giant office complex, Gateway-Newark, linked by an enclosed bridge to Penn Station's western face.

But Stillman's influence extended far beyond Newark, reaching as well into New Jersey's political and public policy spheres. He was the state Republican party's longtime finance chairman and, for 18 years, a member and then vice chairman of the Port Authority of New York and New Jersey. His financial reach and power were critical in overcoming New York's opposition to bond financing for the Meadowlands sports complex and in obtaining financing for the early development of Atlantic City as a major gaming resort.

Those and other influential effects of Paul Stillman's involvements brought broad benefits to Newark and drove its ambitions during the mid- and later 20th century. That some did not survive him would have disappointed him, but he surely would have found some satisfaction in Newark's early twenty-first century progress. ❏

Andre Briod was a Newark Evening News reporter from 1952 to 1961 before embarking on a career in public relations. He got to know W. Paul Stillman well when he ran his own firm in downtown Newark and had First National State Bank and Mutual Benefit Life among his clients and later when he joined First Fidelity Bancorporation as its senior public affairs officer. He has completed a manuscript of a book on Stillman, Newark and the city's private sector in the twentieth century through the 1980s.

⤙ SARAH VAUGHAN ⤚
By George Kanzler

In the early 1970s, the Savoy on William Street in Newark was a not very propitious namesake of the famous Harlem ballroom, merely a slightly shabby bar near enough to City Hall and police headquarters to attract a clientele weighted toward public employees and cops. But it had a great jukebox featuring jazz, R&B and soul, including such Sarah Vaughan 45s as "Tenderly," "Broken Hearted Melody" and "If You Could See Me Now." And Sam Hammock, the bar's owner, had been a bartender at many of Newark's jazz clubs during their heyday in the late 1940s and 1950s, when Newark native Vaughan still lived in the city and would drop by the clubs when back in town from her near-constant touring. So when Sam started closing up early one Saturday night — just after midnight — and said "Let's go down to the Key Club, I bet Sarah's gonna be there," I happily joined him. But I also doubted him; Vaughan had moved to California in 1969 and hadn't officially performed in Newark in years, so why would she be there?

The Key Club, at the corner of William and Halsey streets, just up the block from the Savoy (musicians would catch a fast, cheaper drink at Sam's place in between sets at the Key), was packed that night. Patrons were lined two and three deep around the big U-shaped oval bar, above and behind which the bandstand, dominated by a Hammond B3 organ and drum set, loomed. With Big John Patton performing on the organ, Sam led me around the bar toward the far top of the U where Jean Dawkins, the owner, always sat. Next to Jean, with an over-sized snifter of Remy-Martin and an ashtray in front of her, was none other than Sarah Vaughan, dressed casually in a loose sweater top and slacks, smoking a cigarette and sipping her cognac. Up until then, I'd only seen Vaughan on stage, quite glamorous in the muumuu-like gowns she favored. She was in conversation with Dawkins, but when Sam nudged her she greeted him warmly, and he introduced me as the "Star-Ledger's hip jazz writer." She was friendly, but more interested in catching up with Jean about the soap opera they evidently both watched religiously. Then, when Patton's tune ended, someone handed Sarah a microphone and she honored a request, singing "Misty," one of her signature hits, right from her bar stool and with no accompaniment. When it was over, she was swarmed by people greeting her as "Sarah" and "Sassy." She returned the salutations, addressing many of her admirers by name. They were all of an age to have been part of the crowd that had filled those local jazz clubs when Vaughan still frequented them. For she may have moved to California, but Sarah Vaughan was still, as she sometimes announced on stage, "a Newark girl at heart."

At closing time that night, there was no last call or a clearing out of patrons. The door was simply locked from the inside, shades drawn, and the impromptu party with Sarah continued. When we got to speak again, she warmed considerably when finding out I was also an Aries (our birthdays were three days apart) and that my favorite album of hers was also her favorite — one featuring trumpeter Clifford Brown. A couple of years later, in 1975, Sarah returned to Newark for a Gershwin program at Symphony Hall. Her a cappella, microphone-less rendition of "Summertime" was glorious, like her "Misty" at the Key Club. I sometimes wonder if her voice would have been any better than the rich, contoured tones of the "Summertime" and "Misty" I'd heard in Newark if she hadn't so loved her brandy and cigarettes. I think probably not. ❏

George Kanzler was The Star-Ledger's jazz and pop critic from 1968 until 2002. He reviewed Sarah Vaughan in concert at Carnegie Hall, Lincoln Center, Newark's Symphony Hall and at several New York clubs.

⚞ MARION THOMPSON WRIGHT ⚟
By Clement Alexander Price

For over a generation, beginning in 1981, the Marion Thompson Wright Lecture Series has been among Newark's most durable civic rituals. Mounted during Black History Month, it at once honors the legacy of a remarkable American scholar and acknowledges the pivotally important narrative of African-American history in the larger story of the making of the American Republic. Wright was among the nation's first professionally trained women historians, arguably the first. That the good citizens of Greater Newark consistently demonstrate an enduring interest in historical scholarship through their patronage of the series is important. It underscores an important transformation in public historical literacy and interest in what historian James Oliver Horton has called "the tough stuff" of American history. The tough stuff takes us to stories of race and racism, slavery, prejudice, injustice, and the higher roads not taken. Marion Thompson Wright wrote about such things through the lens of the long and complicated history of Africans and African Americans on New Jersey soil.

Marion Manola Thompson Wright was a native of East Orange, NJ, born there on Sept. 13, 1902. She was the youngest of the four children of Minnie Holmes Thompson and Moses R. Thompson. Little is known about her early life. She moved with her mother to Newark as a child and attended the city's prestigious Barringer High School, from which she graduated in 1923 at the head of the class. "Deeds Survive the Doer" was the motto she chose for her yearbook entry. At 16, before she graduated from Barringer, she was married to William H. Moss. From that union came two children.

The local world in which Wright came of age was largely a segregated world. The long legacy of slavery and the nascent benefits of freedom intersected in ways that influenced her and other African Americans born more than a generation after the Great Emancipation. In New Jersey, and in other northern states, black men and later women were able to vote, and they were largely free to go about their lives without pernicious outbreaks of racial attacks by whites. However, in keeping with the nineteenth-century experience of their forebears, many early twentieth-century blacks, such as Marion Thompson Wright's family, were poor. White racial privilege complicated Wright's youth at a time when European immigration was on the rise and when Northern communities were being settled by Southern blacks joining in the Great Migration. Those two demographic shifts likely influenced Wright's perception of the nation's history and its racial hierarchy. During her childhood, Newark's black population was growing as blacks faced discrimination on multiple fronts, most notably employment, housing and the perception of the race by a cross section of whites and ethnics on their way to becoming white.

Race was permeable in the first three decades of the last century and yet it was not crippling to all blacks. Indeed, Wright was among a select group of black Americans whom the iconic Negro scholar W.E.B. DuBois called the "talented tenth." Her academic talents took her from Barringer to the prestigious Howard University from which, in 1927, she graduated magna cum laude. A year later she earned a master's degree in education there. During the decade that would follow, this brilliant young scholar would return to Newark, serving as a social worker in the city's Department of Public Welfare and the New Jersey Emergence Relief Administration. She later resumed her graduate studies at Columbia University where she studied under the pioneering intellectual and cultural historian, Merle Curti. With him, she completed her dissertation, *The Education of Negroes in New Jersey*, in 1938. She became the first black woman to receive a Ph.D. from Columbia. *The New York Times* book series published her dissertation in 1941 and released it again later as an important contribution to the history of blacks in the U.S. Her writings also appeared in the *Journal of Negro Education*, the *Journal of Negro History*, and *New Jersey History*. In 1940, she joined the Howard faculty as an assistant professor of education, at that time one of only two female assistant professors at the school. She remained on the Howard faculty until her death in 1962.

Professor Wright's scholarship falls within the second generation of the so-called "Negro History Movement," which made its mark around the ending of World War II. The scholars of that time, most notably John Hope Franklin, persuasively argued that racial injustice denied African

Americans secure, racially unencumbered lives in early American history, throughout the decades when the nation became a mature democracy. The Negro History Movement also drew attention to the persistent effort of blacks to improve their status in the Republic and how their agitation against injustice expanded the meaning of democracy. Marion Thompson Wright was especially influential because her writings shed light on New Jersey's seemingly Southern-like racial culture and the eventual willingness of its residents, especially after World War II, to extend democratic rights and liberties to a broad cross sections of its residents, including African Americans.

When Marion Thompson Wright passed in 1962, the Negro History Movement, of which she was an important contributor, had significantly influenced the way American history was researched, written, spoken of and taught to students young and old. Within another generation, the story of African Americans was at the near center of the larger story of American life and culture. The lecture series named in her memory was launched at that time. ❑

Clement Alexander Price was the Board of Governors Distinguished Service Professor of History at Rutgers University in Newark. In 2014, he was appointed Newark's official city historian.

HONORED
NOTABLES

EAST SIDE HIGH SCHOOL
ALUMNI ROSTER OF SUPERIOR MERIT 1914 - 1965

Anthony Ambrose, MD	Medicine and Education
Carl Baccaro, DDS	Dentistry - Civic Affairs
Henry M. Benkert	Athletics - Education
Dominic A. Cavicchia	Law and Government
Ida E. Charles	Early Childhood Education
Walter D. Chambers	Social Service
Janet I. Domino	Art Education
Anthony J. Dopazo	Military Service
Joseph I. Echikson, MD	Medicine
Nicholas T. Fernicola	Law and Government
Donald B. Gomes	Business
Philip E. Gordon	Law and Government
Fred Landolphi	Public Education
Emanuel Liccese, MD	Medicine
Joseph P. Lordi	Law and Government
Joseph Nataro, MD	Medicine
Thomas P. Pannullo	Business
Paul Policastro	Law and Government
Albert Saldutti	Business and Government
George J. Spangenberger	Business and Community Affairs
Robert W. Van Houten, D. Sc.	Higher Education
Ralph A. Villani	Law and Government

SOURCE: Event Program June 23, 1965

ADDED LATER

1966	1970
Domenico Mortellito	Dr. Max Karlen, DDS
Maurice Schapira	Dr. Richard Sable, DDS

1967	1972
Melvin F. Haas	A. Walter Ackerman
Harry Gilroy	Joseph Morano
1968	Dr. Michael Petty
Elizabeth Collins Hoston	Louis M. Turco
Charles Dipace	

1977	**2000**
Golden E. Johnson	Tom Clark
1978	**2001**
Albert Cernados	Stephen Leonardis
1980	**2002**
Andrew J. Naporano Sr.	Susan Teresi
1981	**2003**
Joseph C. Parlavecchio	Ceu Cirne-Neves
1982	**2005**
Diego C. Asencio	Elisabete Oliveira
1983	**2006**
Albert Angrisani	Mario Santos
1985	**2007**
Dr. Emanuel Liccese	Dennis Letts
1986	**2008**
John J. Dios	Richard Errol Wesley
1989	**2009**
Francis J. Giantomasi	Manuel M. Rosa
1990	**2010**
Casimer J. Pomianek	Joseph Maccia
1992	**2011**
Finney J. Alati	Deborah Terrell
1993	**2012**
Joseph Bradley	Elizabeth Aranjo
1995	**2013**
Gerard J. Morano	Michael Cupo
1997	**2014**
Dr. Joaquim Correira	Anthony Tavares
1998	**2015**
Raymond M. Lindgren	Sgt. Harry L. Ettlinger
1999	
Dr. Lawrence A. Armenti	

SOURCE: school yearbooks
(not all years included)

ESSEX CATHOLIC HIGH SCHOOL
ALUMNI HALL OF FAME

1981

Louis P. Allora, '61

Marty McNish, '61

Ron Del Mauro, '62

Jack O'Leary, '64

Joe Mastracchio, '65

John Suminski, '65

Arthur Martin, '66

Mark Murro, '67

Phil Reilly, '69

Pete Westbrook, '70

Rick Cerone, '72

Bro. Francis I. Offer CFC

1982

Jerry Krumeich, '62

Joe O'Dowd, '63

Rich Reinhardt, '64

Barry Washington, '65

Larry Schumacher, '66

Marty Liquori, '67

Jim Hickey, '68

Bob Tortoriello, '68

Eddie Austin, '70

John McCree, '71

Rocco Ferrante, '74

Anthony "Brother Nick" Naclerio

1983

Steve Sullivan, '63

Mike Shannon, '64

Mike Keogh, '68

Bob Molinaro, '68

Gary Mulligan, '68

Al Wujciak, '72

Joe Reto, '79

Samuel D'Ambola MD (fencing coach)

1984

Mike Williams, '62

Jerry Otskey, '63

Dennis Sasso, '65

Dr. Frank Pascuiti, '69

Hugh O'Neill, '72

Ed Hogan, '73

Stan Waldemore, '73

Dave Brown, '75

Joe Garvey (faculty/coach)

1985

Hugh Maloney, '62

Dr. John Petillo, '64

Jim LePore, '65

Craig Courter, '66

Vic Collucci, '67

Charlie McLoughlin, '69

Ken Cubelli, '71

Brian McIntee, '75

Bill Valente (faculty)

1986

Dr. William Gutsch, '63

Walter Krause, '65

Lonnie Monceisi, '66

Tom Mount, '66

Greg Ryan, '66

Jim Harrison, '71

Jim Clark, '76

1987

Robert Coppola, '67

Milton Irvin, '67

Joseph Semler, '69

Tom Reilly, '71

Rocco Collucci, '72

George LaTorre, '74

Dr. James Maguire (faculty)

ESSEX CATHOLIC HIGH SCHOOL
ALUMNI HALL OF FAME (continued)

James McKeon (faculty)

1988

Tom Dubrosky, '63

Al Cifelli, '65

Ed Kwasnik, '67

Bob Jones, '72

Greg Liddell, '73

Joe Re, '80

Bro. Paul B. Whalen CFC

1989

Dr. George Bauer, '64

Lou Constantinople, '65

Jim Doherty, '69

Rudy Guevara, '71

Steve Miller, '73

Joe Furnari, '77

1990

Charles Provini, '64

Alfonse Tobia, '67

Ernest Dickerson, '69

Tom DePoto, '70

James Kirby, '73

Al Uricoli, '77

1991

Harry McLaughlin, '63

Fred Lane, '66

John Lennon, '67

Bruce Soriano, '68

Ray Bauer, '71

Bro. Martin E. Germain CFC

1992

Tom Fuchs, '65

Peter Flannery, '67

Richard Zatorski, '69

Alex DiMeo, '72

Tom McLaughlin, '73

Steve Coppola, '82

Bro. Patrick Duffy CFC

1993

Bert Tobia, '63

Joseph P. LaSala, '65

Wallace W. Hutton, '73

Bro. Arthur A. Loftus CFC

1994

Jack Decker, '71

Cliff Anderson, '75

Robert Taglieri (faculty/coach)

1995

Michael Critchley, Esq., '62

Marcelo Moyano, '76

Bishop Joseph Francis

1996

John Cassese, '62

Frank Norton, '67

Alan Knight, '79

1997

Cardinal Theodore McCarrick

1998

Joseph M. Fowlkes Jr., '67

Paul Schetelick, '67

Stephen N. Adubato, '75

Fred Dwyer (faculty/coach)

1999

Rev. John LaFerrera, '65

Rev. Robert LaFerrera, '67

Dr. Frank Hall, '74

Bro. James R. Kelly CFC

2001

James D. Smith, '61

ESSEX CATHOLIC HIGH SCHOOL ALUMNI HALL OF
FAME (continued)

Martin F. Gleason, '63

Tom Boutsikaris, '65

Louis R. Tomasetta, '66

William T. Connell, '67

Tyrone Garrett, '88

2002

Joseph Romano, '62

Edward Santiago, '68

Duane Dyson, '77

Benson Goodwyn, '87

Mark Dufresne, '95

2003

Henry Prata, '63

Bro. Stephen J. Johnsen CFC, '69

Nick Grosch, '71

Jay Messina, '73

Bro. Howard A. McKenzie CFC

Gloria Pellegrino (staff)

Donald Sullivan (faculty)

Joe Walsh (trustee)

2004

Marc Verzatt, '66

Homer Mosley, '68

Sal Federico, '69

Vick Silva, '70

Ed DeVivo, '71

2005

Michael Witsch, '68

Rick Petersen, '71

Dwayne Reeves, '88

1975 varsity baseball team

John Ennis (faculty)

2006

Joseph Thunell, '66

Roger Desiderio, '67

Larry Iovino, '67

Thomas Miller, '70

1974-75 varsity basketball team

2009

John Nunn, '68

2010

Sean (John) McGovern, '84

2011

Bill Cardone, '71

Rick Fontana, '71

Peter Varsanyi, '77

Tim Walsh, '80

1976-77 varsity basketball team

Gene D'Alessandro (faculty/coach)

2012

Eugene Stefanelli, '62

Tim Reilly, '69

Tim Lee, '71

John Owen Melody, '72

Larry Melillo, '77

2013

Rich Liebler, '63

Vince Otskey, '66

Keith Krauss, '71

Jim Mullin, '73

James Powers, '73

Steve Zirpoli, '76

2014

Steve McCabe, '64

Charlie Dowd, '67

Kevin McGrath, '72

James Foti, '74

Col. Walter Alvarado, '81

SOURCE: Essex Catholic Alumni Association

MALCOLM X SHABAZZ/SOUTH SIDE H.S.
GOLDEN RING OF FAME MEMBERS (with year of induction)

Susana Alvarez	2000	Authur Johnson Sr.	2004
Earnest (Boo Boo) Baron	2010	Marcellus King	1999
Maurice Best	2003	Dr. Keith Kirkland	2000
Dr. Marion A. Bolden	2000	Ronald Kornegay	1995
Joe Brevard	2014	Gregory Latta	1993
Akili Buchanan	2000	Deidre Littles	1995
Reggie Brown	2003	Sam Manigault	2015
Carol D. Campbell	2002	Sheila Manigault	2012
Jonnie A. Cannon	2001	Willie Marsh	2003
Charletta Childs	2013	William May	2004
Greg Collins	2008	Forest McCloud	2011
James Cook	1994	Inez McClendon	2002
Ann Dickey-Kemp	1993	Joe McCollum	2015
Li'za M. Donnell	2007	David McCombs	1997
Maldine Dowdy	1993	Winthrop McGriff	1997
Vincent Finch	1993	Dr. Fred Means	1996
Dr. Leah Gaskins-Fischue	1995	Victor Nelson	1999
Dr. Frager Foster	2006	Frank Padilla Sr.	1996
Bruce Freeman	2009	Autrey Reynolds	1995
Carol Garretson	2015	Hon. Ronald Rice	1995
David Gary	2007	Pamela Ringer	2001
Gloria Gaynor	2005	Akbar Salaam	2014
Safiyna Islam	2013	Alex Sanchez	2015
Hon. John Gibbons	2010	William Tate	2012
Barbara Greene	1996	Katherine Taylor	2008
Marcellus D. Green	2001	Martha Washington	2014
James Harris	2014	Vanessa Watson	1996
Hon. Harry Hazelwood	1992	Alterick White	2009
Tracey Hedgepath-White	2013	Wendy Smith-White	2012
Nathan Himelstein	2000	Hon. Marilyn Williams	1998
Cleo Hill	1996	Kathleen Witcher	1994
Ivan Holmes	2006	Connie Woodruff	1998
Arnold J. Jackson	2001	Lonnie Wright	1994
Hon. Sharpe James	1992	Dr. Don Yee	2008
John Jenkins	1995		
Adele Johnson	1994		

SOURCE: Malcolm X Shabazz H.S.
Alumni Hall of Fame Association

MEDAL OF HONOR RECIPIENTS
WITH TIES TO NEWARK
CIVIL WAR

NAME	BRANCH	BIRTHPLACE	ACCREDITED TO
Edmund English	Army	NY, NY	Newark
Frank E. Fesq	Army	Germany	Newark
Joseph L. Follett	Army	Newark	St. Louis, MO
Gabriel Grant	Army	Newark	Trenton, NJ
William Magee	Army	Newark	Newark
Albert Oss	Army	Belgium	Newark
James Sheridan	Navy	Newark	NY, NY
Andrew Traynor	Army	Newark	Rome, NY
Daniel Whitfield	Navy	Newark	New Jersey

INDIAN CAMPAIGNS

Thomas Sullivan	Army	County Meath, Ireland	Newark

PHILIPPINE INSURRECTION

James Parker	Army	Newark	Newark

CHINA (BOXER REBELLION)

William F. Hamberger	Navy	Newark	New Jersey

WORLD WAR I

Frank J. Bart	Army	NY, NY	Newark
William Sawelson	Army	Newark	Harrison, NJ

KOREAN WAR

Henry Svehla	Army	Newark	Essex, NM

PEACE TIME AWARDS

Henry A. Eilers	Navy	Newark	New Jersey

SOURCE: HomeofHeroes.com

NCE/NEW JERSEY INSTITUTE OF TECHNOLOGY ATHLETIC HALL OF FAME

2010
Tarik Rodgers, '96

Jonathan Ross, '56

Gregory Soriano, '75

2009
Roland E. Barth, '60

Dave DeNure, coach

Jean M. Graziano, '89

2007
David Crimmins, '52

Katherine Eng, '93

Herb Iris, '51

Robert Taetzsch, '52

William Taetzsch, '52

2006
Andrew D. Brown, '63

Nicholas J. Kaminsky, '78

Raymond V. Paulius, '85

2005
Andrew I. Bakun, '82

Carmine P. DeNicola, '78

Paul A. Sarlo, '92

Nevea C. Van Wright, '97

Bob Welgos, '62

2003
Wendy A. Gruenewald, '97

Kenneth W. Hammond, '79

2002
Andrew Handwerker, '63

Paul C. Hausser, '63

John "Gene" Schmid, coach

1996
Raymond E. Blum, '50

Alex Khowaylo, '69

Rudy Romulus, '91

1995
Edward Cruz, '63

Salvatore A. Gagliardo, '85

Elizabeth M. Goldrick Pitt, '90

1994
Charles "Tudy" Lubetkin, '53

J. Malcolm Simon, coach & AD

Myron S. Worobec, '66

1993
Joe A. Dias, '77

Arnold L. Giovannoli, '53

Robert K. Lynch, '84

Warren E. Rodgers, '88

1992
Louis DeVito, '60

Gilbert F. Fehn, '40

Seymour "Zoom" Fleisher, '51

Peter J. Skurla, '41

1991
Myron Bakun, '67

Marilyn E. Dawson, '86

Thomas G. Gallagher, '85

Dan MacDonald, '84

Yoshisada Yonezuka, coach

NCE/NEW JERSEY INSTITUTE OF TECHNOLOGY
ATHLETIC HALL OF FAME (continued)

1990

Thomas Bradley, '78

Yves Etienne, '79

Ali Hubey, '72

Frank Wasniewski, '80

1989

Fred "Coach" Bauder, coach

Hamilton V. Bowser, '52

Raymond P. Kasbarian, '66

1988

Eugene M. Drury, '63

Jay W. Haase, '75

Richard J. Olsen, '69

Jeffrey Tubello, '76

Werner Zorn, '62

1987

Gregory "Egor" Bornako, '70

Fabian Hurtado, '75

Robert Shelby Ketzner, coach

George R. Olson, '77

Lawrence P. Tosato, '56

1986

Hernan "Chico" Borja, '81

Joseph M. Fitzgerald, coach

Robert F. Swanson, department chair

John J. Walsh, '66

SOURCE: NJIT

ST. BENEDICT'S PREPARATORY SCHOOL HALL OF FAME

Elijah Allen, '93

John M. Allen, '54

Vincent Almeida, '95

John H. Anderson Jr., '71

Vincent Aulisi, '52

Frank J. Baader, '15

Anthony Badger, '77

Rick L. Bailey, '78

John Baker, '66

Edward Bals, '52

Joseph A. Barber, '44

John F. Bateman, '34

Rev. Leo Beger, O.S.B. '26

Steven Bercik, '62

Greg Berhalter, '91

Carl D. Biello, '70

Ernest A. "Prof" Blood

E. Thomas Brennan, '62

Matthew J. Bolger, '40

Vincent A. Braun, '35

Nicholas M. Briante, '55

John A. Brogan, '60

Peter R. Brogan, '57

G. Michael Brown, '60

Abbot Martin J. Burne, O.S.B. '32

Rich Bustamante, '92

Lawrence A. Cabrelli, '37

Peter A. Carlesimo, '38

Owen T. Carroll, '21

Michael J. Caruso, '63

John B. Cassell

Salvatore N. Cavallaro, '47

James C. Cavanaugh, '14

Alfred Cito, '38

Harry Coates

George T. Coker, '61

James Colagreco, '48

Edwin "Rip" Collins, '39

John T. Colrick, '25

William A. Conn, '47

Henrique "Hank" Cordeiro, '72

Frank C. Cosentino, '62

Frank Cosgrove, '36

Bishop Joseph A. Costello, '33

William H. Crosby, '57

Gene V. D'Alessandro, '52

John F. Dalton, '44

Edward Deady, '26

Francis E. Delany, '36

James E. Delany, '66

August G. Desch, '18

Charles Deubel Jr., '30

Hugh J. Devore, '30

Ricky D'Innocenzio, '71

Michael DiPiano, H'82

Michael A. DiPiano Jr., '95

J.J. "Jiggs" Donahue, '20

Edward Donovan, '36

Joseph Dooley, '84

Joseph C. Duff, 42

George Dunn, '88

Harry P. Durkin, '49

ST. BENEDICT'S PREPARATORY SCHOOL HALL OF FAME

(continued)

Thomas E. Durkin Jr., '43

Frank Dwyer, '43

George Enderle, '55

William Feaster, '24

Rev. Stephen W. Findlay, O.S.B. '29

Adrian M. Foley Jr., '39

Joseph Fonseca, '67

John A. Ford

Stanley Frankoski Jr., '73

Tramond French, '91

Leslie A. Fries, '19

Brian P. Froelich, '64

James Furey, '51

Alexander S. Garry, '35

William S. Garry, '36

Michael A. Genevrino, '42

Benjamin R. Geraghty, '32

John J. Gibbons, '42

Edward J. Gilhooly, '13

Bernard Greene, '73

Paul J. Griswold, '69

Vincent J. Healy, '34

Michael J. Hearn, '35

George F. Hewson, '26

Frank J. Hill

Rev. Matthew Hoehn, O.S.B. '17

Derek Hoff, H'96

William J. Jackson, '27

Richard S. Jacobs, H'90

Edwin W. Jamieson Jr., '62

Peter D. Jones, '11

Vernon June, '84

Joseph M. Kasberger

Jerome "Jeep" Klemm, '56

Richard "Spike" Kochansky, '61

Rev. William Koelhoffer

Michael Laughna, '68

Rev. Edwin D. Leahy, O.S.B. '63

Thomas A. Leahy, '77

Thomas E. Lenney, '61

Wayne T. Letwink, '53

David Liddell, '35

Ralph Lilore, '64

Joseph J. Locascio, '60

Maurice "Horsey" Lonergan, '37

Rev. Thomas S. Long, O.S.B. '27

Pedro Lopes, '90

Rev. Maurus J. McBarron, O.S.B. '26

Francis F. McDermitt, '15

Leo J. McGlynn, '29

Philip A. McLaughlin, '21

William C. McLaughlin, '39

Edward W. Madjeski, '27

John J. Magovern Jr., '25

Al "Boomie" Malekoff, '43

Peter Mattia, '66

William J. Mealia, '56

William Meister, '48

Frank A. Milbauer, '21

Peter Mocco, '60

ST. BENEDICT'S PREPARATORY SCHOOL HALL OF FAME
(continued)

William Monaco, '50	Eugene F. Schiller, '50
Christopher F. Monahan, '57	Scott Schweitzer, '89
Kenya Moncur, '91	Anthony J. Scotti, '57
Russell S. Monica, '35	Benjamin J. Scotti, '55
John E. Mulvihill, '28	Rev. Cornelius Selhuber, O.S.B. '93
Francis J. Murphy, '46	Bernard M. Shanley, 1886
Pat Napoli, '87	Bernard M. Shanley Jr., '21
Richard Nazareta, '58	Robert W. Sherry, '50
Herb Neilan, '24	Harry F. Singleton, '27
Leo V. Norton, '23	Rev. Dunstan Smith, O.S.B. '32
Frank O'Brien, '61	Most Rev. John M. Smith, '53
Paul "Bucky" O'Connor, '55	William Sweeney, '34
Michael Ondiro, '37	Paul B. Szem, '57
Eamon J. O'Reilly, '62	Richard E. Tarrant, '60
Ralph W. Pellechia, '52	Paul E. Thornton, '63
Rev. Bernard Peters, O.S.B. '18	Frank S. Torok
Rev. Thomas R. Peterson, O.P. '47	Rev. Boniface Treanor, O.S.B. '47
Edward J. Quinn, '36	Rauhn Turner, '96
Philip E. Rafter	Andre Van Drost, '82
Tabare Ramos, '84	James Waldron, '71
Rev. Boniface Reger, O.S.B. 1892	Thomas Glynn Walker, '19
William J. Reilly, '18	Frank P. Walsh, '43
Albert Reinoso, '59	Jim Wandling, '92
Claudio Reyna, '91	Richard Weisgerber, '34
Peter Rhatican, '63	Arif Welcher, '96
Clarence Richardson, '79	William "Mugsy" Whelan, '27
Matthew J. Rinaldo, '49	Thomas J. White, '57
Justo Rosario, '92	John H. Yauch Sr., '17
Peter Rubas, '54	Andrew F. Zazzali, '18
James A. Scarpone, '58	SOURCE: St. Benedict's Prep

SETON HALL LAW SCHOOL DISTINGUISHED GRADUATE AWARD RECIPIENTS

2015
Paulette Brown, '76

2014
William J. Palatucci, '89

2013
James Crawford Orr, '64

2012
Liza M. Walsh, '84

2011
Patrick C. Dunican Jr., '91

2010
Kevin H. Marino, '84

2009
Robert L. Baechtold, '66

2007
Mitch Baumeister, '72

2006
Timothy Rothwell, '76

2005
Gov. Christopher J. Christie, '87

2003
Karol Corbin Walker, '86

2002
Edward B. Deutsch, '71

2001
Hon. Dennis M. Cavanaugh, '72
Hon. Joel A. Pisano, '74

2000
Robert G. Rose, '74

1998
Hon. Katherine S. Hayden. '75

1997
Ambassador Clay Constantinou, '81

1996
Gov. Donald T. DiFrancesco, '69

1995
Vivian Sanks King, '85

1994
Michael Critchley, '72

1993
James F. Mulvihill, '71

1992
Frank J. Vecchione, '64

1991
Joseph P. LaSala, '72

1990
John F. McMahon, '65

1989
Nicholas R. Amato, '64
Hon. Daniel J. Moore, '57
Hon. Robert T. Tarleton, '57

1988
Rosemary T. McFadden, '77

1987
Cary Edwards, '70
Thomas Greelish, '71

1986
Barbara Curran, '77
George L. Schneider, '66

1985
Bernard M. Hartnett Jr., '55

1984
William B. McGuire, '58

1983
Daniel A. Degnan S.J., '54

1982
W. Hunt Dumont, '67

SOURCE: Seton Hall Law School

RUTGERS-NEWARK ATHLETIC HALL OF FAME

Frank Adinolfe, '86	Michael Faulkner, '73
Ihor Akinshyn, '95	William Finkle, '90
Jim Andrich, '85	Asmar Fortney, '08
Andrew Awad, '97	Jim Fredo, '90
Steve Ballerini, '06	Burton Geltzeiler, '50
Robert Blunt, '72	Aaron Green, '50
Emily Bock-Russo, '93	Donald Harris, '59
Henry Bodner, '59	Willie James Heard, '77
Bill Boericke, '88	Steve Herman, '63
Raymond Brienza, '57	Dr. Jeremy Hoff, '02
Donald Cameron, '54	Jose Holguin, '83
Robert Castronovo, '70	Michael Hopton, '83
Jason Celentano, '94	Taras Hunczak, coach
Mary Coleman, '80	Burton Ironson, '51
Dr. Tim Coleman, '80	Jerry Izenberg, '52
Robin Pearce Cook, '05	Stephanie Jackson, '83
Carla Cusate, '84	Ed Janiga, '83
Irene Darmochwal, '82	Vangela Crowe Johnson, '94
Dr. Carl DeFronzo, '82	Ronald Jones, '81
Jayne M. DeMichele, '96	George Kane, '65
Sue DeAlesandro, '90	Jeffrey Karlin, '69
Al DeCicco, coach	Ed Kasbarian, '67
Donna Del Rosso, '90	Jerome Kasper, '51
Brian Dena, '00	Alherd Kazura, '81
Roselyn Desroches, '91	Michell Koss, '82
Fred DeVesa, '68	Monroe Kritchman, '59
Walter Egnatuk, '57	Flo Labenski, administrator & coach
Sheena Eldred, '06	

RUTGERS-NEWARK ATHLETIC HALL OF FAME
(continued)

Domini Lanzone, '94	Steve Senko, administrator & coach
Troy Longo, '02	Richard Serratelli, '51
Danny Lopes, '98	Alka Shah, '95
Jim Lopez	Jerry Sherman
Carl Mackerer, '63	Dave Sica, '07
Joseph Macula, '78	Anthony Spezzaferra, '91
Larry Manochio, '62	Gabriela Tacun, '96
Larry McClure, '67	Jack Throckmorton, '65
Robert Mizerek, coach	Al Trank, '81
David Monisera, '94	William Tyson, '68
John Murphy, '50	Marc Volpe, '73
Christopher Olsen, '90	Luz Zambrano, '93
Mike Oropollo, '67	Jake Zeidwerg, '56
Donald Parrish, '05	SOURCE: Rutgers-Newark
Patrusia Kotlar Paslawsky, '79	
Charle Pezzano, '52	
Sanford Pollack, '51	
Joseph Pucillo, coach	
Jen Raido, '09	
Paul Reid, '80	
Edward Reilly, '87	
Michael Richards, '88	
Rosalyn Roberts, '55	
Laura Salinardi-Murphy, '79	
Denise Cadmus Saywack, '96	
Rich Scalabrini, '95	

RUTGERS-NEWARK DISTINGUISHED ALUMNI
(all degrees)

Shah Ali, 2005

Hayford I. Alile, '69

Mark Angelson, '75

Frank Askin, '66

Cynthia Augustine, '82

Gloria A. Bachman, '70

Richard H. Bagger, '86

Keith Banks, '77

Orville E. Beal, '54

Felix M. Beck, '53

Candace Beinecke, '70

Marc E. Berson, '68

Fannie Bear Besser, '20

Annabelle Bexiga, '98

Dennis M. Bone, '84

Adriana Bosch, '77

Raymond Brienza, '57

Bob Busse, '38

Joseph Cali, 2010

Robert E. Campbell, '62

Michael Patrick Carroll, '83

Mason N. Carter, '74

Raymond C. Chambers, '64

Ronald K. Chen, '83

Mei Wei Cheng, '99

Lawrence R. Codey, '75

Gary M. Cohen, '83

Barbara Bell Coleman, '74

Christopher J. Connors, '88

Anthony Coscia, '84

Sam Crothers, '62

Peter James DaPuzzo, '66

Kathleen A. Donovan, '74

Frank P. Doyle, '75

Tashni-Ann Dubroy, 2011

Amanda A. Ebokosia, 2008

Marianne Espinosa, '74

Zulima Farber, '74

Alvin Felzenberg, '77

Louis J. Freeh, '74

William M. Freeman, '83

Rosalind Fuse-Hall, '83

Albert R. Gamper Jr., '65

Anna Marie Gewirth, 2006

Nia H. Gill, '75

Mary Jo Green, '70

Wade Henderson, '73

Richard J. Hughes, '31

Burton Ironson, '53

George E. Irwin, '72

Jerry Izenberg, '52

Ralph Izzo, 2002

Natalie Jesionka, 2007

Annette Juliano, '65

Maryann Keller, '66

James P. Kelly, '73

Irwin I. Kimmelman, '52

Sandra King, '69

Alfred C. Koeppe, '69

Barry Komisaruk, '65

Michael J. LaPolla, '78

Jaynee LaVecchia, '79

RUTGERS-NEWARK DISTINGUISHED ALUMNI

(continued)

Suzanne Lego, '65

Irwin J. Lerner, '58

Helena D. Lewis, '94

Donna Lieberman, '73

Gerald H. Lipkin, '63

Virginia Long, '66

Soichi Matsuno, '81

Sherilyn McCoy, '88

Rosemary McFadden, '73

Catherine M. McFarland, '80

George E. McPhee, '92

William Mendello, '72

Robert Menendez, '79

Frederick A. Morton Jr., '93

Ozzie Nelson, '30

Arthur B. Newman, '65

Eileen Newman, '65

Elizabeth M. Norman, '73

Michael Norman, '72

U. Joy Ogwu, '75

Eugene M. O'Hara, '62

Hazel R. O'Leary, '66

Olena Paslawsky, '76

Julius L. Pericola, '56

Alex J. Plinio, '60

Miguel A. Pozo, '98

Victoria F. Pratt, '98

Sylvia B. Pressler, '59

Joan M. Quigley, '79

William F. Rasmussen, '60

Taji Reisch, 2014

Thomas A. Renyi, '68

Ronald L. Rice, '79

Matthew J. Rinaldo, '53

Peter W. Rodino Jr., '37

Richard W. Roper, '68

Esther Salas, '94

Vivian Sanks-King, '70

Ninfa Saunders, '79

Yvonne Smith Segars, '84

Elizabeth Blume-Silverstein, 1911

David T. Sloan, '76

Gail Thompson, '88

Robert Torricelli, '77

Luis Valentin, '89

Nancy M. Valentine, '69

Lois Van Deusen, '77

Judith Viorst, '52

Harry J. Volk, '30

Elizabeth Warren, '76

Vincent Warren, '93

Lois Whitman, '76

Tracey Scott Wilson, '89

Donna Lee Wong, '70

SOURCE: Rutgers-Newark

WEEQUAHIC HIGH SCHOOL HALL OF FAME

Alvin Attles, 1955: basketball player & coach

Sid Dorfman, 1937: sportswriter

Les Fein: basketball coach, 1956-67

Dr. Max Herzberg: principal, 1933-57

Sandra King, 1965: journalist

Benilde Little, 1976: author

Robert Lowenstein: chair, foreign language dept.

Hilda Lutzke: English teacher, 1937-75

Seymour "Swede" Masin, June 1938: all-around athlete

Dr. Victor Parsonnet, June 1941: pioneering cardiologist

Philip Roth, Jan. 1950: Pulitzer Prize-winning author

Ron Stone: principal, 2002-07

SOURCE: Weequahic H.S.

To Newark

The day a modern city celebrates
Her age, and wonders what her life may mean,
Long dead philosophers could come to her,
Poets and scientists should throng to her,
And the most noble thoughts of men and women
Alive and dead, should quicken in her mind.
The clouds and stars should speak, nor should the fields
Be dumb; and the procession of the years
Should bring her many a richly 'broidered word
Taken from the loom of time.
What would they say?
Newark, the years would bring the self-same words
They brought of old to Baghdad and Peking
And many an elder city now forgotten,
The same-self words they bring to San Francisco,
London, Berlin; for they would say to you
That though the gardens of the distant past
Are in fair memory, and though the dust
Of ancient times came to consummate flower
In many a beautifully bodied girl
And boy, in many a tender-hearted woman
And stalwart man, this life of ours to-day
Is quite as fair, and animated dust
As precious. They would say to you that still
Apples of the Hesperides are bright
And waiting to be picked, and days are fresh,
And dogwood still is white in early May.
And they would say that never any town
Was more beloved to eternity
Nor given a more golden chance. Newark,
You have the only stuff that ever was
Of glory, for you have the souls of men;
The dream of love and justice which you weave
Out of the faces in your thoroughfares, —
A girl-like sunlight on the tasseled corn;
Beside her, eager with his love, a youth
Whose stride is music and whose laugh is wine, —
The dream you weave of them, the dream you weave
Of all your children and their hopes and fears,
Will be a prophecy of time to come,
When, in the wisdom of his ageless heart,
Mankind shall build the City Beautiful.

Haniel Long
Reprinted from *The Newark Anniversary Poems* 1917

Newark Sunday Call

PHOTO CREDITS

Photos courtesy of The Newark Public Library: Hugh J. Addonizio; William Ashby; Louis A. Bamberger; James Baxter; Seth Boyden home; Cockloft Hall; Stephen Crane; Stephen Crane home; Charles Cummings; John Dryden; Connie Francis; Kenneth A. Gibson; Julius Hahne; Elias G. Heller; Charles Evans Hughes; Kearny homestead; Gottfried Krueger; Wynona Lipman; Clara Maass; Seymour "Swede" Masin; Franklin Murphy; Marcus Ward; Marcus Ward home; Samuel A. Ward, and Edward Weston.

Photos by Glen Frieson: Homes of William J. Brennan Jr.; Joseph DiVincenzo; Savion Glover; Sharpe James; Gottfried Krueger; Jerry Lewis; Effa Manley; Donald Payne; Joe Pesci; Ralph Rainger; Peter Rodino; Philip Roth, and Paul Simon, and Grace Church.

Photos from Corbis Images: Photos of Fanny Brice; Betty Carter; Bob Fitzsimmons; Whitney Houston; Harold Lockwood; Shaquille O'Neal; Eva Marie Saint; Ted Schroeder; Wayne Shorter; Willie "The Lion" Smith; Horace Stoneham, and Sarah Vaughan.

Photos from private collections: Andre Briod (W. Paul Stillman); Sheriff Armando Fontoura (self); Warren Grover (Amelia Moorfield); Dr. Victor Parsonnet (self); Clement Price (Marion Thompson Wright); Michael Redmond (Maria Jeritza); Guy Sterling (George Clinton; Newark Sunday Call); Johanna Wright (Lonnie Wright).

Photo courtesy of The Newark Museum: John Cotton Dana

Photo by Z. Risasi Dais: Amiri Baraka

Photo courtesy of Northrop Grumman: Jack Northrop

Photo courtesy of the Charles Stewart Mott Foundation: Charles Stewart Mott

Photos courtesy of the U.S. Dept. of the Interior, National Park Service, Thomas Edison National Historical Park: Thomas Edison and his shop

Photo of Queen Latifah: Sony Pictures Television

Photo of Chris Christie: Governor's Office/Tim Larsen

Photo courtesy of Rodgers & Hammerstein: Jerome Kern

Photo courtesy of Michael Thornton: Frances Day

In memory of Dr. Clement A. Price, Newark historian

CPSIA information can be obtained at www.ICGtesting.com
Printed in the USA
LVOW10s1212100116

469981LV00002B/395/P